# Praise for *Half-Life of a Secret*

"Strasser's prose reaches beyond the straits normally reserved for academic presses in which this book was published, and her patience against some of the biggest ethical questions humans face is a thing of great strength. A profound debut of memory, research and imagination that mines conflicts of heart and intellect."

—Kerri Arsenault, *Star Tribune*

"With a detective's focus, a philosopher's yearning, and a granddaughter's devotion, Strasser deftly fuses memoir with biography, lyricism with hard truths, and a hidden history with the forgetful present. This book is intimate and epic, harrowing and healing. It chases the phantoms of America, reveals the contamination of secrecy, and finds grace in a fraught inheritance: hers and the nation's."

—Dan Zak, reporter for the *Washington Post* and author of *Almighty: Courage, Resistance, and Existential Peril in the Nuclear Age*

"Emily Strasser's *Half-Life of a Secret* offers not only a fierce literary vision but also a profoundly ethical one. This work of investigation and self-investigation is the rare book that becomes more beautiful the more you read. Audacious in her insistence on care and her refusal of easy answers, Emily Strasser engages fearlessly with the biggest questions of living in a debut as urgent as it is timeless."

—V. V. Ganeshananthan, author of *Brotherless Night*

"A well-researched, poignant journey of discovery, Emily Strasser's *Half-Life of a Secret* interrogates and reveals the secrets, stories, and human and emotional cost of the Oak Ridge nuclear weapons facility. From Tennessee to Hiroshima, Strasser's weave of historical fact and the story of her grandfather brings a much-needed truth and relevancy to a difficult and ever-present topic: the devastating legacy of nuclear weapons and the choices we face to the present day. A must-read."

—Kristen Iversen, author of *Full Body Burden: Growing Up in the Nuclear Shadow of Rocky Flats*

"Emily Strasser's book reads like several detective novels at once—except that the stories and secrets she unearths are her own family's, wrapped inside the larger secret of the development of the atomic bomb in Oak Ridge, Tennessee. Beautifully detailed and impeccably researched. Strasser proceeds with unrelenting curiosity and patience, 'breathing in history' and exhaling poetry. Brava!"

—Cristina García, author of *Dreaming in Cuban*

"*Half-life of a Secret* presents a family, a city built to build the bomb, consequences, and the painful, time-transcending tentacles of war. The story is profound and cleverly crafted, but if you love to see perfect words in startling yet perfect places, you will love Emily Strasser by the end of page one."

—Steve Leeper, former chairman of Hiroshima Peace Culture Foundation and cofounder of Peace Culture Village

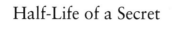

Half-Life of a Secret

# Half-Life of a Secret

## of a Secret

*Reckoning with a Hidden History*

Emily Strasser

UNIVERSITY PRESS OF KENTUCKY

Published by The University Press of Kentucky

Scholarly publisher for the Commonwealth, serving Bellarmine University,
Berea College, Centre College of Kentucky, Eastern Kentucky University,
The Filson Historical Society, Georgetown College, Kentucky Historical Society,
Kentucky State University, Morehead State University, Murray State University,
Northern Kentucky University, Spalding University, Transylvania University,
University of Kentucky, University of Louisville, University of Pikeville, and
Western Kentucky University.
All rights reserved.

*Editorial and Sales Offices:* The University Press of Kentucky
663 South Limestone Street, Lexington, Kentucky 40508-4008
www.kentuckypress.com

The Library of Congress has cataloged the hardcover edition as follows:

Names: Strasser, Emily, author.
Title: Half-life of a secret : reckoning with a hidden history / Emily Strasser.
Other titles: Reckoning with a hidden history
Description: Lexington : The University Press of Kentucky, 2023.
Identifiers: LCCN 2022043824 | ISBN 9780813197197 (hardcover) |
    ISBN 9780813197203 (pdf) | ISBN 9780813197210 (epub)
Subjects: LCSH: Strasser, George Albert, 1918-1984. | Oak Ridge National
    Laboratory—Employees—Biography. | Oak Ridge National Laboratory—
    History. | Manhattan Project (U.S.) | Atomic bomb—Social aspects—United
    States—History—20th century. | Nuclear weapons industry—Tennessee—
    Environmental aspects. | Nuclear industry—Employees—Health and
    hygiene—Tennessee—Oak Ridge. | Strasser, Emily—Family. | Chemists—
    United States—Biography. | Oak Ridge (Tenn,)—Biography.
Classification: LCC QC789.2.U62 O257 2023 | DDC 331.7/623451190976873
    [B]—dc23/eng20221230
LC record available at https://lccn.loc.gov/2022043824

ISBN 978-1-9859-0150-6 (paperback)

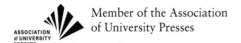

Member of the Association
of University Presses

ASSOCIATION
of UNIVERSITY
PRESSES

*For my family*

# Contents

# FIRE

It began with a bloom of fire on an off-white wall. The light swelled, blinding yellow darkening to a smoldering orange, all of it surging up from a nest of angry black smoke. There it burned; even the night singed red around the fireball, suspended, frozen in its incandescence within the dull rectangle of a plastic picture frame.

At the center of the bright, billowing thing was the darker shape of a man, arms loose at his sides, stance relaxed. He blocked the light, stood unchanged by it, only the shiny parts of him admitting to some anomaly in the landscape—a glow of firelight on his glasses, a gleam on his bald head.

Bald like my uncle. Like my father. Like the men of my family. He was George, the grandfather I'd never met. The man who'd died of a heart attack a few years before I was born, in the room next to where I now lay under yellow flowered sheets, transfixed by his image.

I could see the photograph by the amber light of the security beam over the driveway below, the light that burned all night long because out here in the country, night by itself was too dark. I stared and stared, a clenched thrill in my stomach. I felt myself floating, unmoored from time and space, drawn by my grandfather's eyes, eyes that knew everything yet said nothing, drawn to the desert where fire blossomed in silence, sprouting from a great, featureless plain that could have been the end of the world or the beginning.

When I shut my eyes, the fireball lingered like the impression of a bright light just switched off, branded red behind my eyelids.

Mornings at my grandmother's lake house—Meemaw's—I woke before dawn. I didn't look at the photograph as I crept downstairs without waking my parents to find the kitchen lit like a lantern in the dark morning. Together, Meemaw and I ate cereal—she, Raisin Bran; me, Cheerios—and watched for rabbits on the dew-slick front lawn. As dawn broke gray and clouds of mist lifted from the mirror-still lake out back, a heron rose like a ghost from the opposite shore, crossed the distance with steady, slow wingbeats, and landed on our dock, surveying his realm.

The sun burned the mist off the lake, climbed hot and high, pinked my shoulders and bleached my beach towel. I spent the entire day in my bathing suit, hurtling up and down the weedy hill between house and dock to fetch snacks, sunscreen, floaty toys. There were cousins and my little brother to play with, an aunt or uncle or parent on duty to drive the boat or supervise swimming. We fished off the dock, mostly catching little sunfish we threw back, or took the canoe out to search for turtles in the quiet, shaded coves where the trees hung low and felled branches in the soggy shallows made critter hidey-holes. The grass baked yellow, and the lake water heated warm as a bath. The photograph, like the morning dew, was gone as if it had never been. Gone, until bedtime.

The photograph is the first image I remember of my grandfather. It hung in what we called the cubbyhole—the small space off the upstairs living room, sharing the same musty smell and seventies-era multicolored shag carpeting. The space was deemed ideal for a child. Sometimes my cousin Julia shared the futon with me.

"First person up!" one of us would scream before turning out the light.

"Wakes up the other!" the other would respond, pledging not to miss a single moment of our time together.

On those nights, I didn't look at the photograph, the spell of it broken by our whispers, our mussed curls tumbled together on the pillows. But when I was alone, I couldn't keep my eyes from the unearthly orange searing out of the dark edges behind my grandfather's oddly unconcerned face.

I knew only vaguely that the photograph showed my grandfather standing in front of the thing he had built. I have the faintest memory of my mother telling me. I can almost see her, sitting on the edge of the futon, face aglow in the yellow light, turning to that terrible burning behind glass. Tucking me in. And then I'm alone.

If she said the words *atomic bomb*, they floated away, sounds unhinged from meaning, or sunk so deep in my subconscious that it would be years before I could dredge them up again. *Atomic bomb* was the province of the rat-tailed boys at school who were obsessed with military history and wrote bloody Civil War battle scenes during freewriting—interests our pacifist Quaker school failed to persuade them away from. Those boys knew about atomic bombs, but to me, the words meant nothing.

I was an anxious child. Afraid of robbers under my bed, of the house catching fire, sick with guilt, already, for the toll that humans put on the earth with all of our trash, building, and cutting. I cried for boiled lobsters and trees chopped down for new construction. If I had understood what was in the photograph, I would have been inconsolable.

Grandpa George, and what he did, existed wordlessly, a hum below articulable thought. The photograph was more feeling than concept, a delicious, chilling sense of myself small before something great and fearful.

We spent evenings at Meemaw's around the hexagonal picnic table overlooking the water, still telling stories after our plates lay empty except for a few crusts of bread, spindly fish bones, and soggy lettuce leaves. Meemaw held quiet reign over a rotating company: some combination of her four children—Karin, Kurt, Nellie, and my father, Dale—and their spouses and children. "Twenty-nine ninety-five!" she'd declare of a meal she particularly enjoyed, then, smacking the table, "No, thirty-nine ninety-five!" and I knew I was one of the lucky ones, wealthy in what couldn't be bought.

I was happiest then, quiet at the table beside my brother and cousins, listening to my parents and aunts and uncles talk politics or tell stories of their youths, only occasionally piping up to request my favorites—"Tell about the time when Nellie dumped a milk-shake down Meemaw's back while she was driving!" or "Tell about when you taught my dad to waterski when he was four!" I watched the adults under the light of the moon, the glow of lightning bugs winking around us, the lake below a tarnished silver.

I loved family stories. They were my way of orienting myself in the world, evidence that I was a part of something larger—history, family, the passage of time, a shared mythology. They made me feel safe, buoyant on love.

It wasn't until I was older that I began to notice the stories we didn't tell. If Grandpa George was invoked around the dinner table, it was with wry humor and affection. The portrait conjured by my family's stories was of a bearded, energetic farmer, always getting himself into messes with haphazard and ambitious projects.

"A caper," announced my aunt Karin, all of five feet tall, hands on hips in the carport as her husband, Paul, and brother Kurt wrestled an air conditioner up the deck stairs, "is supposed to be easy but usually ends up involving moving a refrigerator somewhere along the way." Capers, I understood, had been George's specialty, one inherited by the men in my family, who never hired anyone to fix something until they'd broken it more completely in their own attempts. What was meant to take half an hour always took the better part of a day or more and ended, often as not, with a mess and a missing tool part.

I'd seen the George of capers, the George of the farm, in other photographs: soft-bellied in overalls and red plaid, grinning beneath an unruly beard beside a bandy-legged colt or hoisting a fishing line heavy with a gaping bass or whiskered catfish. This was the George who'd bought and tended the acres of farmland down the road from the lake house, where a neighbor now ran cattle and we filled buckets with tart, wild blackberries. This was the George who fit into the place I loved best.

In time, I outgrew the cubbyhole, passed it on to my little brother and younger cousins. Some part of me was relieved—a shadowy residue clung to that space, like the feeling after an uneasy dream. Instead, I slept on the golden couch in the next room or in Meemaw's bedroom, where the total darkness was punctured only by the red numbers on the alarm clock. I barely thought of the photograph anymore.

Then, on a spring day in Atlanta, tenth grade, the classroom bright with afternoon sun, I glanced down at my American history textbook to see the words "Oak Ridge" printed under a segment about the Manhattan Project. I froze.

Oak Ridge was the name of the place my father had grown up in, twenty miles east of the lake house. Sometimes on rainy days at Meemaw's, we ventured into Oak Ridge to pick up pizzas or go shopping. The drive was a pleasant half hour on quiet roads lined with rusting barbed wire fences swallowed by wildflowers, past run-down trailers and country churches, but the town itself was a graying, low-slung stretch of strip malls and grim apartment buildings hiding winding neighborhood streets lined with neat little homes. Once or twice we visited the science museum that displayed full-body hazmat suits but whose real draw was the glass orb you could touch to make all your hair stand on end with static electricity.

I'd heard stories about Oak Ridge from my father. It was a strange town. Nearly everyone worked at one of three government laboratories. "Until I went to college," he told me, "I didn't know that fathers could be anything other than scientists. All the fathers I knew were physicists, chemists, biologists . . . oh, and engineers." George was a chemist and worked in a lab whose anonymous name, Y-12, revealed nothing of its function. My father never visited his father's office—none of the kids did—and George never spoke of his work, though sometimes he carried home papers in locked metal boxes.

One summer during college, Karin got a job doing administrative work at Y-12. The spring before, black-suited security investigators showed up at her North Carolina dorm to question her roommate and friends. Flustered, excited, her friends reported: "Karin, there were some men here, asking all about you!" Karin was unfazed. It was the sort of thing that was common in the Oak Ridge of her childhood, during the height of the Cold War.

Oak Ridge, to me, was this sprinkling of family anecdotes. Karin's children, who grew up in the city, would joke about seeing barrels of nuclear waste left to rust in a parking lot. My father reminisced about catching lightning bugs and selling them to one of the labs for some kind of experiment, twenty-five cents for every hundred bugs. The rumor was that they were being monitored for radiation. I accepted these strange stories without much curiosity.

But now, the name of this nondescript place, my father's hometown, glinted on the thin page of my history textbook.

The entry explained that Oak Ridge was one of three secret cities, along with Los Alamos, New Mexico, and Hanford, Washington, built to develop the atomic bomb. I don't remember what else it said. Probably it outlined the basic history: How on the eve of World War II, the discovery that atoms could be split introduced the possibility of a fearsomely powerful new weapon. How refugee scientists in America, who'd fled Europe to escape spreading Nazism, feared the power of this new weapon in Hitler's hands. How Hungarian Jewish physicist Leo Szilard had implored his friend Albert Einstein to write to President Roosevelt urging him to put the nation's industrial and scientific muscle to work building an atomic bomb before the Nazis could get one. And how the result of that letter was the Manhattan Project—a massive, covert effort involving hundreds of thousands of people working in secret sites across the country, including Oak Ridge.

What I do remember, viscerally, is the shock of recognition at those words, "Oak Ridge," the acid-tinged drop in my stomach. Long tables were arranged in a horseshoe opening toward the whiteboards and our teacher's desk at the front of the room. I sat center, shy in social settings but eager in the classroom. During the previous unit on the Depression, I'd been loudly perplexed—"But how can money that doesn't exist be traded? How can something without material equivalence lose value? How can it have value at all?" Now, I wanted to say something, to name my relationship to this history. "I know about that place," I wanted to say. But my tongue felt heavy, my throat tight. I sat silent, the hot ember of a secret in my gut.

We devoted the next several days to discussing the bombings of Hiroshima and Nagasaki. We went over reasons historians argue the bombs were or were not justified: they ended the war and saved the lives of tens of thousands of American soldiers as well as Japanese civilians that would have been lost in a land invasion; the cities were civilian rather than military targets, and the war was over already, Japan on the verge of surrender.

Our teacher gave us handouts detailing the immediate and long-term effects of the bombings—people incinerated where they stood or dying in agony in the hours, days, weeks, and months after, suffering from severe burns, fever, vomiting, diarrhea, hair loss, hemorrhaging. Buildings collapsed and burned for miles, radioactive black rain, and melted glass. For those who survived the initial blast: disfiguring keloid scars, cataracts, leukemia, and other cancers years later. The estimated death toll from both bombings was between one and two hundred thousand from August 1945 to the end of that year.

I hadn't slept in the cubbyhole in years, but I could see the photograph as if it hung before me. As my class discussed the bomb, I lined up the pieces that had been there all along but just out of reach, like the dregs of a dream you can taste but not describe.

George, my grandfather, helped build an atomic bomb. That bomb was dropped on noncombatants—on children and teachers and gardeners and nurses—in Japan.

Until that moment in the classroom, I hadn't imagined how, in the minutes after the shutter clicked, the fireball behind George must have risen and cooled to gray. Before that moment, I couldn't

have said that *mushroom cloud* was the name for the shape it took
as it ballooned into the sky.

By then, I'd caught hints of another George in the offhand comments of the adults. More complicated than the hapless farmer,
this George had had "problems," but mainly they were due to the
medicines not being right. "The medicines are better now," they'd
assert. This was relevant because an aunt and cousin had some of
the same "problems" George had, but they were going to be okay,
thanks to medicine. George's "problems" had to do with "brain
chemistry," which I learned was a family matter, an inherited thing
that the adults in my life were watchful for.

Various family members told me, "If you are ever having a
hard time, don't try to go through it alone. There's family history
here. It's brain chemistry," and I knew they meant George. And
when they said, "The longer you go, the worse it gets, the harder it
is to manage. Don't wait to ask for help. There's no shame," I knew
they meant that George had been ashamed, that he had waited too
long, that it hadn't been managed.

If in some families therapy and antidepressants are a stigma,
in mine they were a first line of defense. "I stuck her little butt in
therapy in high school," my aunt said of her youngest daughter, the
one who had what George had. "That's why she's done so well."

That cousin told me she'd understood me as a child, wondered
if we were similarly wired. In time it became clear that I did not have
what George had, but I still understood my own heightened anxiety, which made the world funnel to a dark vortex around a single,
arbitrary pin—a homework assignment one day, the destruction
of the rainforest the next—as the diluted, milder echo of George's
demons. I had vulnerable genes. When I finally started therapy and
medication in college, the decision was greeted by my parents with
some sort of relief.

I got a name for George's problems when my father's youngest sister was diagnosed with bipolar disorder, an official, clinical
explanation for her unspooling crisis inflamed by alcohol and a bad

marriage. But despite evidence of an inheritance that continued to shudder through the generations, the prevailing narrative was that the family had come out intact. We were a competent, professional bunch, lawyers and doctors and teachers and scientists. We children did well in school, were expected to follow a functional, successful path.

Once, I found George's wallet slipped down sideways in a drawer upstairs at the lake house, the leather worn dark and smooth. It contained a handful of cards: a hunting and fishing license, a couple of health insurance cards, instructions for CPR, and an almost blank business card for Strasser Farms. Also, a flimsy yellow card reading: "I am taking Eskalith. Slurred speech, staggering gait, dizziness, or unconsciousness may be due to the drug. Please see that I get prompt medical attention."

What I didn't know then, but suspected, was that Eskalith is a medication for bipolar disorder. What struck me though was the evidence of George's humanity. The family only spoke of his mental illness by way of necessary explanation—for the dangerous thread of heredity running through the generations and for the other reason he might be found staggering in dizzy circles, slurring his words, or passed out heavy in the middle of the day. But the card was a glimpse into his lived reality, his vulnerability. At any moment, George might have had to depend on the kindness of a stranger to make sure he received necessary medical attention. He couldn't trust himself to know when or how to ask. This was the same man who could pose unmoved before a nuclear explosion.

I was stunned to touch the thing, the worn wallet that he had actually slipped into his back pocket daily for months or years. He seemed to me, then, more a person than he ever had before. Though George's mental health issues were not a secret, I still felt as though I had found something forbidden. The family spoke of George with a studied carefulness, an attitude that mirrored the placement of that photograph, tucked away but in plain sight, as if the very casualness of its presentation might render it unremarkable. How easily it could all be acknowledged and dismissed in the same breath. "Oh yeah, I mean he drank a lot, but it was of an era. All the guys out here drank." A shrug, half a laugh. "He never talked about work. That wasn't allowed. But you know, it was the Cold War. These guys really thought they were keeping the Soviets from bombing us! It was a different time." A sip of wine.

I laid the cards out on the carpet and looked at them amid the swirls of disturbed dust, lit golden by light escaping from the corners of the curtains. When I heard footsteps on the stairs, I shuffled everything back into the drawers.

Clinical as the family's treatment of mental health might have been, it was a significant evolution from my grandmother's close-lipped attitude. As a child, I experienced my grandmother's independence as a kind of grace and competence. She was wiry, tough, loving, and stubborn. She traveled the world and lived alone at the lake house, out on a gravel road surrounded by woods and farmland. She refused her children's pleas to quit smoking and proved her point by out-hiking my parents in the Smoky Mountains, enjoying the view with a cigarette as they caught up. She adored her grandchildren, but she did not live for us; my parents had to schedule visits months in advance to accommodate her travels, weekly bridge games, book clubs, and church meetings.

She led an active, structured, independent life, a life kept safe and ordered by clear rules and full calendars. Everything had its proper place and appropriate behavior. Her dogs, large, loping country mutts, had the run of the land but were never allowed in the house. Children were to be indulged but well behaved. It was my grandmother, not my parents, who unfailingly insisted that I use the "magic words."

As she aged, the appearance of health, of life as it had always been, became a mask behind which she hid her slipping mind, her failing body. After hitting sixteen parked cars in a church parking lot, she bought a brand-new BMW, which she quickly totaled when she ran into a parked truck, insisting the sun had blinded her. After a couple of scary falls—a slip as she stepped from the tub, a tumble on the long gravel driveway—the family hired a caretaker to check on her weekly; Meemaw locked her out. Helplessness made her desperate and entrenched.

She refused help until she was physically incapable of doing so, until, after she suffered a stroke, my father drove the three and a half hours from our house in Atlanta, strapped her in the car, and delivered her straight to the hospital. We transferred her to a rehabilitation hospital near our home in Atlanta, and there, after suffering another stroke, she cursed for the first time in a decade when her sons suggested she move in with one of them.

She got her way, and her children arranged for full-time care in her house at the lake. She spent the last months of her life at the kitchen window, gazing out at the water as her caretakers spooned soft foods between her lips. Every weekend for the last year of her life, one of her kids flew or drove in from Atlanta, DC, or Connecticut. They sat with her as she struggled to swallow, as she lost strength and words. We kids played in the lake as we always had and then moved carefully through the hush of the house.

Still, she greeted each new level of care, each loss of independence, as an attack. *No* was the last word to go. "No" to chocolate Ensure. "No" to a blouse picked out by the caretaker. "No." The word formed with effort, the single syllable drawn out, loud and clear despite the strain. "No." The niceties had all gone. The please and thank-yous, the magic words she'd insisted I use. At the very end, she held fast to her ability to refuse, to set the boundaries of her world.

I never asked my grandmother about George. She died when I was fourteen, before I had become curious, before I had connected the burning thing in that photograph with the horror of Hiroshima. Before I had begun to suspect that her rules were the scaffolding that gave shape to a life that was largely unspeakable. It is difficult now to imagine what she would have told me of the husband whose work was secret and whose personal darkness she had guarded so fiercely during his lifetime.

The quiet rhythm of the last months of her life blur together in my memory. The light through the kitchen window. The soft-spoken caretakers in loose scrubs. The parade of pureed foods in bright plastic bowls. Her vacant stare from a face more and more skull-like.

But one memory stands out with sharp clarity. One afternoon, after she'd eaten lunch, I sat with her in the kitchen holding her hand, the loose skin like silk sliding over bird bones, the flesh of her palm oversized beside a shrunken wrist. Suddenly, her fingers clenched mine with a startling strength, and she turned to me, eyes wild.

She opened her mouth, her lower lip turned down, quivering, to reveal its veiny underside, her yellowed teeth. Her tongue worked, a clumsy protuberance, and a sound came from deep in her throat, groping, urgent, incomprehensible. Her grip tightened, crushing my knuckles together. Strings of saliva flew from her lips.

There was something fearful in her eyes; she knew I couldn't understand. She tried again, repeating the sounds, my hand in hers now moist with sweat; I couldn't say whether it was hers or my own. I barely dared blink or breathe for fear I would miss something.

Just as suddenly, she stopped, her grip slackened, and she turned again to face the window, silent and calm, as if she'd never tried to speak.

2

# ASH

In the last months of her life, Meemaw drew us back to the lake, the home she'd chosen at the very end. Where before we had mostly baked in the unsubtle heat of summer, in those months we saw the lake's seasons—the fiery crunch of fall, the gray still of winter, the whirring exuberance of spring.

That time solidified the lake house as a physical and emotional anchor for the family, and after she'd gone, my father and his siblings decided to hold the house in common. We continued to gather there for summers and holidays as we had during her lifetime. The house would sit empty for months at a time, then overflow with kids running in and out, dripping lake water across carpet; teenagers stretched out sunning on the dock; adults napping in hammocks or busy with dinner prep. Aside from necessary repairs, everything remained the same—the closets filled with worn flannel shirts and faded down coats abandoned by children and grandchildren, the shelves stacked with classic board games: Chutes and Ladders, Clue, Candy Land, Sorry! It was a sort of living time capsule.

Best of all, there were drawers full of the photographs, letters, and newspaper clippings Meemaw had collected over a lifetime. She had saved ticket stubs, paper napkins from airplanes and hotels, notes from Bible study classes. I spent many afternoons kneeling on my towel in front of the mahogany dresser upstairs, thumbing through the browned corners of newspapers, squinting at gray photographs and sepia snapshots, looking for nothing in particular, but thrilling to touch these talismans of the past.

Watts Bar Lake is a reservoir formed by the damming of a seventy-mile section of the Tennessee River. The lake house sits on a little thumb of land on the Emory River, a widened tributary of the lake, near the confluence with the colder waters of the Clinch River. Other than rainy days, and the two hours of adult-enforced shade time during the hottest part of the afternoon, we were in or on or by the lake—swimming, fishing, waterskiing, reading on the dock.

Like many lakes crowded with vacation homes and buzzing with motorboats, Watts Bar isn't, I suppose, all that special; the water is murky, and the landscape is pastoral but not remarkable. But like many who've had the good fortune to have a family home, a place to return to, a place that can hold our many selves, I have loved that lake like no other place.

I know it intimately—the bottom of small sharp rocks and tiny twirled shells, the smell of the water dried on my skin and hair, the exact shape of the tree line against the sky. I know the way the water feels under my water skis on a calm day, like butter under a blade. I know the way it churns under a restless wind, pewter and perturbed. Thunderstorms turn it into a pocked tin roof. Misted at dawn, blued at dusk.

I know the body of it—the thick torso of the channel and its tributary arms thinning between steep forested banks. I know how the water goes cold in the Clinch and still in the Little Emory. I know the clearings on public lands where families park pickups and camp, string hammocks and rope swings, burn beer cans in campfires. I know where the water stretches wide and flat to lap against vast, manicured lawns beneath towering new colonnaded estates. I know the turnoff to a hidden rope swing from which the brave can drop twenty feet into deep water. I can spot the yawning mouth of a cave hiding behind trees on undeveloped land. I know—I love—the wind lifting my hair and blurring out sound below a shout as the motorboat zooms over the water. I know the unpleasant surprise of a gnat landing in the back of my throat, and I know, now, to keep my mouth shut when my face turns into the wind.

I know, also, the signs that rupture the idyll. On cleared shorelines, enormous transmission towers stalk rolling fields, hulking giants stringing power lines as thin as thread across an otherwise unbroken sky. Above the lake, the power lines bear large orange beads like suspended basketballs to warn planes away.

As a kid, seated in the bow of the motorboat, I would bend my head back to fixate on those bright orange spots and feel myself unglued from gravity, swimming up into the sky. It was the human anchor between sky and water that impressed me, the height of the power lines, the size of the transmission towers, a middle distance I could clap onto and feel my own smallness beside; what was awesome out here wasn't nature—this was a mellow, comforting landscape—but the mark of industry.

Even this lake isn't natural; it was dammed by the Tennessee Valley Authority in the early 1940s to control flooding and provide electricity to the region, and its level still rises and falls seasonally with the storage and release of water.

The most prominent signs of industry visible from the lake house, though, are the twin smokestacks of the coal-burning Kingston Fossil Plant that taper a thousand feet into the sky just over the shore opposite. They serve as a landmark by road or water; when I see the thin cylinders pointing above the tree line, I know we are almost home. At night, red lights blink from their tops, two fierce eyes keeping watch.

When I was a kid, we sometimes went fishing beneath those smokestacks, perched on the skimmer dam separating the main body of the lake from the plant. It was called a skimmer, my uncle Kurt explained, because the wall extended only partway to the bottom of the lake, thus skimming warm water off the top and allowing the cooler, denser water to sink down where it was drawn under and into the plant. "If you fall in," my cousin Julia told me, "you'll get sucked under." As I stood on the concrete wall, warm in the sun, my eyes traced the fishing line ten feet or so until it disappeared into the lazy current. I felt my stomach swoop.

Once, I handed my pole to Uncle Kurt, walked to the end of the wall, climbed down a muddy hill, and wandered the strange landscape behind the dam. I stood at the lip of a small, violently churning man-made waterfall, frothing white; farther on was an eerie still pond covered in shiny gray scum, dirty foam clumping against the shore. A heron picked its prissy way past. Unnerved, I ran back.

When I was nine years old, I saw a movie at a friend's house that sent me into a spiral of insomnia, then depression. I spent weeks in mounting panic as bedtime approached, and no sooner would my parents leave the room than I would sit up screaming, equally terrified that I would fall asleep and that I never would. I spent days in a sleep-deprived haze, wondering how everyone else carried on with the cheerful noisiness of life when death was next.

My mother, in worried desperation, asked if I wanted to "talk to someone," a prospect I was horrified by despite my family's apparently enlightened attitude toward mental health. I didn't see a therapist, but some weeks later, the depression gradually lifted on its own.

Into adulthood, though, I would remember that time with deep fear, a glimpse of where my mind might go if I let it. I had seen something I was unable to unsee, and I worried that my capacity to operate in the world depended on my staying just so far above that dark place.

The film that sparked the episode was a typical disaster movie: a quiet, idyllic town nestled beneath a long-dormant volcano ignores signs of new volcanic activity until it is too late, and then it's the scramble of escape, the heroism of rescue, the drama of destruction under the fiery rush of lava and an ash-dark sky. One image in particular sent me rearing from my bed, gasping in panic: an old woman on the shore of a lake, legs mangled to bloody stumps, left by her family to die. She was a grandmother who had attempted to save her grandchildren by pulling a boat across a lake turned acidic by the volcano. As soon as I shut my eyes, she appeared there, acid-eaten legs gleaming with blood and pale face pained, but most terribly, resigned.

The fear that set in, that began to infect my daylight hours too, was the sudden sense that the world wasn't as it appeared; a mountain might be a secret volcano, a placid lake might boil and burn. And while the urban sprawl of Atlanta didn't offer many possibilities for hidden volcanoes, I thought of the wooded hill across the cove from Meemaw's house. Like the grandmother in the movie, my grandmother lived alone in the woods. The film seemed prophetic. Though my mother assured me there were no volcanoes anywhere near us, I wasn't assuaged. I had learned that threats may lie in plain sight, unperceived.

On the longest night of 2008, in my childhood bed in Atlanta, I slept the exhausted, dreamless sleep of a college student post finals. After midnight, a man one hundred and fifty miles north of me but less than two miles from the empty lake house woke to a thunderous roar and peered out his window to see trees surging into the cove behind his house. It was a scene from a nightmare, but he wasn't dreaming. Trunks cracked against each other as they crashed onto the shore, carried by a heavy gray sludge. Everything was dark but for the blinking lights atop the smokestacks of the Kingston Fossil Plant. *A landslide*, the man thought at first, then he attempted to describe what he saw to the Roane County 911 dispatcher on the phone. *An earthquake*, thought another man, a plant worker called from his bed to address the disaster, as he watched a bottle of water shiver in the cupholder of his car.

It wasn't an earthquake or a landslide or a volcano or any other natural disaster, though many compared it to a tsunami, the 5.4 million cubic yards of gray sludge that burst from a waste containment pond at the Kingston Fossil Plant that midwinter night. It splintered docks, blanketed roads and a railway, pushed homes from their foundations, and buried others up to their porches so that residents had to escape through windows into a strange new landscape, hundreds of acres covered thigh-high in dark, glinting swirls and clumps and ragged masses of heavy wet slurry.

In the days after the spill, my family learned what had happened from the safety of our Atlanta kitchen. Clutching mugs of strong coffee, we read about the disaster, how a wall in the waste containment pond at the plant had suddenly ruptured, releasing 7.3 million tons of sodden coal fly ash—a toxic by-product of coal combustion containing radioactive elements and heavy metals including arsenic, lead, chromium, mercury, and selenium—into the surrounding land and water.

We knew the plant by its twin towers rising above the lake, blinking away all night long; that morning, we learned how it worked and how it broke. Built by the federally owned Tennessee Valley Authority (TVA) in the 1950s to serve the increasingly demanding energy needs of Oak Ridge's Cold War nuclear weapons operations, the Kingston Fossil Plant generated energy by burning coal to heat water to create steam to turn a turbine. The ash left over from the combustion process was stored wet in ponds to keep it from becoming airborne, held behind simple earthen dikes despite environmentalists' recommendations that coal fly ash be buried in lined landfills.

For decades, as the ash pile grew, the TVA built dikes around dikes, cleaned up leaks, patched walls. There had been major repairs as recently as 2005, though engineers noted weaknesses in the dikes as early as the 1970s. The 1.1 billion gallons of toxic muck that exploded into a quiet December night were more than twice the amount authorities said the pond contained, enough to fill sixteen hundred Olympic swimming pools, one hundred times the amount of oil spilled into Alaska's Prince William Sound by the *Exxon Valdez* in 1989, and five times that which would be released by the Deepwater Horizon oil rig explosion less than two years later.

We spotted the lake house's thumb of land, just south of the ash pond, on the aerial photograph printed in the *New York Times*. When we were able to reach a neighbor, he reported that the cove beside the house was clogged with debris, but the house and dock were untouched. The mass of sludge had gone north and east, into a valley and through the Swan Pond community, damaging or destroying dozens of homes but miraculously taking no lives that night.

The following winter, a year after the spill, cleanup was ongoing. The grass was pale, and bare treetops hunched in a bluish haze. From Emory River Road, directly across the water from the plant, I looked down to see shiny gray scum frothing in the curves of the bright yellow booms—long inflated tubes stretched across the channel to collect and contain the ash. Across the river, bulldozers sat idle on barren fields of red mud. Warning signs on the shore advised: "Striped bass from this body of water contain contaminants at levels thought to increase the risk of cancer or other illness in humans. THESE FISH SHOULD NOT BE EATEN."

Many of the houses along the road sat empty. After the spill, the TVA purchased 180 properties affected by the spill or cleanup, most of them private homes. The nets on the basketball hoops hung still.

The air was chill and smelled of slate. I walked past the empty houses and thought about how slowly things happen and how quickly. The previous winter had been wet and cold. Some said later it was the weight of too much water, soggy ash, then the bite of freezing rain that compromised the dike, releasing decades of improperly stored toxic waste. I suppose if it hadn't been that night, that winter, it would have been another. We never know until it is too late that the last patch won't hold.

One afternoon, I walked in on a conversation between an old family friend and my uncle Paul, Karin's husband, who'd followed his father-in-law into a career in nuclear weapons. Paul, now retired, reclined in a leather chair, one hand on his belly, the other holding a sweating gin and tonic. He set his drink down to gesture as he spoke. "Everybody's got their panties in a twist over these heavy metals. They say—oh, arsenic, lead, those are poison! But the thing is, these heavy metals, they're not water-soluble. All they do is sink to the bottom and stay there. I might not like to eat a catfish, but otherwise, it don't make much difference to the water."

"Maybe," said Valerie, "but my students have been complaining that when they're in the shower, the water stings."

"Probably just the power of suggestion." Paul sipped his drink.

"Probably." My family had stayed out of the lake the summer after the spill, but Valerie had decided it was safe to swim. She is a child of Oak Ridge, not unduly disturbed by such things.

I hadn't thought of the photograph of George for ages, but in the year after the ash spill, I found myself remembering the darkened cubbyhole and the glow of unearthly fire with a nagging insistence. It struck me, for perhaps the first time, that it was very odd to have such a photograph. Who posed with a nuclear explosion, and who displayed such an image in a family home?

It was a remarkable departure from how I'd been raised and how I understood my family. We had no veterans, no soldiers. Neither my father nor his siblings even hunted, though they might have, growing up in East Tennessee. Yet here was this glorification of the most devastating violence, hung above a child's bed.

In almost every other way, my parents were extremely conscientious with my brother and me, careful about what we consumed, what we were exposed to. We were a health-food-eating, public-television-watching kind of family. My brother and I attended Quaker school, where overzealous pacifists banned keeping score at recess soccer on the grounds that competition bred violence. School days were punctuated by moments of silence and interminable discussions aimed at obtaining consensus. At home, we weren't allowed to have water guns that resembled weapons—they had to look like dolphins spitting from their mouths, happy frogs, seahorses.

And my mother had even been an antinuclear activist in the 1980s; she was one of the founders of the Chicago chapter of Women's Action for Nuclear Disarmament and had single-handedly organized a month of readings and performances in Chicago to commemorate the fortieth anniversary of the bombing of Hiroshima. But after entering this family, she must have learned to accept what was extraordinary and disturbing; otherwise, she wouldn't have put me to bed beneath that photograph. That George had been a nuclear weapons scientist wasn't a secret, not anymore, but to make a fuss over it would have been to upset a careful equilibrium.

My grandmother must have been the one who hung the photograph in the cubbyhole, a gesture both defiant and ambivalent—it would be seen but not by many, displayed but out of the way, an ambiguous symbol of regard for her husband and his work. I remembered that afternoon at the lake, when she'd crushed my fingers with her sudden grip and labored, so desperately, to speak.

About to graduate and faced, for the first time in my life, with the decision of where and how to be in the world, I felt my mind pulled back to the lake, the place I had always felt most loved, most innocent. A place that, after the spill, felt fragile and perhaps not so innocent anymore.

Sitting on the bed in my sun-bright room, I wrote in my journal: "lake, George, Fossil Plant, atomic bomb?"

By *lake*, I meant family and home. I meant my grandmother. I meant the feeling I'd had as a child sitting around that picnic table after dinner, cocooned in stories.

On the cusp of entering the adult world, I was neurotically idealistic, and scared, deeply concerned with the problem of how to live a good life. I lived in constant compromise and constant guilt at the compromise. As a white person in America, I knew my comfort was already founded on murder, genocide, stolen labor and stolen land, the destruction of the earth. To contribute more good than harm became an all-consuming, paralyzing order at times. How was it possible to tread lightly when my every choice, my every movement, harmed the planet, benefited from or reinforced an unjust power system? Where could I even begin?

I ached for a clean slate, an innocent beginning.

Love was meant to be an uncomplicated goodness, home a place from which you could set your compass. But there was George—the dimmed center of that photograph, the human before the absurd, indifferent destructiveness of that deadly light—stuck like a knot in my throat. How do we love what is tainted?

I had been looking away. That day in high school when I learned about Oak Ridge and Hiroshima, I did not rush home to ask my parents about George's work. The photograph was an incarnation of everything I feared to know.

But if goodness required denying uglier pasts, then goodness was fragile indeed, a real hypocrite. If I couldn't face this original sin of my family, how could I navigate any of the rest? If the ash spill taught me anything, wasn't it that what was hidden would come out anyway, seep from cracking walls or explode into a midwinter night?

Those four phrases—"lake, George, Fossil Plant, atomic bomb"—seemed points on a map to something I needed to understand. I didn't know then that my attempt to unravel what that photograph meant about history, my family, my home, and the bomb would consume the better part of ten years, find me elbow-deep in archives, see me lob Freedom of Information Act requests at a byzantine labyrinth of government agencies, and send me not only back to Oak Ridge but also to the deserts of Nevada and the islands of Japan. I knew only that I needed to begin by looking at what was in plain sight.

3

# STILL BURNING

I checked out books about the Manhattan Project from my college library and scanned the indexes for Oak Ridge. I learned that, within months of Roosevelt green-lighting the Manhattan Project in June of 1942, fifty-nine thousand acres of rural land were seized from small farmers in East Tennessee; fields were cleared, roads laid, laboratories built, and prefabricated houses assembled. In 1943, workers recruited by the thousands flooded in from around the southeast, while scientists disappeared from laboratories and universities across the country, relocated to this hastily erected town.

Secrecy and speed were of the utmost importance—speed because scientists thought Germany was well on its way to having its own bomb, and secrecy because they feared American scientific knowledge and processes would aid German production. Oak Ridge was one of three secret cities built by the Manhattan Project; the other two were Hanford, Washington, responsible for plutonium production, and Los Alamos, New Mexico, responsible for bomb design and construction. Oak Ridge, the primary site of uranium enrichment, was known as Site X.

The perimeter of Oak Ridge was enclosed with barbed wire fences hung with signs warning, "Military Reservation No Trespassing," periodically interrupted by observation towers. To enter the gates of the city, Oak Ridgers had to present a resident's ID and submit to an armed search. Once inside, movement was further constrained. Around town, residents could be stopped and asked to show their IDs at any time, while shopping, heading to the movies, or picking up a child from school. The gesture became so automatic that sometimes churchgoers would flash their badges as they greeted their ministers or husbands would reach for their IDs as their wives opened the front doors.

Inside the plants, an elaborate security apparatus policed who was allowed to go where and ensured everyone stayed within their designated territory. Workers wore color-coded badges, each corresponding to one of the five levels of security clearance that granted access to certain areas accordingly. By my best guess, George, as a midlevel scientist, would have been a level three, perhaps moved up to a level four when he took on greater managerial responsibilities toward the end of the war. The vast majority—some 95 percent—did not know what they were doing; they saw only dials to be monitored, beakers to be cleaned, hallways to be swept, pipes to be welded. Even among the scientists and military officials with the highest level of clearance, called Q clearance, information was doled out on a need-to-know basis.

Compartmentalization, I learned, was the official name of the policy restricting both worker knowledge and project-wide communication, ensuring that no one group or individual could gather enough information to form a complete picture of the enterprise.

One billboard in the townsite depicted the "see no evil, hear no evil, speak no evil" monkeys, beneath the words "What you see here, what you do here, what you hear here, when you leave here, let it stay here."

I began, too, to ask about George. I wanted to understand what kind of man he was. My father was pleased by my interest but responded to my tentative questions distantly. He'd never really understood what his father did and never thought much about it; such was the secretive culture of Oak Ridge. As a father, George had been interested in but a bit puzzled by his children. He wanted to connect but didn't know how to play, so instead, he put his kids to work, rallied them to chores on the farm or projects around the house. About George's mental health, my father responded with the same restraint I'd heard throughout my childhood. *I guess he drank too much, but you know everybody did at that time. It really was a chemical issue. Things were better after they got him on the right medicine.*

He suggested I call D. H., a family friend I'd known all my life. D. H. was a large, gentle man who lived with his wife, Barbara, in a cozy log cabin opposite Meemaw's long gravel driveway. His tall, bent form coming down for a drink was a familiar sight throughout my childhood. I'd snack on chips, listening to him tell stories in his soft North Carolina drawl, peppered with fantastic phrases like "cold as whiz" and "blotto drunk."

More than a neighbor or friend, D. H. was an extension of the family. He lent us his motorboat, helped my uncles with repairs on the house, and kept an eye on Meemaw as she grew weaker and more entrenched. Time and again, he called my father in Atlanta to tell him to drive up despite Meemaw's protestations that she was fine. Once, D. H. spotted a blood-smeared newspaper crumpled at the end of her driveway. He hurried down to the house. When no one answered his knock, he broke in. Meemaw had fallen while getting her mail, dropped the newspaper, and managed to get back down the long driveway and lock the doors on her shame. Without D. H., she might very well have died years earlier than she did, lonely, frightened, and in pain. My father suggested this was not the first time D. H. had played such a role for the family.

D. H. had been close to George. He'd known him both socially and professionally, worked under George at Y-12. D. H. might be able to give me a perspective the family could not, my father told me. What he didn't say, but what I half-suspected, was that D. H. might be less constrained by the family's habitual carefulness. Perhaps also, I might find it easier to ask him what I needed. I, too, was bound by fear and caution.

I called him one afternoon. He was glad to hear from me and quickly warmed to the subject. "You know about how I met

George?" he asked. "It was one of those pig roasts out at the lake. We sat up from ten p.m. till four a.m., talking about everything under the sun." He laughed. "You should have seen how he sat around the fire, Emily. On his haunches, his head resting on his knees, all folded up. He didn't need a chair."

By the time D. H. met George around the pig roast fire, George was assistant plant manager at Y-12. D. H., as he told it to me, was a reluctant recruit. A week after he'd declined the initial job offer—he was working on his master's degree and intended to go on for his PhD—he received an order of induction into military service, bound for Vietnam. He'd be mixing Agent Orange. His brother, already over there, told him not to come if he could at all avoid it. So he called the Y-12 recruiter and said he was interested in the job after all. He completed his master's thesis in three weeks, defended it, and began work two days later.

After their fireside conversation, George took an interest in D. H. He made sure the younger man met the scientists visiting from Los Alamos, insisted he make trips to the Nevada Test Site to see nuclear tests, and clued him in on internal politics that could be the pitfalls of a young man's career.

Outside of work, George began seeking D. H. out as an accomplice. For weeks or months at a time, George burned with excess energy, barely slept, and looked for anyone or anything to keep him company, to help him pass the blazing hours. D. H. was an early riser and game for whatever George threw his way.

"When I heard that knock before six o'clock in the morning, I always knew it was George!" D. H. laughed. They'd visit a country diner at dawn and order greasy plates of sausages and grits or drive out to a tract of forest George had bought for the lumber and count trees or chop firewood.

D. H.'s first wife wasn't wild about George pulling her husband out of the house early on weekend mornings. "He kept me in a lot of trouble!"

D. H. told me a story I'd heard from my father and Uncle Paul, one that everyone seemed to think encapsulated George. On a winter's day, Paul, D. H., George, and my father were driving back from Crossville, some fifty miles west of Oak Ridge, where they'd been surveying trees on the tract of forest George and Paul had purchased. Freezing rain slicked the road, and at the bottom of a steep hill, the jeep lost traction and began to roll. My father watched timber axes and chain saws float through the air in a sort of circular dance, inches from his face. He felt calm and curiously removed, amused, almost, by the absurdity of the situation.

The vehicle landed with a lurch upright in a ditch, and the tools fell to the floor, somehow avoiding the passengers. A passing tractor helped pull them out, and they drove back to Oak Ridge in a jeep that now listed to the right. It wasn't until they were back in town that they noticed that George's right arm was swollen huge. He hadn't uttered a word. D. H. and Paul insisted he go to the hospital, where doctors had to cut off his jacket sleeve to examine the arm, which was broken. Like my grandmother, George was not one to voice, or perhaps even notice, his own pain.

What my father and uncle hadn't told me was that three or four weeks after the accident, my grandmother called D. H. and Paul to drive a drunk and depressed George to the mental health center in town. "He resisted," said D. H., "but eventually he went in there. Stayed for three weeks or a month. And I found out then that he'd been treated there before, more than once. And he'd spent a long time at a hospital in Virginia. And I was surprised—he was second-in-command at the plant, a man held in very high esteem. How had he managed to maintain that?"

Though D. H. was at first astonished to learn that his mentor and boss had been repeatedly hospitalized, this scene would become a regular occurrence—Paul and D. H. wrestling a cursing and liquor-soaked George into the car and then driving him to the mental health center as he raged. At least once, he resisted so violently they used a leather belt to strap him down.

I thought of Meemaw, some decades later, locking the nurses out of her house, refusing to get in the car to go to the hospital until my father threatened to carry her.

After we'd talked a while, D. H. lowered his voice to say, "Well, you do know how George died, don't you?"

"Yes. A heart attack." It was one of the first things I'd known about George. I'd written it countless times on health history forms. The reason he died young, the reason I'd never known him.

He paused, then said, "Emily, he drank wood alcohol. I caught him, behind the shed."

I felt hot suddenly, vaguely nauseous.

"He was a chemist. He knew what that would do to him. It was poison. He essentially committed suicide."

After we hung up, I sat for a few minutes, my cell phone hot on my bare leg. I traced the stitching on the quilt with my fingertip. Same room, same quilt, same bed. I waited for the conversation to reveal itself as a dream, but it did not. The sun was now too bright. I rewound our words. I felt as if I'd just watched a movie of myself making a devastating mistake. Maybe I would do something different this time. But there was no way out, no unhearing.

If what D. H. said were true, either my family had been lying my entire life or they didn't know. And if they didn't know, who was I to tell them? What would it do to them? To all of us?

I'd stumbled into a dark fairy tale, some ancient lesson against curiosity and disobedience—Psyche holding the lamp above her lover's head, a drip of hot oil waking him, her banishment and heartbreak. Briefly, I considered not telling my father, not telling anyone, quietly backing away, no sudden movements. But if this was a fairy tale, I had already broken the rules. I could not go back.

I called my father. I told him what D. H. had told me.

He received the revelation calmly. "Hmm," he said. D. H. had recently been diagnosed with early-onset Alzheimer's, he told me. "He gets confused. He mixes things up."

Still, he promised he would call his siblings and ask whether they had any doubts about how their father had died. I didn't know how to feel—some measure of relief at my father's reassurances beside confusion that he thought it possible his father had committed suicide and none of his kids had known. I'd had no idea it was all so bad. I waited, imagining the conversations my father was having with his siblings, doubt ricocheting through the family like shrapnel.

He called me back a few hours later. He thought he knew the incident D. H. was referring to, but it had occurred many years before George died. "I was in Brazil, during my gap year, or I was in college. And yeah, Dad drank antifreeze. But later, at the hospital, it looked like he didn't drink as much as he said he had."

My father thought, and his siblings agreed, that this was the incident D. H. had mistaken for the end.

"I saw my dad two and a half weeks before he died, and he was doing better."

I let out a long-held breath. The air seemed to settle around me, the light gold before dusk, gentler now.

I'd been given a back door out, and I took it. Permission to set this question aside. And yet, D. H.'s insistence lodged in the back of my mind like a tree root in asphalt, swelling and cracking the smooth surface. It mattered, I thought. What D. H. remembered meant something, even if it wasn't true.

Around that time, on a visit to the lake, I returned to the cubbyhole upstairs in search of the photograph. I wanted to study George's face, test it against my memory. I wanted to see if the photograph still held the same power over me.

But where the photograph used to hang, I found a large formal portrait of George, one of those whose color was touched up after the fact, flesh almost plastic, cheeks shined to a high polish. He wore a controlled almost-smile, one brow furrowed over a squinted eye. A professional photo, I guessed, something taken for his job, not his family; this distant and inscrutable man was most definitely George the scientist, the same one who'd stood before that fearsome fire.

I assumed that my aunt Karin, now mindful of her grand-children who slept in the cubbyhole and built blanket forts among the couch cushions upstairs, had removed the bomb photograph in favor of this one. With four families cycling through the house, things were always getting shuffled around. I didn't ask where it had gone; I was sure that when I had the time and motivation to search, I'd find it paper-wrapped in a drawer or tucked in a closet, still burning.

4

# HOMEPLACE

Oak Ridge. Oaggridge—that's the way I've always heard it. The heavy grunt of industry. But stop, roll the words over your tongue, feel them separately. See the oaks, proud and weathered, softening the narrow, rolling ridges that distinguish this part of East Tennessee. From above, it looks as if someone had absentmindedly drawn fingers through the earth, wrinkling the land between the Smoky Mountains to the southeast and the Cumberlands to the north. The land stretches out long, the slope of a hip, the curve of a waist, sinking down into the grass as days roll into seasons, roll into years, the moss appearing first between toes, in the dark hollows at the backs of knees, and so on until the body of the earth is covered in a patchwork of forest and cleared fields stitched together by unhurried, winding roads with names like Sugar Grove Valley and Turpin Hollow and Clax Gap. This land has been worked a long time, its hard edges worn smooth by patient cultivation. It is a land to dream yourself to sleep in. And despite the dark weight of that name—Oaggridge—it is this Oak Ridge that you see first when you approach the city from the west.

It was early December. I'd graduated from college the previous spring. This was the first time I had returned to the city since I knew what Oak Ridge was. I turned the name over in my mind—Oak. Ridge. Oak. Oak. Ridge. Ridge. Oaggridge—unsure, this time, of what I would encounter.

Nearly seventy years before, in the fall of 1943, my grandparents pulled through the gates of the brand-new settlement and began to unpack their lives into the spare prefabricated house assigned to them. My father and his siblings knew little about their parents' lives during the war, but they knew that their father had been recruited from the chemical company where he worked and that he and Doris had married just months before. They were young and patriotic, eager to serve.

Outside the fences, the hills, forest, and farmland looked much as they do today but softer, the roads brown and unpaved, the rough wooden farmhouses melting back into the green. As I dipped in and out of the valleys, wound around the hills, I thought of how their eyes might have sought the shadowed spaces between the trees for clues to their new lives. War jobs, they knew. Decent pay. On-site housing.

George, the son of a farmer, had recently finished his master's in soil chemistry. He'd been declared 4-F by the draft because both feet were broken in an automobile accident on a snowy night in upper East Tennessee a year or so before. Or he'd been too short, or his eyesight too poor; that's what his kids remembered, their father thoroughly unsoldierly by multiple measures. But now, at last, George—the farmer's son, the soil scientist, the army reject, already bald and wearing thick glasses at twenty-five—was wanted by his country. Wanted for what? The recruiters couldn't say exactly. But of course he went.

Doris couldn't have been so certain. Her children say the young woman huddled in worried conference with her mother. She'd been married just five months before, no time at all to start a life and a home, and now her husband wanted to take her to a town that was still being built for a job he couldn't explain, more than three hundred miles from her childhood home on the Mississippi floodplain of West Tennessee. Doris adored her home and family—gentle but determined parents who'd sent three fiercely loyal daughters through college in the midst of the Depression. With the mystery of it, the unspoken why and what, three hundred miles might have been three thousand. Did it unnerve her, the way these hills hunched in on themselves, disclosing nothing but the next bend in the road?

I can't say how many times I traveled this road as a child—the landscape is embedded deeper than conscious memory. The back-and-forths from my childhood home in Atlanta, the hot August days at the lake house twenty miles west of Oak Ridge.

I am six, curled in the back seat beside my little brother, half-zipped bags, pairs of shoes, and stale Goldfish tossed on the car floor. We have played every game. We have been driving forever. Our little white Jack Russell terrier has long since resigned himself and is curled into a lump on the middle seat. But when we exit the highway, he knows—he leaps up and begins a frenzied dash from window to window, scratching our legs with his too-long nails, piercing our ears with his high-pitched bark. I crack the window and press my nose to the glass. As we cross the white bridge over the Clinch River and the sound of the tires on the asphalt goes hollow with all the air beneath, I feel a loosening in my chest, a lifting, an opening from the inside.

I am eight, ten, thirteen, and everything is the same—brother, dog, snacks, the elation of arrival. My eyes seek the deer appearing with sudden stillness at the edge of the forest at dusk, their deep hush a wordless accusation against our human intrusion. I don't know that when those same deer are killed during the fall hunting season, they will be tested for radiation, and a few will be confiscated.

I have been dreaming through this place my whole life.

That December day, though, I leaned forward over the wheel, driving slowly. The trees were bare, branches lacing against the gray sky. The forest looked like any other but for yellow cattle gates here and there, signs reading "Closed to Public. US Department of Energy. Call for Entry," blocking otherwise unremarkable gravel roads disappearing into the woods.

I'd spent the previous year reading about the "secret city" from the comfort of my college suite, riveted on the couch while my roommates read their neuroscience and philosophy homework. I was trying to understand how this place had made George a man who would pose unflinching for a snapshot before a nuclear blast. How this place had made a family who would display such a photograph without question or explanation. Most of all, though, I read to understand how this place, despite its tenuous and dark beginnings, had become home. Because of all the places I had ever known and loved—Atlanta, New York City, even a little town in the foothills of the Indian Himalayas whose name means "sanctuary"—this was the landscape that filled me with the ache of home.

The lake house owed its origins to Oak Ridge, the land purchased and house built by my grandparents in the early 1960s as a summer and weekend getaway from the city where George still worked at the nuclear plant he'd joined as a young chemist during the war. By then, the city was no longer secret, its name revealed to the world in newspaper headlines and radio broadcasts in the days and weeks after the bombings of Hiroshima and Nagasaki. But Oak Ridge had become a linchpin in the nation's nuclear weapons industry, the plants remained secured by layers of fencing and armed guards, and a learned reticence alongside official policies protecting ongoing weapons work conspired to maintain a culture of secrecy in the city. My father grew up in a city no longer gated but flanked still by empty guard towers, where everyone's dad was a scientist, and no one knew exactly what that meant.

Now, I saw it unfold before me, here all along for the looking. As I approached town, signs began to appear indicating the directions to "Y-12 National Security Complex" and "Oak Ridge National Laboratory." My pulse quickened. I felt charged, on the edge of something.

During World War II, even the most mundane details of city life were protected for fear that such fragments would aid spies in surmising the size and nature of the operation; rosters of high school sports teams were not shared with opponents, and residents could not mail church bulletins to relatives out of town. A woman writing to her mother about the number of appendectomies performed at the city hospital was purportedly hauled in for questioning by security.

Personal journals were forbidden, and mail was censored, sometimes arriving so heavily redacted as to be inscrutable. Residents recruited as informants recorded the names of those who seemed too nosy or too talkative and dropped them in envelopes addressed to the nonexistent Acme Credit Corporation of Knoxville. It was rumored that as many as one in four residents were informants.

Site X was omitted from area maps. Now it seemed impossible that I could just drive in following printed directions.

The road spilled abruptly onto the wide, flat Oak Ridge Turnpike. A billboard emblazoned with an American flag advertised in-home nursing to uranium workers. Once, uranium was named only in code in this place. A few minutes later, I passed between two empty white guardhouses. Oaggridge.

A beginning. In the spring of 1942, Manhattan Project scouts bounced along dirt roads, past ragged farms, modest schoolhouses, and simple churches. They were searching for a place to hide a secret whose ultimate size was unknown. The site needed to accommodate three nuclear production plants, as well as housing for all those required for the effort: scientists, construction workers, secretaries, electricians, military personnel, as well their children and spouses, and the teachers, nurses, doctors, and shopkeepers needed to ensure the town's self-sufficiency.

The men searched for what they knew would be necessary, ticking through the requirements. Water: plenty, cool, and continuous. A railroad that could carry labor and supplies from across the country without drawing too much attention. Electricity: How much? More than most rural areas could supply. And—in case something went wrong—the site should lie at least ten miles from the closest major population center. Finally, but perhaps most important of all, it must be hidden from view; no one could know or even guess its purpose.

In the bursting green of a southern spring, the men's eyes alighted on the parallel tracks of the Louisville and Nashville Railroad on the snaking curve of the Clinch River, and on the TVA's hydroelectric Norris Dam, sixteen miles upstream. They liked the hills too: each tucked in its separate valley, the nuclear plants would be shielded from prying eyes, while the ridges provided natural protection for the townsite, in case of an accident.

In a photograph, the men—engineers and scientists flown down from New York—stand on a railroad track between steep, scrubby hillsides. In rumpled suits, they're stiff and out of place, squinting beneath the felt brims of their hats. Another photograph, without the men, shows a silvered expanse of water, a grassy shoreline, and a tree on a finger of land, its shadow pooling in the water below.

For a time, the Tennessee site was weighed against a stretch of land in Illinois, forty miles from Chicago. A report stamped SECRET considered the relative merits of each: Chicago offered better access to medical facilities and proximity to laboratories researching radiation, desirable due to the presence of "unusual occupational hazards" including "the dangers of uranium poisoning" and "the hazard from the gamma rays and neutrons" inherent in the work. Tennessee offered more room for expansion if the needs of the project should grow. And it was feared that a large nuclear plant forty miles outside of Chicago was likely to be spotted by picnickers disembarking from the New York Central Railroad, while there was "no reason why the [Tennessee] site should ever be noticed except by the local inhabitants." In the end, size and secrecy were decisive.

The report described the homes of these inconsequential local inhabitants as "scattered houses" and "very small settlements" with a few churches and cemeteries. The engineers did not name the farm towns within the proposed site—Scarboro, Wheat, Elza, Robertsville, and New Hope—but they did map the geologic makeup of every ridge and valley, drawing thick, color-coded stripes in bright green, orange, blue, and pink across the tight black swirls of their topographical maps. The land, as they saw it, was nearly empty.

These ridged woodlands had been beloved and lived in by Native peoples for thousands of years before the Spanish, and then the English and French, marched in, bringing disease and genocide.

Hundreds of years of settler encroachment, warfare, coerced land cessions, broken treaties, and forced removal decimated the population and stripped the people from land. Though the 1791 Treaty of Holston had "solemnly guarantee[d] to the Cherokee nation, all their lands not hereby ceded," the Cherokee were once again forced to renegotiate in 1798, ceding the land that would become Oak Ridge in the First Treaty of Tellico on October 2.

By 1942, most of the thousand families counted for removal for the bomb project were poor farmers. They learned they'd be evicted that fall, when they answered their doors to grim government officials or returned from their fields at dusk to find notices tacked to front doors or to the old oak trees that shaded their porches—"The War Department intends to take possession of your farm." No further explanation would be given.

Thirty years after what was done could not be undone, one local explained in an oral history interview: "It was always the 'homeplace' that they spoke of you see. Among people in East Tennessee the connotations of the term 'homeplace' are rather profound. I know that personally, you see . . . because I have that in my makeup and my character. I love the mountains and the hills and the earth and the rivers and so forth. No place else is home and I can't make it that way and don't really want to."

As the government prepared to take possession of the existing houses inside the new townsite, appraisers photographed each structure: every house with flaking or fresh paint, every smokehouse, springhouse, tenant cabin, and poultry house. No matter how fertile the fields, how well-kept the houses, appraisal reports described the homes as "poor," "unattractive," "inconvenient," and "very ordinary." Sometimes families posed somberly in front of their homes, arrayed barefoot on dirt driveways. Some were given as little as two weeks to leave and, in the rush, abandoned cellars full of canned vegetables, fields ripe for harvest, shoes, pans, mementos, even wandering livestock. They left as thousands of construction workers flooded in, ready to dismantle their homes, flatten their fields, chop down their orchards.

Yet even the photographs, poor consolation though they were, marked a privilege extended only to those who could lay formal claim to the land. Tenant farmers and sharecroppers, many the descendants of enslaved people, were never counted nor compensated, as many as three thousand people excluded from the official reckoning. If they are seen in the photographs, they are at the edges, accidental: a child playing in a yard, a woman crossing a field.

How many erasures this place was built on. Poor farmers evicted from their homes, sharecroppers with no legal claim over the land they worked, African people forcibly torn from their homelands, the Indigenous Peoples—including the Cherokee, Yuchi, and Shawnee—who'd loved and lost this land long before Oak Ridge was ever dreamed of. What is it to love a home founded on such violence for the sake of further violence?

On that December day, I drove through town past strip malls and car dealerships, reading what was once hidden behind fences and cloaked in coded language announced on local business signs. The Y-12 Federal Credit Union. Atomic City Computers. Secret City Auto Sales. Most of the signs carried the same symbol—three or four overlapping ellipses representing the paths of zooming electrons orbiting a heavy nucleus. At the Catholic church, a beatific Mary balanced barefoot atop an orb bearing the image of this city's pride.

In the official Seal of the City of Oak Ridge, a variation of the stylized atom, an acorn serves as the nucleus. What story does the city want to tell about itself? The nucleus is the anchor that holds the electrons in orbit, the vital center that makes the atom more than just a handful of free-floating particles. An acorn suggests roots, organic growth, respect for land and history. But in a nuclear bomb, it is the nucleus that splits, the fracturing of that heavy center that blazes into the God-defying energy that melts deserts and disappears cities. It was the splitting of the nucleus that made this city possible.

In early 1943, officials from the Manhattan Engineer District, the Army Corps of Engineers division created to build and manage all aspects of the nuclear effort, approached the civilian architectural firm Skidmore, Owings & Merrill to design the townsite. Though it would have been easier and cheaper to build an army base, the District judged that happy workers would be more likely to stay on the job. The design needed to be pleasant enough for a civilian population; the town needed to feel like home.

The architects were given topographical maps with identifying labels cut out and asked to design a town in an unnamed location for an undisclosed purpose. Population approximately thirteen thousand. While the Army Corps may have been concerned with resident comfort for purely practical reasons, the architects allowed themselves to dream. They drew roads that wound along the hills and neighborhoods with centrally located schools and shopping centers, positioned houses to take advantage of natural light, and imagined the trees and flowers that would grow in generous yards and parks. The blank slate was an architect's dream. One of the architects, Nathaniel Owings, admitted: "All we wanted was a series of homely little American villages tied together with a road to take care of the long-distance traffic and permit the men to be on time to work." Every single-family house was to have a porch and a fireplace.

On paper, the plans were lovely; the site stretched long and narrow, seven by seventeen miles, and the roads turned and branched among the hills, following no regular pattern but mimicking, rather, some organic logic, the houses like so many leaves lining tangled vines.

"In theory," Owings reflected, "this terrain offered the perfect opportunity: a kind of clean, uncluttered, uncommitted area with nothing to stand in the way of an ideal plan."

The army and the architects designed a system of roads that would curve with the land but adhere to an ordered rationality. The avenues would be named after states, moving alphabetically from east to west: Arkansas, California, Delaware, Florida, with Illinois toward the middle of the city and Wisconsin to the western end, a deconstructed national map overlaying the once-rural landscape. Roads, lanes, and circles branching from the avenues would take the first letter of the avenues' names; from Arkansas Avenue would come Albany Road, Atlanta Road, and Aspen Lane. It was the perfect scheme for a city that would welcome scientists from across the country, whose purpose was national despite its backwoods location.

Yet as the architects carried their papers into the field, climbing the hills to mark the paths of roads and locations of buildings, they kept running into little country cemeteries, humble gravestones peeking through fallen leaves or unmarked fieldstones above soft depressions in the earth. The living had been dispensed with neatly, but the dead proved more awkward. Everywhere, the architects had to adjust their plans around these little plots scattered across the land.

By the summer of 1943, the estimated population of Oak Ridge had increased from thirteen thousand to forty-two thousand; the city's population would rise to seventy-five thousand by the spring of 1945. Careful plans were abandoned as the architects and the army scrambled to house the rapidly growing population. The roads remained gravel and mud, the sidewalks rough wooden boardwalks, and only the most important scientists and highly ranked military personnel were given homes with porches and fireplaces. Trailers, dormitories, and flimsy flattops were added to accommodate common soldiers, construction workers, and plant employees, crowding into open spaces set aside for fields of wildflowers, even into Gamble Valley, which hugged Y-12, land meant to remain empty in case of an accident.

The day before George and Doris were set to arrive—November 21, 1943—George was informed by telegram that no housing was yet available for him and his wife. "Quarters can be had in city of Knoxville provided you come immediately," the telegram advised. They would live in several places, first in Knoxville and then inside Oak Ridge, before finally being transferred to a little flattop house on a steep lot in June 1944, a place they could call their own.

At the height of construction, a house was completed every thirty minutes. Residents joked that there were two ways to get to Oak Ridge: take the bus or stand in an empty field and wait for the city to be constructed around you. The second method might prove more reliable—the roads changed so rapidly that bus drivers often got lost and had to ask their passengers for directions.

Under the strain of constant construction, the land melted into mud that ran in ruddy rivulets down the streets, sucking shoes off of feet, staining the hems of skirts and cuffs of pants, and creeping up the stoops to paint the town brown. Women tramped to dances in evening gowns and knee-high rubber boots and carried clean shoes into Knoxville so they wouldn't be identified as residents of *that government town.*

What was left of the people who came before—squash vines and cornstalks, flecks of rust from old farm tools, the frayed end of a rope swing—was mashed down into the earth, smoothed indistinguishably beneath the mud, all soon to be covered with the stony dust of new construction. A country church, a couple of log cabins, some weathered farmhouses were repurposed as storage or overflow housing, strange and soft beside the severe modern lines of the new buildings. And the fences were reused; curls of barbed wire salvaged from cattle fields were stretched across the edges of the site. Inside, the city appeared to be a world reborn in all of its primordial muck.

Though Doris's heart may have sunk when she saw the muddy, half-built town, she was the kind of woman the city needed—hardworking, self-sufficient, and committed to the appearance of cheerfulness. George, I imagine, was grateful for a new beginning. His childhood had not been a happy one. His father was a stern and unkind taskmaster who valued work above all else. With long days dictated by the rhythms of the farm—up before dawn for the milking, in the fields till dusk—there was little time for joy or play in the Strasser household. George, short and bookish, was not the sort of strapping, hardworking laborer his father respected. Oak Ridge was the fresh start he craved, the rural farmland of his childhood wiped clean for something new and better. And so he would report for work in a brand-new lab on a sprawling campus of stark buildings bristling with pipes and wires.

As a married couple, George and Doris escaped the dormitories many of their single peers were assigned to. While their tiny flattop, set on stilts with plywood walls and a tar-covered canvas roof, left something to be desired, they were far more privileged than many.

In the planning of the city, the architects had designed a separate "Negro Village" on the east side of town. Though segregated, the village was to be composed of the same types of homes as the rest of the town and would have its own school, stores, church, and cafeteria. Yet in the frenzied rush to find housing for the ballooning population, the site set aside for the Negro Village became another white neighborhood. One official even suggested that Black workers would not be comfortable in the nice houses originally planned for the Negro Village, that they would prefer inferior conditions similar to what he claimed they were used to.

The housing area for Black residents was instead shunted to a swampy, low-lying area adjacent to Y-12, in blatant disregard for the safety policy requiring plants to be separated from residential areas by ridges that could shield homes from hazardous releases. There, Black workers—who made up some 10 percent of the Oak Ridge workforce—lived in flimsy plywood "hutments," five or six beds crowded into a 256-square-foot box around an oil stove. The dirt-floor shacks were dark, uninsulated, and poorly ventilated, without running water or electricity. Due to these poor conditions, the majority of Black workers lived in Knoxville and commuted into the city for work.

Compromises in living conditions—from the little indignities white residents had to put up with to the outright injustices Black residents were subject to—were justified under the logic that everything was temporary, that there was a war to be won, that sacrifices must be made. No thought of what it all would cost or of what would come after.

Businesses in the town could secure leases only for the duration of the war, and even the sturdiest houses—called cemestos for their lightweight frames of cement mixed with asbestos—were given a life expectancy of just twenty-five years. Optimistically named Victory Cottages, made of prefabricated plywood walls and roll roofing, they held two families and were built to last no more than three years.

During the war, Oak Ridge had no free press, no free assembly, and only the shell of local government. Production workers within the plants worked long hours under hazardous conditions, and union activities were severely restricted. Those who complained might be visited by a security agent, even terminated.

In a September 1944 memo titled "Number of Deaths at the Oak Ridge Hospital," the chief of clinical services in Oak Ridge, Dr. Charles E. Rea, reported an average of 8.8 deaths per month during the ten months the hospital had been open. He went on, "The question has arisen as to whether it is desirous to have a funeral home in the Area. If there is a funeral home, there probably will have to be a cemetery."

Perhaps he was thinking of the cemeteries from the displaced populations that still dotted the city. A cemetery would prove inconvenient when it came time to pack up after the war. It was decided that "with the adequate facilities for embalming in the surrounding towns a funeral home on the Area is not necessary at this time."

Instead of bodies, they buried barrels of radioactive waste in shallow, unlined trenches and drained contaminated wastewater into local creeks.

Although few signs are left of the people who called this land "homeplace," the cemeteries lie there still, more than seventy of them scattered throughout the city. Some have only a couple of family graves, others more than a hundred; some have no gravestones at all, are the resting place of an unknown number. They are tucked behind housing complexes, in patches of woods, off of busy central roads, and on restricted land. When the Atomic Energy Commission

(AEC), the civilian agency created to manage America's growing nuclear industry after World War II, took control of Oak Ridge, they inherited the odd duty of maintaining some of the Oak Ridge area cemeteries. The Department of Energy (DOE), the AEC's successor, continues this task. With a security escort, the descendants of those buried in secured areas within the plants' fences can enter the gates and honor their dead.

I realized I'd been driving past one of the cemeteries on my way into the city from the lake. One afternoon, I slowed as I approached the brown sign for the African Burial Ground. I made a sharp turn onto a nearly hidden gravel road and drove up a steep incline. The road leveled before a black iron fence, softened by green mold, surrounding what looked at first to be just an empty patch of woods, thick-carpeted in leaves. It took a moment before I could spot the lichen-covered gravestones—small, rough-chiseled, and unmarked. A white plaque bearing a stenciled number two was nailed to a tree. Bark lipped over the top edge, slowly consuming the sign. Atomic Energy Commission Cemetery #2.

A gleaming block of marble dedicated the site to the African people who "lived, worked, and died in bondage" in the old farming town of Wheat. On a smaller, gray slab of marble, there was a short historical description of the cemetery listing the names of the area's slave-holding families. There was little information about the estimated ninety to one hundred people buried in this ground. I knelt to examine the offerings scattered around the base of the marble: a handful of pennies, a couple of faded silk flowers, a small cross fashioned from two sticks held together by a hair band, a metal bangle, a golf tee, a crayon, a guitar pick, a sprig of lavender, two tins of snuff. A couple strands of Mardi Gras beads, faded purple and gold, draped across the top of the monument. I lifted one and let it drop back against the cold marble, heard the clack of plastic against stone.

The air was chill, the day neither bright nor dim, sunshine filtering through white clouds. Beside the fence encircling the graves, a yellow gate, US Department of Energy 5-P, blocked a road vanishing into the woods. Judging by the fallen leaves, the road had not recently been used.

Through the trees, I glimpsed the site of the K-25 gaseous diffusion plant across the turnpike, where my grandmother took a job as a clerk toward the end of the war. Inside that massive building, as she filed memos or checked charts whose meaning she could only guess at, her belly began to swell with her first pregnancy. Oak Ridge was not the home she had imagined for her future children—when did she begin to suspect she might never leave?

Uranium enrichment processes at K-25 were shut down in 1985, and decommissioning began in 2002. By the time I stood above the whispering highway on that December day, K-25 lay half demolished, bricks, pipes, and crumbled concrete bagged and buried in the Oak Ridge nuclear waste landfill or shipped to the Nevada desert. From my perch, all I could see was a long, low brick building and an imposing white tower.

I searched for some kind of lesson, some logic in this convergence—a cemetery for enslaved people beside one of the world's first nuclear weapons plants. "We will never know the names of those buried here," read the historical description. I thought of how, in the chaos after the bombings of Hiroshima and Nagasaki, a full accounting of the death toll could not be made. At Hiroshima's memorial, there is a stone tomb containing a blank book dedicated to the unknown dead. So many lives erased on both sides of this American history.

A funeral home opened its doors in Oak Ridge in 1950. By the time a cemetery was established in 1955, George was working as the assistant plant manager of Y-12, supervising the production of fuel for hydrogen bombs. Doris was raising three kids, soon to be four, in a still-sturdy cemesto house.

Seventy years after they were built, many of the cemesto homes, meant to last only twenty-five years, still stand, though their sameness is hidden now beneath fresh paint, brick walls, gabled roofs, and new additions. You can still spot them, though—the same repeated shape, same angled orientation on the lot, same distance from the road.

Today, the 120-acre Oak Ridge Memorial Park, the city's first cemetery, promises "perpetual care" to the eleven thousand graves placed there in the last seven decades.

The DOE also ensures perpetual care to the hazardous waste landfill covering 120 acres in Bear Creek Valley west of Y-12, known, inelegantly, as the Environmental Management Waste Management Facility (EMWMF). Opened in 2002, the EMWMF is the disposal site of contaminated soils, dismantled buildings, and radioactive scrap materials, as the DOE undertakes the Superfund cleanup of the Oak Ridge site. The landfill is nearing its capacity of more than two million cubic yards, and a new landfill of similar size is being planned at an estimated cost of $700–900 million.

At a much smaller cost, the DOE still maintains thirty-two historic cemeteries. "Perpetual care" means that when the landfill is capped, the DOE will monitor and maintain the lined cells against leakage and decay, forever.

5

# KIN

Like my grandparents, Colleen and Dot were Oak Ridge originals; they'd moved to the secret city during the war, full of patriotism and young energy, and never left. Though they didn't meet my grandmother until after the war, they became some of her closest friends, the moms who shared carpooling and babysitting duties while their husbands worked long hours at the plant doing God-knows-what. Perhaps most crucially, they shared a weekly bridge game, adhered to with an almost religious regularity.

I met them at their assisted living home on Laboratory Road in Oak Ridge. Colleen intercepted me in the lobby, her face pale between a red beret and purple sequined scarf, and steered me to a hospital-bright room, optimistically called the Coffee Shop, where Dot, with her close-cropped white hair, was waiting. I must have met them in passing when I was little—Dot and her husband owned the house next door to ours at the lake, and my father speaks of Colleen like a beloved and eccentric aunt—but I don't remember. They greeted me with an easy familiarity; they didn't know me, but they knew my people.

"Now, remind me, honey—are you Dale's daughter?" asked Colleen.

"Yes, that's right."

She nodded, satisfied to place me within her map of my family. We sipped burned coffee from Styrofoam cups.

"And how nice you're learning more about your grandparents and Oak Ridge." Colleen nodded approvingly. Her accent, with its warm, lilting vowels, comforted me, reminding me of my grandmother's. "Now holler if you need anything!" Meemaw used to call out when I went to the bathroom; it always made me giggle—what could happen to me in the bathroom? My world was looked after, contained.

"You know," Colleen continued, "me and George, we kinda kin." In response to my puzzled expression, she added, "Well, sometimes we say we kin to the same thing or we kin to each other. George and I, our families in Nashville, we kin to the same thing."

I understood she meant that she and George were distant cousins of some sort. I was familiar with this southern preoccupation with kinship—my great aunt Nell, Meemaw's older sister, would greet strangers by interrogating them until she could find a common relation or at least an acquaintance. It was a sort of game, to see how quickly she could find a connection, her way of orienting herself in the world. My father recalled taking her to the Second City comedy club when she visited him in Chicago; after settling in and looking around apprehensively at the packed club, she turned to the startled businessman sitting next to her, stuck out her hand, and said in her sweet-as-honey accent, "Hi, I'm Nell Lafon, and I'm from Jackson, Tennessee."

And so with Colleen, I was not only the granddaughter of an old friend but also a distant relation. One of hers.

Oak Ridge, under military rule, curated a very particular sort of family. To pull off the massive project, efficiently and in secret, the city needed people who were hardworking, obedient, and unquestioningly loyal. Before letting George into the inner sanctum, security agents had to find out what sort of man he was. Was he loyal? Could he keep a secret? Could he be blackmailed? Would he turn spy?

Strasser. The name came from his father, a man of German ancestry, raised on American soil by his immigrant parents. Initially, this heritage caused some consternation among the agents overseeing George's security clearance. The Germans were the enemy, after all. Still, the plant needed scientists, and a longtime neighbor attested on a security questionnaire: "His father is of German parentage but entire family are fine loyal American Citizens." It was decided that George could be trusted to serve the country embraced by his grandfather.

The question of loyalty thus satisfied, George's security clearance was authorized in a memo dated November 10, 1943: "Since this report would indicate that applicant would make a satisfactory employee we are giving him our approval." Among Mr. Strasser's "satisfactory" qualities were the facts that he was married, resided in a "reputable section" of Nashville (read: white, middle class), and was a man of "good moral character, habits and reputation, known as honest and dependable." His personal references all testified to his "reputation for honesty and integrity" and confirmed that he did not drink.

One step remained before George would be allowed to enter the top-secret uranium enrichment plant where he would serve as "Jr. Chemist #2." On November 22, 1943, he signed his employee's agreement, which stipulated total silence on his work both during and after his employ with Tennessee Eastman Corporation, the government contractor engaged to run the plant. *I will not at any time disclose either orally or in writing, or otherwise . . . any knowledge or information which I may have acquired while in the employ of Tennessee Eastman Corporation. . . .*

George's security clearance was granted on November 24.

Claims of kinship tug on our loyalty, coaxing us to duty or sacrifice in the name of familial love. "Whose son will die in the last minute of the war?" asked one Oak Ridge wartime billboard in bold black letters beside a grisly painting of a battle scene—a tangle of limbs, a man flopped over on the forking trunk of a tree, and one soldier still upright, back to an explosion, casting a gaunt face skyward. "Minutes count!" the billboard admonished.

Another showed a soldier resting beneath a tropical tree, face scrunched in pain or concentration, a thought bubble billowing from his head, holding the image of a stiff-smiling woman and dark-eyed baby. "Just what are you doing to make this dream come true?" the text implored.

The workers of Oak Ridge, of course, did not know just what they were doing. To protect the secret at the center of this vast enterprise, each saw only what they needed to see and spoke as little as possible. The lack of information led to wild rumors, speculation, and jokes. One woman, whose job involved collecting urine samples from potential employees during their physicals, was convinced that urine was the essential ingredient in whatever was being built. Others thought they were making fourth-term campaign buttons for FDR or a special kind of paint that would be poured on the ocean to cover the periscopes of German U-boats; unable to tell that they had surfaced, the subs would continue to rise out of the water and expose themselves. When faced with questions from curious locals outside of the city, Oak Ridgers answered with playful evasion.

*What are you making out there?*

"The bottom half of horses."

"Windshield wipers for submarines."

"Eighty cents an hour."

*How many people are working out there?*

"Oh, I guess about half of 'em."

Anyone who was too curious or persistent would be visited by a security agent.

As they welded pipes, sorted papers, polished concrete floors, all without a clue about what any of it added up to, the Oak Ridge workers needed to be taught that they, too, were soldiers fighting to preserve what was most precious. *Minutes count.*

"Loose talk helps our enemy," warned another billboard.

As we sipped coffee under fluorescent lights, Dot and Colleen told me how they'd come to Oak Ridge. Colleen's family moved to the city when she was eighteen, after one of her brothers went into the army. "My mother wanted all of us to come and go to work and win the war, go back home, and get back to normal," she recalled.

Colleen worked as a leak test operator, climbing around the immense pipes in the basement of the plant, running a probe over every inch and welded joint. Inside the maze of pipes, gaseous uranium hexafluoride was pumped through a series of porous barriers that gradually sifted uranium-235 (U-235) from uranium-238 (U-238). Colleen wasn't told that, though; she was just warned to evacuate if she ever smelled "anything funny."

Dot had lost a brother at Pearl Harbor and was eager to join the war effort. But she also had her own reasons for jumping at the chance to work in the secret city, motivated more by the life she dreamed of than the one she'd come from.

Dot had grown up in a rural West Tennessee farmhouse without plumbing or electricity, using the pages of a Sears, Roebuck and Co. catalog for toilet paper. As soon as she graduated high school in 1944, she left the farm and set out looking for a job in Oak Ridge. "I came actually to meet a nice man who was well educated. 'Cause I came from the farm and I was smart enough to know I didn't want to marry a farmer," she said.

After six weeks of training, she began her job as a cubicle operator at Y-12, the uranium enrichment plant where George worked as a chemist. There, Dot sat on a high stool for eight hours a day, six days a week, monitoring a number of dials as she'd been instructed. "We just had a certain job like turning knobs, which anyone that was bright would be able to do. And then if the machine started acting up and making noises, real bad noises, then we would call in the technical guy."

The machine was a calutron, used to enrich the uranium that would wind up in the Hiroshima bomb, but Dot didn't know that. What she knew was that the varying hours of her shift work allowed her to juggle three men at once. "I had the cutest little guy—I loved him. I had to give him up, though, for Paul. I don't know if he had any money." Paul was Dot's technical supervisor and would become her husband. "I decided the day I saw him that he was gonna be mine. I wrote on his shirt in shorthand, 'I love you.'"

"That same day that you met him?" asked Colleen, arching her eyebrows.

"Well, it wasn't—it was the first week, somewhere," conceded Dot.

I could see why, of the two, Colleen was the one regularly tapped for interviews. While Dot reveled in irreverence, playing her audience for startled laughs, Colleen was concerned with accuracy, her delivery practiced and smooth. By the time I met her, she was something of a prom queen of Oak Ridge history, her memories and interviews featured in history books, documentaries, radio stories. When Dot strayed from the topic at hand, Colleen reeled her back in. From time to time, she'd glance at my notebook as if to say, *Okay now, let's get back to your homework.*

"So, when we first came to Oak Ridge, it was very crowded. And what else? It was seventy-five thousand people here. And you couldn't get housing. In order to get a house, you had to qualify to go on a list, and you got it from your employer, didn't you, and you didn't just go and look around and find a house." She rattled off the basic facts with an easy rhythm and looked over to make sure I was taking notes.

Both vividly remembered the mud everywhere. And the lines—the lines for rations, for laundry. The shortages. "It was hard to be a glamour girl because everything had gone to war." Colleen shook her head mournfully, the light winking off her sequined scarf. Bobby pins, metal curlers, elastic, and nylons, all repurposed for parachutes, bullets, airplanes. In place of hose, Colleen drew a seam up the back of her leg with makeup. "If it rained, look out!" Still, despite the hardships of life in wartime Oak Ridge, Dot and Colleen mostly remembered the excitement of being young and single in the secret city.

By war's end, the average age of the Oak Ridge population was twenty-seven. And for those young people, this strange and barren city was full of opportunity, a chance to begin lives their parents couldn't have imagined. Because most Oak Ridgers were young and new to the area, separated from family by distance, fences, and the code of secrecy that prevented frank communication with the outside world, they quickly formed close bonds. "In this climate," writes anthropologist Janice Harper, "kinship based on ancestry and biology was replaced with a new form of 'kinship' based on marital alliances and fosterage among families who quickly came to depend upon each other for exchange of information (limited though it was), access to suitable housing, strategic resources, and childcare." So, too, being an insider of the secret city created a sort of conspiratorial closeness among its residents.

"Everyone was more patriotic then," Colleen told me. "I came here, and they said, 'You're not to tell anybody anything.' And I didn't know. I mean, I had never studied chemistry or any of that stuff, so I didn't even know what they were doing." Colleen shook her head, eyes wide. "And I didn't ask. I know that's strange, but we weren't supposed to ask. We knew it was a secret."

Dot was too busy dating and securing a husband to wonder much about what she was doing. Later, she understood that had been part of the plan all along. "They wanted these little high school women that could be bossed around."

Previously, only PhD scientists had operated the calutrons, but the scale of operations at Oak Ridge demanded other labor, and managers found that recently graduated high school girls did as well or better than the PhDs. They were diligent and dexterous, and because they didn't understand what they were doing, they didn't fuss with the settings to optimize output like the PhDs did; abiding by the rules without understanding purpose or consequence proved to be the most efficient strategy.

"The little high school girls, they would fit right in there and do exactly what they were told," Dot said, remembering what her husband told her after the war.

"In everything the District built was imbedded the philosophy that those who lived and worked there should be utterly alienated from their work, ignorant of its significance, yet willing and efficient, perfect machines, in all that they did," writes historian Peter Hales.

"We were so stupid we didn't know anything else," said Colleen. "Isn't that crazy? We were programmed for doing that."

Years after the gates of Oak Ridge were opened for good, residents would recall how the fences had made them feel safe. Everyone on the inside had been vetted, shared the same patriotic purpose. Many didn't feel the need to lock their doors. "We were all part of a family that lived here, and it was like you could go anywhere, you could do anything," recalled a woman of the childhood she'd spent in wartime Oak Ridge. "There was no crime, you could go on vacation, leave your doors open. You know, if somebody needed to go in and borrow a cup of sugar while you were gone, they were free to do that."

There is a common narrative of Oak Ridge as a great equalizer, a kind of utopia. It was a place where poor farmers' daughters like Dot could find college-educated husbands. Where the schools were excellent, health care was universal, and a free, extensive bus system could whisk one to an abundance of recreation and cultural activities, including a symphony, theater, sports leagues, and the South's largest swimming pool. Prefabricated houses curtailed ostentatious displays of wealth. Some Oak Ridgers liked to call themselves "class-unconscious." The city's first church, where both Dot and Colleen would be married, was a modest but graceful white clapboard structure shared by Catholic, Protestant, and Jewish worshippers called the Chapel on the Hill. Some would remember wartime Oak Ridge as "a beautiful enclave," even a "Camelot."

A commemorative booklet celebrating Oak Ridge's twenty-fifth anniversary glowingly recounted the wartime community spirit: "People from every walk of life and from all parts of the world were bonded together in a great effort and a great adventure." My father still remembers the lyrics to a catchy song from a musical produced to commemorate the same anniversary: "Oak Ridge is a place for the whole human race!" One nuclear family.

Yet Oak Ridge was not a Camelot for everyone. "I just thought it was the worst place though when I first come up here," recalled a Black woman named Kattie Strickland in an oral history video interview. She was regal in a maroon velvet hat and fur-collared coat.

Military propaganda may have touted unity and sacrifice, but housing, assigned based on job type, marital status, and race, enforced strict hierarchies. Married white couples like George and Doris lived in tidy apartments or flattop homes, while single white women lived in dormitories governed by strict rules, and single white male laborers lived in trailers or stuffy plywood hutments. Sturdy, single-family homes running along a ridge housed top civilian and military officials beside world-renowned scientists; popularly, Knob Hill was known as "Snob Hill."

Lowest down the ladder were the Black workers, some seven thousand of the Oak Ridge workforce, who were recruited from throughout the southeast to serve as maids, janitors, truck drivers, porters, and construction workers. Promised high-paying jobs, they were given one-way bus fare or loaded onto train cars bound for an unknown destination.

In 1941, President Roosevelt had issued an executive order that there would be no discrimination in the defense industries. However, Black workers arrived in Oak Ridge to find that, despite Roosevelt's decree, this place would not be so unlike others. The Fair Employment Practices Committee had inadequate legal power and did little to protect Black workers in the secret city, where security restrictions and lack of media presence obscured blatantly discriminatory practices from scrutiny.

On paper, Black residents were not limited to the miserable, swampy hutments, but since housing was assigned based on employment, and Black people were hired only for the lowest-ranking positions, they did not qualify for anything better. Even the handful of workers in positions considered more skilled, such as Black nurses, were given barely-livable accommodations in cramped Victory Cottages. Brilliant Black scientists who'd been working on the

Manhattan Project in Chicago and New York were not allowed to transfer to Oak Ridge with their teams.

Though segregation in that era and region was widespread, this was something worse. Housing for Black workers was separated by gender, and there was no place even for married couples to live. Kattie could visit her husband's hut, shared by several other men, but had to return to her own before curfew at 10 p.m. The women's housing area, dubbed "the pen" by those confined there, was encircled by barbed wire and an electric fence and patrolled by armed guards who could enter the women's hutments at any hour without warning. Purportedly, this was meant to "protect" the women.

For Kattie, though, it wasn't the crowded hutments, the mud and rats, or even the fact that her time with her husband was regulated by a curfew that made her call this the worst place she'd ever seen. It was that she had to leave her four daughters behind because Oak Ridge offered no accommodations for Black families until close to the end of the war, when a small number of hutments were converted to shoddy family housing. "I said, 'Lord have mercy.' I thought like I was going to the back side of the world from my kids," she recalled.

Determined and resourceful, Kattie put up with it all for the sake of the high paychecks—she made nearly double sweeping floors, scrubbing bathrooms, and polishing tanks at K-25 than she'd made cleaning the library in Auburn, Alabama. She supplemented her wages by selling beer and cigarettes to eager neighbors and extra sugar to diners at the cafeteria. "I didn't like the place, but I just liked what I was making," she said, then let out a low, dry chuckle, "the money."

When the cafeteria food made her sick, she resolved to find a way to cook for herself, her husband, and her friends over the oil stove in her husband's hutment despite the rules forbidding it. She asked a construction worker to weld her a biscuit pan from scrap metal, and a taste of her perfectly browned biscuits was enough to convince the guards to look the other way.

Her pragmatism and frank humor remind me of Dot, and I imagine, at another time, in another place, in another world, these two might have hit it off. Yet it's unlikely they ever crossed paths. Black and white workers rode separate or divided buses, began work shifts by punching in at separate "clock alleys," worked under separate foremen, and ate in separate cafeterias. Even the road connecting the Black housing area to the town center was fenced off from the white housing area.

In the months following the war, Enoch Waters, a reporter from the *Chicago Defender*, a weekly African American newspaper, wrote a series of damning articles about the disgraceful conditions for Black residents in Oak Ridge. "It is the first community I have ever seen with slums that were deliberately planned. . . . [It] is as backward sociologically as the atomic bomb is advanced scientifically," he wrote.

The federal government justified the segregation by declaring that it could not "afford to sponsor social experiments" and claimed to defer to local custom regarding race relations. In fact, Waters wrote, East Tennessee had always been one of the more liberal parts of the state; the hilly landscape was not conducive to large plantations, so slavery had never been a major part of the local economy, and a significant number of East Tennesseans had sided with the Union in the Civil War. By 1800, there was a thriving community of free Black people in Knoxville; Black residents founded the city's first fire department, and worked as policemen and public officials as early as the late 1800s. "It is apparent," wrote Waters, "that the government, far from adopting 'local custom,' has introduced at Oak Ridge a social pattern that is actually foreign to the area."

In the climate of unquestioning loyalty demanded by Oak Ridge, to name the hypocrisy was unpatriotic. In the summer of 1944, a group of Black residents, who'd organized themselves as the Colored Camp Council, petitioned for some modest, equitable accommodations for Black families. Addressing a colonel, they appealed, "We feel that you, as a high official in the American

Army in which so many Negro youth are fighting and dying for democracy and the preservation of America, will sympathize with the requests of those of us who are laboring on the home front to supply the battle front." The petitioners were not granted houses, but they were subjected, without their knowledge, to detailed security investigations.

"If through the work done here America has advanced science, it is equally true that in the way it has forced Negroes to live here America has retarded the cause of democracy," wrote Waters. "And this is ironical because it was to preserve democracy that this whole project was brought into being."

Early on the morning of March 24, 1945, a car of six Black workers bound for the K-25 plant pulled around a stalled government vehicle and crashed head-on into an oncoming dump truck in a chaos of screeching metal and the smell of burned rubber.

The workers were taken to the Oak Ridge hospital. One of them, Ebb Cade, a middle-aged cement worker, had broken both legs and an arm. Of interest to the doctors was that he was a "colored male," "well developed" and "well nourished." He would be called HP-12. HP stood for "Human Product."

The doctors delayed setting his bones for nearly three weeks. Letters circulated between Los Alamos and Oak Ridge. Nurses collected Ebb's urine, stored the samples. Detailed instructions arrived, along with a glass vial of plutonium. On April 10, a doctor filled a syringe with the contents of the vial, pressed the needle into the skin of Ebb's left arm, and plunged 4.7 micrograms of plutonium into his bloodstream, nearly five times what was then considered a safe dose.

The following day, the Sixth Armored Division of General Patton's Third Army marched into Buchenwald, one of the largest concentration camps within German borders. They were greeted by the cheers of some twenty-one thousand emaciated prisoners. The brutal labor camp had imprisoned some quarter million political dissenters, Jewish people, Roma, German deserters, and foreign prisoners of war, killing those too weak to work. Nazi scientists had also used prisoners to test vaccines for infectious diseases and treatments to "cure" homosexuality.

The Manhattan Project was justified in the name of securing a more righteous world order. The experiment on Ebb was justified in the name of developing safety standards for the nuclear workers who were, even then, being exposed to radiation and toxic hazards without full knowledge or adequate protection.

Ebb was told nothing. After being discharged, he returned to Greensboro, to his wife. He was a beloved uncle who brought bags of oranges to his nieces and nephews on Sundays. He died eight years later, at age sixty-three, apparently of heart failure.

Ebb Cade was the first of eighteen people to be injected with plutonium by Manhattan Project doctors in the name of medical research and one of thousands to be subjected to government-funded human radiation experiments without their consent during the Cold War. "Almost without exception," writes Eileen Welsome, an investigative journalist whose work was instrumental in uncovering these stories, "the subjects were the poor, the powerless, and the sick." They were inmates in state prisons, developmentally disabled children, poor pregnant women and their unborn children, working-class and Black patients checking into hospitals for cancer treatments.

Decades later, it would be difficult to ascertain how many knew about the human experiments. Paper trails disappeared into thin air. Many denied knowledge and responsibility. Welsome attributes the widespread justification of the experiments by doctors well aware of their ethical responsibilities to the culture of secrecy born of the Manhattan Project and solidified in the Cold War.

Decades after Ebb's injection, one Dr. Howland claimed he had performed the procedure against his own objections only when pushed by an order from his superior, Dr. Friedell. Dr. Friedell denied he'd ever given such an order and said that the injections had not been performed by Dr. Howland at all but by one Dr. Dwight Clark.

But this is not the story of the doctors and researchers who knew about, advocated for, and performed the injections on Ebb Cade and the others. This is not the story of the scientists who knew what it meant to build an atomic bomb, the generals who chose the targets, or the pilots who flew the planes. It is the story of the air around them, of the ordinary people who didn't know, who didn't ask, who looked away. Because serving, serving well, meant sticking to your business, meant cultivating a lack of curiosity about the work, about the town, about the lives of those unlike you. It meant sacrificing for a righteous fight while ignoring the injustices at your doorstep.

The month of Ebb Cade's car crash, Dot was married in a small evening ceremony at the Chapel on the Hill. As Ebb lay in his hospital bed, unaware of the plutonium slipping through his blood and bones, Dot lay awake in the little flattop house she'd moved into with her husband.

While the propaganda signs in Oak Ridge prompted residents to imagine the sufferings of soldiers on faraway battlefields, compartmentalization taught them not to extend such empathy to their neighbors. Later, as a result of the segregation that rendered the lives of Black residents invisible, or of simple denial, many white residents would claim ignorance of the conditions endured by their Black counterparts.

In his memoir published seven years after the war, General Leslie Groves, the Army Corps officer who oversaw the entire project, described the advantages of compartmentalization: "Adherence to this rule not only provided an adequate measure of security, but it greatly improved over-all efficiency by making our people stick to their knitting."

After the war, Kattie and her husband, Willie, stayed in the city, drawing a network of family and friends from Alabama to them. When housing opened up for Black families, they brought their children and eventually settled in Scarboro, the Black neighborhood established after the war in the still-segregated city, tucked into a valley adjacent to Y-12.

Valeria, Kattie's granddaughter, who grew up in Scarboro, moved away, and moved back, told me that Oak Ridge offered her grandparents a better quality of life than did the economically depressed and underdeveloped Alabama they'd come from. Here were good jobs, new houses with washing machines, electricity, running water, and a tight-knit community bonded by the hardships and injustice of the war years and solidified through the decades of segregation that followed. Oak Ridge, she told me, was "an opportunity to take whatever was given to you and make a community and a home for yourself."

Valeria loved growing up in Scarboro, where, cocooned by a loving family and strong community, she had everything she needed. "We knew that there were white people across town and what have you, but it was a wonderful place to grow up in. We played with one another. We had our school, and everything was good. I didn't know that I was poor. I felt like I was rich!"

By the end of the war, Dot was married to her college-educated husband. Colleen's family did return to Nashville, as their mother said they would, but Colleen never did. She'd been ambivalent about marriage, refusing her boyfriend's repeated proposals, but when news of the Nagasaki bombing reached Oak Ridge, she knew the war would soon be over, and, fearing her GI boyfriend would be shipped away and her mother would make her return to Nashville, she reversed that no to a yes. She was married three months later.

"It didn't take you guys long!" I laughed.

"That's right," laughed Colleen. "That's right. Got the job done."

Their stories always circled back around to this—not to the bomb, the end of the war, patriotism or victory or pride or guilt, but to the lives they began in the strange circumstances of the secret city. For these women, this was not a war story but an origin story.

In my family too, only one anecdote has survived from the day Oak Ridge learned of the bombing of Hiroshima: "Ma'am," my grandmother's boss purportedly told my pregnant grandmother after they'd heard the news, "your baby will be born in peacetime." Nine days later, on August 15, Emperor Hirohito announced Japan's surrender, and the formal agreement that officially ended World War II was signed two weeks after that. My aunt Karin was born in November. These were potent beginnings.

In Meemaw's drawers upstairs at the lake house, I found a tiny black-and-white picture of her standing with a group of eleven other women, all white, all holding their infants and toddlers. From her penciled note on the back, I gathered that this photograph was taken in February of 1946, when my aunt Karin was three months old.

These children are the pre-boomers, conceived before the assurance of peace but born in the blissful months after the war ended. The women's hair is curled and coiffed into soft and bouncy waves, and they wear straight-cut suit dresses and bold lipstick. Only about half look at the camera—the other half are engaged in trying to get their crying, squirming, or sleeping babies to look up.

Psychology tells us that our earliest lives instill patterns, fears, and insecurities we may not even be able to remember or articulate. What did those babies, wriggling in their mothers' arms, learn of silence before they could even speak? A father at a dinner table, brooding on some incident at the plant—a spill maybe, a technical puzzle, or his own nagging suspicion that he knows what they are building. Or a nurse who's noticed something strange about the treatment of the Black cement mixer, who knows three weeks is too long to leave bones unset, who feels in her gut what she will not speak even to herself. Or the wife cooped up at home with the baby, only rumors and her own imagination for company, because in this town, even gossip, even guesses are policed. And so there's just the click of silverware on ceramic, the smacking of lips, the rustle of napkins.

6

# Countdown

One proud Oak Ridge retiree read an early draft of my writing about the city. He marked up the margins with corrections and additions. In a portion in which I expressed uneasiness over the city's legacy, he reminded me emphatically, "We were at war!" He urged me to account for other instances of mass killings on both sides.

Beside a lyric, emotional passage, he wrote, "Poetry! Not reality!"

Though I'd finished college with a longish, meandering essay about George and Oak Ridge, I felt as if I'd barely begun to understand this history. The retiree's accusation of poetry landed like a punch. I worried that he was right—that in my preference for the emotional and metaphoric, I'd missed some essential grittiness, some solidity of fact. I worried that I, living on the other side of this split screen of history, had unfairly judged those who lived before.

So I resolved rigor. I'd wind myself back to the beginning to ask: How did this moment come to be? Where, *exactly*, did George fall in all of this? For what was he responsible? I resolved to know the numbers, to count them.

### Forty-Three Seconds

The design for the first atomic bomb sounds simple: a hollow cylinder of uranium, the projectile, was fired at very high speed into a solid cylinder of uranium, the target. When the two collided, they began a nuclear chain reaction, and a fraction of a second later, the bomb exploded, forever splitting history between the time before the atomic bomb and the time after.

In the hour before, the weather plane sent to scout for the *Enola Gay* radioed to report favorable conditions above Hiroshima. The morning was bright, the sky blue; the plane set its course for the city, cradled in the Seto Inland Sea on the southwestern edge of Japan's largest island. The target was a T-shaped bridge in the center of the city, spanning the bifurcation of the Ota River. At seventeen seconds past 8:15 a.m. on August 6, 1945, the *Enola Gay* released the bomb from a height of 31,600 feet.

The crew counted the seconds. One thousand one. One thousand two. They held their breath against the possibility that the bomb might not explode after all.

On the ground, an eight-year-old boy playing hide-and-seek with his friends closed his eyes and began to count.

The crew was nervous, and they counted too quickly. "I think we had all concluded that it was a dud," Theodore Van Kirk, navigator of the *Enola Gay*, would later recall of the forty-three seconds before the plane's cabin filled with the blinding white light of the bomb's explosion.

### Three Neutrons

A chain reaction begins when a stray neutron thrown from the nucleus of an atom runs into another nucleus, causing that atom to split apart, dislodging two more neutrons to collide with two more atoms, which break into more pieces, and so on. When atoms split—a process called fission—some of their mass (the $m$ in the equation $E = mc^2$) is converted to energy. When many atoms undergo fission all at once, as in a nuclear chain reaction inside a bomb, you get an enormous $E$ of fire and heat and light and wind.

Only some atoms are suited to splitting. Recall—an atom is a nucleus made of positively charged protons and neutral neutrons orbited by negatively charged electrons. Uranium, as the heaviest naturally occurring element on earth, is inherently unstable, with ninety-two positively charged protons straining against each other. Imagine trying to hold ninety-two magnets with all of their mutually repellant north poles facing inward. They would push against your hands, and some would find gaps between your fingers and go shooting out. So, too, uranium throws off bits of itself, little clumps of protons and neutrons called alpha particles. That's radioactive decay.

Inside the body, those stray pieces can knock electrons out of atoms, disrupt chemical bonds, and cause tissue damage, genetic errors, and cancer—but alpha particles are too big to penetrate the skin, so they're not hazardous to humans unless ingested or inhaled. When an atom undergoes fission, though, it breaks into smaller atomic fragments and shoots out radiation in the form of beta particles and gamma rays, which can go right through human skin and wreak havoc on our cells.

U-238 is the most common type of uranium, an isotope containing 92 protons and 146 neutrons. But though U-238 decays naturally, it rarely undergoes fission. My uncle Paul, a nuclear physicist, told me that as long as you don't lick it, you can keep a paperweight of pure U-238 on your desk without harm; he did.

U-235 is a rare isotope that makes up less than 1 percent of naturally occurring uranium. U-235 is exactly the same as U-238, except it has three fewer neutrons.

Even multiplied by three, the mass of a neutron is unfathomably tiny. But three neutrons make the difference between a mildly radioactive paperweight and an atomic bomb. Neutrons, which have no electric charge, act as a kind of buffer between the crowded, positively charged protons. Ninety-two protons squeezed into a nucleus are restless neighbors but take out three neutrons and the nucleus is volatile, ready to fly apart at the slightest provocation.

Uranium with a high concentration of U-235 atoms is known as highly enriched uranium. The purpose of Oak Ridge, or Site X, was to produce highly enriched uranium.

Here's a family story: On George's first day at work in the brand-new 9203 chemical building at the Y-12 uranium enrichment plant, his foreman instructed him not to move a certain box past a line painted on the concrete floor.

"What will happen if I do?" George asked.

"It will go critical."

"What's critical?"

Critical is when there is enough unstable material to sustain a nuclear chain reaction. Critical is the point of no return.

## A Hypothetical Number of Casualties

The primary argument used to justify the bombings of Hiroshima and Nagasaki is that a land invasion of Japan would have cost tremendous casualties on both sides. The Allied plan for the invasion was called Operation Downfall; some half a million American soldiers would have been killed or wounded, the bomb's defenders claim—more than a million, even.

Men repeat these numbers to me. I should be proud of my grandfather, they tell me. I am startled by the ease with which some people can deploy hypothetical numbers like a cavalry of the truth against actual immeasurable suffering.

In fact, casualty estimates of a potential invasion varied widely at the time, and historians have spent decades debating which numbers Truman and his military leaders actually believed. Most likely, they thought some tens of thousands, not millions, might have been killed or injured. After the war, higher numbers were cited by those who had a stake in justifying a decision called inhumane and unnecessary by even some of the highest-ranked military leaders at the time, including General Dwight Eisenhower, supreme commander in Europe, and General Douglas MacArthur, supreme commander in the Pacific.

It is unclear, though, how much Truman even knew or cared about the estimated casualties of an invasion; he was probably most concerned with bringing the war to a close as quickly as possible.

But the claim that the bombs were the lesser of two evils—the war continuing or the war ending—also depends on the belief that the bombs did, in fact, end the war. The day the US bombed Nagasaki, the Soviets also invaded Manchuria, ending, without warning, their neutrality pact with Japan; Japan surrendered six days later. Some historians argue that the Soviet betrayal was the more decisive factor. Others contend that it was probably a combination of the bombs, the Soviet invasion, continued conventional bombing, general war weariness, and political tension. Some even insist that the primary motivation for using the bombs was to ensure victory before the Soviets joined, to intimidate this ally now emerging as an enemy, and to gain an upper hand postwar.

In any case, many historians now agree that while the war would not have ended as quickly as it did without the atomic bombs, it probably would have ended before the planned invasion, scheduled to begin November 1.

I do not know how many volumes, how many pages, have been written to justify or condemn or explain or contextualize the bombings of Hiroshima and Nagasaki. We cannot know how many lives might have been lost or saved in an alternate history. No one then could see the future, and no one now can know what might have happened in a different past.

### 500,000 *Purple Hearts*

In English, *count* has meant "to tell" for as long as it has meant "to enumerate." *To tell* also once meant to make a list, to name items in order, or to count. These etymologies suggest that we understand stories as a way of making numerical sense of the world, a way of balancing the books.

To tell a story, one must decide what counts and in what order.

There is an oft-repeated, though contested and inconsistent, claim that, in anticipation of the casualties that would result from the invasion of Japan, the US government manufactured some five hundred thousand Purple Heart medals. Because of the sudden end to the war, because of the nuclear bombings of Hiroshima and Nagasaki (so the argument goes), there was no land invasion of Japan. According to the story, American military casualties since then have not yet exhausted that supply of Purple Heart medals, and the surplus was so great that field commanders in Iraq and Afghanistan kept a stock on hand to award immediately in the field of combat.

This story is repeated by those who want to justify the atomic bombings by invoking the presumed human toll avoided by using the bombs. But I did not understand that the first time I heard it. Instead, I thought about how the United States justified the 2003 invasion of Iraq—there were supposed to be nuclear weapons there. The US was the first country to build a nuclear bomb and is the only country to have used one in war. As it turned out, Iraq did not have nuclear weapons, but American soldiers were awarded more than thirty-five thousand Purple Hearts there.

Between 2003 and 2011, some one hundred thousand to one million people died, directly or indirectly, as a result of the US military invasion of Iraq; the vast variation in numbers is due to the difficulties of conducting accurate surveys in conflict zones, different calculation methods, who is doing the counting, and whose deaths count. Some estimates only include direct violent deaths, while the majority of wartime deaths are usually the consequence of destabilized infrastructure, hunger, contaminated drinking water, and reduced access to medical care, among other strains prolonged violent conflict puts on people and land. Though the Iraq war officially ended in 2011, civilians and combatants continue to die there.

Do these deaths count in this reckoning? But now I am out of order.

*To reckon* also means both "to count" and "to tell" but carries an additional moral weight. In a religious context, a reckoning is both a tally of one's good and bad deeds before God on Judgment Day and an avenging of past injustices.

### *How Many Uncounted Miners*

Go back to when atoms were just atoms and rocks were just rocks, to when uranium was just some potent dirt, rose pink or pollen yellow or ebony black or some blazing mix, hidden among other minerals considered more valuable—vanadium, cobalt, copper, radium.

Then, the hot crash of war, the shaking of hands and passing of papers by powerful men, and miners were sent into dark shafts in the earth to dig out the now-precious rock. The uranium bound for the bombs was buried in the high desert of the Colorado Plateau and on the shores of Canada's massive Great Bear Lake, but by far the greatest supply came from the open-pit Shinkolobwe mine in the Katanga region of the Congo, where the ore was two hundred times more concentrated than that found anywhere else in the world. There, under Belgian colonial rule, Congolese miners chiseled and hauled and sorted and packed the ore without protection from the radioactive dust that clung to their skin and clouded their lungs.

No bomb without those miners working for starvation wages under a system of forced labor; no bomb without mine managers enforcing quotas with whips, without colonial armies firing on striking workers. Even when not working, the miners walked on ground saturated with uranium, drank contaminated water, lived in houses made of radioactive stuff.

While estimates suggest that miners could have received the equivalent of a year of radiation exposure in the course of just two weeks of work, while recent studies found elevated levels of uranium and other metals in urine samples of those who live in the area today, and while locals tell of unexplained illnesses and children born with birth defects, there have been no comprehensive medical studies. The secrecy surrounding the mine, the fear that negative publicity about the hazards of uranium mining could impede production, and, more than anything else, a brutal and extractive colonial rule that saw Congolese lives as expendable, ensured that there would be no account of the lives stolen here in the name of a "righteous" war.

Now, the Shinkolobwe mine, officially closed since the Congo gained independence in 1960, is a honeycomb of makeshift tunnels where thousands of freelance miners take their chances to collect valuable copper and cobalt, still mixed with uranium, to sell on the black market. Everywhere the smuggled minerals go, they leave an invisible, radioactive trail.

## *1,152 Calutrons*

By train and ship and plane, uranium ore made its way from the mines to uranium mills, refineries, and laboratories in the US and Canada to be pulverized, roasted, boiled, and chemically treated. From Mallinckrodt Chemical Works in Missouri, the uranium, now in the form of orange uranium trioxide, was sent to Y-12. There, it was converted to gaseous uranium tetrachloride and fed into calutrons, D-shaped tanks that whirled the atoms in a semicircular arc through a magnetic field; the heavier U-238 atoms traveled in a slightly different path than the lighter U-235 atoms, and the two were deposited in separate collection spots.

Nimble-fingered girls like Dot, just out of high school, operated the calutrons. They sat on four-legged stools for eight-hour shifts, twenty-four hours a day, in front of wide, gray control panels, watching needles waver and adjusting dials if they dipped out of a desired range.

To achieve the necessary concentration of U-235, uranium had to cycle through two sets of calutrons: the alpha, then the beta. The alpha calutrons were fifteen feet high, arranged in ovals called racetracks. The betas were half as tall, arranged in rectangles. There were 1,152 calutrons in nine buildings.

## *Sixty-Four Kilograms of Highly Enriched Uranium*

My father tells a joke: A farmer's chickens have stopped laying eggs. He asks a physicist for help. The physicist furrows his brow, scribbles some calculations, and finally says, "I have a solution! Assume a spherical chicken in a vacuum . . ."

The joke was particularly funny to a child of Oak Ridge, familiar with the impractical brilliance of the theoretical physicist, one of the four personality types that my father calls "the Myers-Briggs of Oak Ridge." Engineers were the most practical, engaged with the visible, physical world. Biologists were political. Chemists were levelheaded and detail-oriented. And physicists were dreamy and detached, sometimes failing to notice where theory did not precisely align with a messier reality.

Ideally, the enrichment process lost no uranium; the full amount inserted into a calutron would be extracted at the other end, now separated neatly into its various isotopes. In reality, however, a lot of uranium got stuck on the insides of the calutrons, and the machines had to be painstakingly dismantled, the uranium leached off with acid and then purified and reprocessed into a form that could be fed back into the machines.

Those responsible for reclaiming the uranium from this acidic solution were the six or eight young chemists of the 9203 lab. This is where I found George in the fall of 1943.

The person who told me he was there was Bill Wilcox, the Oak Ridge retiree who happened to have worked beside George in that lab. The one who accused me of poetry.

Bill called their work "complicated chemistry stuff" but humored me by recounting how the acidic solution—clear blue or yellow—arrived at the lab in big glass carboys. In the chemists' hands, clear liquid became a yellow substance, "just like New York cheesecake," that, when heated in an oven, decomposed into a bright-orange powder, "very pretty, nice and pure." This—uranium trioxide—the men of 9203 sent to the lab up the hall to be transformed into dull-green uranium tetrachloride, which would be fed into the beta calutrons.

By the end of 1944, the chemical operations had outgrown the 9203 lab, and Bill and my grandfather parted ways. Bill, who excelled in the technical areas, moved to a small experimental troubleshooting laboratory. George was promoted to shift foreman, supervising, by Bill's estimation, some hundred people on three shifts in the new 9206 chemistry building. The planners had failed to anticipate just how extensive was the need for this particular type of high-level chemical janitor. George's job was necessary because the scientists' equations could not account for the textures of the world, the warmth of human hands, and the coolness of steel pipes, because some things are not, finally, calculable.

When the desired concentration of U-235 was reached, the blue-green crystals, now uranium tetrafluoride, were packed into gold-lined cylinders and carried in briefcases handcuffed to the wrists of armed and suited couriers via passenger trains from the hills of Oak Ridge to the mesas of Los Alamos. Beginning in early 1945, the deliveries accumulated until Los Alamos had enough of the precious substance to form the critical mass of the world's first uranium bomb. The bomb contained sixty-four kilograms, or 141 pounds, of highly enriched uranium.

### 4.5 Billion Years

Before uranium ore was wrested from the ground in the Congo, Canada, and Colorado, before Germany invaded Poland, before the Japanese bombed Pearl Harbor, before the formation of our solar system, Earth's naturally occurring uranium was formed by exploding stars more than 4.5 billion years ago. It has been here all along, sprinkled through corals, seawater, bones, buried deep in the earth, just waiting.

When did it become critical?

Uranium wasn't discovered by humans until 1789 and its radioactivity until more than a century later. But the time from the discovery of fission at the end of 1938 to the manufacture of the first atomic bomb was less than seven years. Forty-three seconds for the bomb to fall and one-millionth of a second for it to explode.

The Los Alamos physicists who designed the bomb used the term *shake* to describe the speed of the reaction, from "as fast as two shakes of a lamb's tail."

## 878 Sailors

The uranium projectile and other components of the bomb left Los Alamos on July 14 in a black truck escorted by seven security cars. From Albuquerque, the components were flown to San Francisco and loaded onto the USS *Indianapolis*. The crew did not know what the three crates, holding thousands of pounds of cargo, contained.

Altogether, the bomb's journey from Los Alamos to the Pacific island of Tinian took ten days. The day the ship arrived, the uranium target left Albuquerque by air. To avoid total loss of the precious material in case of accident or attack, it was divided into three pieces to be carried on three separate planes.

Four days after the USS *Indianapolis* delivered its secret cargo, a Japanese submarine torpedoed the ship while it was en route to Leyte Gulf in the Philippines. The ship was not reported missing, and the surviving 850 of the crew's 1,196 men floated in shark-infested waters for nearly four days before they were accidentally spotted by a bomber on a routine patrol. By the time the rescue ships arrived, only 318 of the crew survived. The 878 killed are incidental to this reckoning. Aren't they?

## Twelve Airmen

There were twelve men aboard the *Enola Gay*, and the flight from Tinian to Hiroshima took six and a half hours. At 3:00 a.m. Tinian time, Captain William S. Parsons descended into the bomb bay of the *Enola Gay* midflight to arm the weapon while Second Lieutenant Morris R. Jeppson held a flashlight. The procedure lasted twenty minutes. Just over four hours later, they descended into the bomb bay one last time to replace the green plugs blocking the firing signal with red ones.

"Maybe I was the last one to touch the bomb," Jeppson would later reflect. He was twenty-three years old at the time of the bombing.

### .7 Grams Uranium

The $c$ in the equation $E = mc^2$ stands for the speed of light, a number so huge that when squared and multiplied by even a tiny amount of mass, the resulting E will be tremendous.

One thousand forty-two. One thousand forty-three.

Of the sixty-four kilograms of uranium in the bomb, less than one kilogram underwent fission, and all the energy of the explosion came from just over half a gram of matter that was converted to energy. That is about the weight of a butterfly.

### Sixty-Seven Cities

Bill's point about other wartime atrocities, I suppose, was that the bomb was just one of the many ways humans have killed each other cruelly and in great numbers.

It's true, and the war in the Pacific was an exceptionally brutal one, fueled by racist propaganda that flourished on both sides of the Pacific, depicting the enemy as vermin, as devils, as subhuman. Atrocities committed by both the Japanese and the Americans inflamed and perpetuated, writes historian John Dower, "an obsession with extermination on both sides—a war without mercy."

It was within the context of such a war that the US reversed its previously held policy of not targeting civilians, beginning with the Allied bombing of German cities in 1944 and culminating in relentless and widespread targeting of Japanese cities; ultimately, American firebombing devastated sixty-seven Japanese cities and killed hundreds of thousands of people between February and August of 1945. Within this context, perhaps the atomic bombs were not all that remarkable. It was no great leap from firebombing cities to nuking them. But I do not think that because something is unremarkable, it is not wrong.

Sixty-seven is also, by one count, the number of Oak Ridge Manhattan Project scientists who signed a petition to the president urging him not to use the bomb without first giving a public demonstration and offering the Japanese a chance to surrender with full knowledge of the new weapon's power. Introducing the atomic bomb to the world, they insisted, carried a "special moral obligation."

Military authorities halted the circulation of the petition on security grounds, and it never reached President Truman, who did not even know of the existence of the bomb until he was sworn in after the death of Roosevelt. He was not asked whether the thing should be used; it was presented as a military matter, already decided. The order was issued by some general acting in the stead of another general, who was elsewhere at the time.

Among the estimated 67 percent of Hiroshima's buildings that were destroyed was the school building in which a boy named Tanemori Takashi was playing hide-and-seek with his friends.

### *1,968 Feet*

"There was no 'decision to use the atomic bomb,'" insists nuclear historian Alex Wellerstein. It was a bad and long war with lots of people making lots of decisions that added up to Hiroshima and Nagasaki. The bomb was made to be used. What was set in motion when the Manhattan Project began in 1942 would not be stopped.

And so, forty-three seconds after being released from the B-29, the bomb called Little Boy exploded 600 meters, or 1,968 feet, above the city. The height of detonation was calculated to ensure as much damage as possible to wooden Japanese civilian homes, the precision enabled by a specially designed fuse. A report on the optimal height of explosion even discussed how to ensure that enough firefighters would be killed to allow a firestorm to whip through the city, engulfing buildings and humans not destroyed in the initial blast. The whole point was to kill as many people as possible as efficiently as possible.

### Five Cents

Bill showed me two basketballs. One of them had a nickel glued to the outside, and the other had nothing. This weight, he told me, is the only difference between U-238 and U-235. Bill carried these basketballs to local schools and explained the basics of nuclear science to bored fourth graders. What did they see in the apparent innocence of a nickel?

I see a lesson almost too cliché to mention. It is the tiny, inconsequential things that make the fatal difference: eighty-two thousand pairs of hands in Oak Ridge, six chemists in a lab, twelve men aboard a plane, a clear sky over Hiroshima on August 6, forty-three seconds to fall, and a butterfly's weight of uranium.

The entire Manhattan Project, including all three secret cities, as well as laboratories and offices in Chicago, Berkeley, New York City, and elsewhere, probably employed some half a million people over the course of the war. Though Oak Ridge was mainly an industrial site compared to Los Alamos, where the scientific luminaries worked out the technical puzzles of the bomb, it employed by far the greatest number of workers and accounted for more than 60 percent of the project's total expenditures.

The bomb needed Oak Ridge. It needed the janitors and electricians and secretaries and calutron girls. It needed Dot and Colleen, young, patriotic, and distracted by all of their ordinary worries and dreams. It needed Kattie Strickland, putting up with racist indignities for the sake of a high paycheck, a better future for her children. The bomb needed the chemists of the 9203 uranium processing laboratory. It needed midlevel scientists like George. They pulled the lever, cleaned the pipe, stuck a cake of uranium in the oven, and went home to feed their children.

The day I spoke to Bill, it was raining, hard—one of those southern summer thunderstorms that falls with a vengeance, the sky turning steely dark, the rain coming in buckets, pounding roofs, drowning fields, rising in curtains as the tires of the cars hit the streams rushing by the curb, an impossible amount of water that briefly transforms this mild, gentle landscape into something violent, inescapable.

I would never be able to ask George how much he knew, whether he regretted his part. But I could ask Bill.

"Hell yes," he said, punching the air with his fist. "I knew exactly what we were doing—damn right. It didn't make any difference whether we were eventually gonna build an ocean liner . . . or whatever the hell it was."

We sat in the formal living room of his wartime cemesto. The house shuddered under a deafening roar of thunder, and I turned to the window to see the tree branches outside lit bright as bones against a gray sky. Bill didn't seem to notice, barreled on.

"I knew what my job was, and that's what people don't realize . . . Well, no, I didn't know I was building a bomb. I knew I was building some kind of a military weapon for sure and hoped like hell it was gonna do something to help shorten the darn war."

### *80,000 Lives and Counting*

The numbers that might have died in an Allied invasion of Japan are based on hypotheticals, of course, and therefore highly uncertain. But the actual dead from the bombings of Hiroshima and Nagasaki cannot be counted accurately either. Hospitals, fire stations, and police departments were destroyed, corpses reduced to ash in fires that raged through the cities, and records of the pre-bomb population were incomplete to begin with. Some of the more reliable sources of information were school attendance rosters and work details recording the names and locations of students assigned to clear firebreaks or labor in war factories; officials could estimate other casualties by counting the dead and injured schoolchildren.

Estimates for total deaths from the two bombings range from one hundred thousand to more than two hundred thousand from August through the end of the year.

Around eighty thousand is one estimate for the number of those who died instantly in Hiroshima. That was also about the population of Oak Ridge at that time. That number does not account for those who died in the subsequent months, years, and decades due to radiation-related cancers and other health effects. And how do we count the psychological burden of the survivors? We'll never know the size of it.

A reckoning implies that the world may be set right with some sort of calculation; good and evil measured, justice meted, balance restored.

I cannot make this equation come out. I count too many different kinds of things; my units are all mixed up.

I need a new kind of arithmetic.

# RESTRICTED DATA

August 5 was a warm evening in Oak Ridge. Children pulled up chairs to dinner tables, single women left dormitories for a cafeteria meal, hair coiffed and lipstick bright, and across the reservation, workers donned uniforms or stripped them off as they began and ended shifts or worked straight through the dinner hour because this was a wartime schedule, and the whirring and thumping and buzzing of the machines never stopped. By the time the children were tucked into bed, what was done was done, Oak Ridge's purpose made manifest above a coastal city seven thousand miles away.

The night was nearly moonless.

Before lunchtime on August 6, 1945, President Truman's voice crackled over the radio, announcing, "Sixteen hours ago an American airplane dropped one bomb on Hiroshima. . . . It is an atomic bomb. It is a harnessing of the basic power of the universe. The force from which the sun draws its power has been loosed against those who brought war to the Far East." Before he named Oak Ridge, Truman spoke of massive production facilities where "over 65,000 individuals are even now engaged in operating the plants."

"Few know what they have been producing," he said. "They see great quantities of material going in and they see nothing coming out of these plants, for the physical size of the explosive charge is exceedingly small." As he broadcast their task to the nation, those "even now engaged" did not hear him. It was the housewives, children home from school, nurses clustered around a radio, shift workers already finished or not yet begun their day's work who heard the news first.

Hiroshima had been burning for sixteen hours when the phones at the plants started ringing. *It's happened*, they said. *We know what you've been building.* Some scientists, alarmed by this breach of secrecy, not yet understanding, hung up on their wives.

At first, people gathered in neighbors' homes and spoke in low voices. There was a buzzing excitement, but quiet, tentative. *Was it now? Was this it?* For all they had been instructed in secrecy, there had been no preparation for this moment. Then, it was as if the volume had been slowly turned up. People poured out of houses and plants. Within a few hours, the streets were full and loud with whistles, horns, laughter, and cheers. Scientists began to call out words that had been forbidden, and then others took up the cries without knowing what they meant—"Fission! Atomic! Radiation! Uranium!"

Oak Ridge went from being a city that whispered to a city that shouted.

Doris, whose tiny frame now swelled in pregnancy, could not dance, but she could raise her arms above her head and clap, elbows flying, shouting, "Hallelujah."

One of the most iconic photographs of Oak Ridge, reproduced in history books, tourist brochures, and museum displays, was taken on the day of Japan's surrender, 1945. Jubilant white residents crowd forward into the frame, beaming, hands raised in the air. Many hold up the *Knoxville Journal* with the foot-high headline "WAR ENDS." The crowd, packed together, seems to tilt to the left slightly, moving as one body. A girl in a striped dress sits on someone's shoulders. A woman in glasses holding a rolled newspaper throws back her head in a wide-mouthed laugh. A few wave flags; others raise two fingers in a V for victory.

The crowd wears an almost wild exhilaration. Put aside, for a moment, what we now know about Hiroshima and Nagasaki.

This crowd does not yet know what we know. The deaths are distant; the first official statements about the bombings did not even mention casualties but emphasized military and industrial targets. And when the deaths come, they are just numbers, more numbers in a war of already incomprehensible numbers. What the crowd knows is that the war is over, that their fathers and brothers and sweethearts can come home. What they know, or what they're told, is that by their loyalty and diligence, they have played an essential part in the victory. And they are exultant, too, with their sudden freedom from long months of oppressive silence.

Most popular historical treatments of the secret city end here, with victory and the promise of peace. And I suppose Oak Ridge did end here for many of the residents. The fate of the new weapon not yet decided, the city began to empty abruptly as people left to return to their other lives and homes. Some feared the city had no future now that its wartime purpose had been fulfilled, and others had been laid off as production slowed. By June 1946, the city's population had dwindled from seventy-five thousand to forty-three thousand. Those who left could celebrate their part in the victory and later say, *I didn't know. I had no idea.*

But Oak Ridge did not disappear. Life continued. Production continued. By the end of 1946, uranium enrichment at Y-12 was shut down as the gaseous diffusion process at K-25 outstripped the efficiency of the calutron process at Y-12. Instead, Y-12 took up the machining of uranium weapons parts, work previously performed at Los Alamos, as the Cold War demanded increased production.

For midlevel scientists like George, those who might have guessed something but only learned the full extent of the project along with the rest of the world, the end of the war was the first moment they could consciously choose whether to continue to be involved in nuclear weapons work. It was the first real moment of conscience. "WAR ENDS" was another beginning—for nuclear weapons and for George himself. He did choose, and his career, fueled by the arms race, would flourish.

In the photograph, women crowd the foreground, smiles dark with lipstick, eyes glittering. The men in the shadowed background wear smiles that are more tempered, hesitant. Further back, some can be seen only by the light reflecting off their glasses, lit points pricking the darkness like cat's eyes.

I imagine George and Doris just outside the frame. Doris with soft rolled curls, one hand protectively over her swelling belly, smiling brightly. But I cannot see George's expression. Could he yet fathom the weight of this new creation in the world?

Not everyone is smiling. Some have been caught blinking or looking the wrong way. A soldier grimaces as if someone's just stepped on his toe. But my eye is drawn to a young woman in the front left-hand corner. While the rest of the crowd faces forward, she stands sideways, utterly still, head turned over her left shoulder to meet the camera's gaze with a dark stare. There is no hint of a smile. She seems to be looking out of the frame, like one of those self-portraits the old masters would sneak into their paintings, the small, shadowed face at the feast, serious amid celebration, the canny gaze beneath a felt cap, looking out of history, straight at me.

The overwhelming narrative of wartime Oak Ridge reinforces the elation of the "WAR ENDS" photograph: energy, patriotism, hope, and youth. But in one of my history books, I came across a reference to a psychiatric service set up in Oak Ridge during the war. Psychiatric care was not originally among the social, recreational, and health services the city deemed necessary for the maintenance of a healthy and efficient workforce, but within months of the first residents' arrival, it became clear that the psychological burden of life on the townsite—the isolation, the sparse and restrictive living conditions, the long hours, and all that was unsaid or unknown, guessed at or dreamed of—posed a threat to morale and productivity.

From the day the psychiatric service commenced in the spring of 1944, need overwhelmed capacity. The psychiatrists and social workers found that residents suffered from "social problems," including juvenile delinquency, illegitimate pregnancies, alcoholism, and depression, but "our greatest problem," wrote Dr. Eric Clarke, the chief psychiatrist, "was the acute anxiety neurosis, comparable to battle fatigue encountered in overseas units." Such symptoms, often accompanied by perplexing physical ailments, were most common among patients in supervisory positions, those with the most knowledge, responsibility, and pressure. The best treatment was extended leave from the city. Many other residents, including those holding lower-level jobs, likely did not seek treatment for fear it might threaten their employment.

In the records of the psychiatric service, I saw a way to peer past the cheerful facade of wartime Oak Ridge, to see the beginnings of what such a life might have cost. I was searching for the first blush of the bruise of secrecy, for what the dark-eyed woman in the "WAR ENDS" photograph knew.

From a history book, I copied the citation of a letter from the chief psychiatrist of the wartime reservation to the head of the Oak Ridge hospital. I meant to begin here, to touch the thing itself, to see what else I could find.

The letter was supposed to be housed in the AEC collection in the National Archives at Atlanta. The AEC archives house the onetime secrets of the nation's nuclear complex that are now deemed acceptable for public viewing. One would imagine that finding the original letter cited in my history book would be a simple matter. But the organizational system had changed since the authors cited the letter in the 1980s, the collection was massive, and the finding aids were a convoluted mess.

The reading room was gray carpet, white tables. The only sounds were the soft swish of turning pages and the occasional wheels of a cart across the carpet as the archivists ferried boxes in and out of the cool dark vault. Three or four other researchers were already at work.

Shane, the archivist in charge of the collection, said the letter might well be at this facility, yet it was possible that it had been removed after subsequent reviewers in the 1990s determined the file to be "restricted," or containing sensitive nuclear weapons data.

"Yes, it's possible someone could have looked at files which were later removed. Unfortunately, we have no way to definitely determine if that was the case," Shane confirmed. There was nothing for it but to dive in.

I requested random boxes with names that seemed promising or mysterious. I sifted through yellowed and transparent onionskin memos, printing fuzzed by time; waxy brown folders with the words "To Remain Classified" marked out with a single squiggling pen line across their fronts; memos with dry titles such as "Financial Requirements of the Oak Ridge Disaster Program"; folders with ominous titles such as "Criticality Experiments"; charts of radiation levels in various test animals: mice, rabbits, dogs . . . The hours stretched on. Within the steady white light of the room, time seemed not to move. I forgot to eat. By four o'clock, I was shaking with hunger.

I came and went, and the days blurred into each other. I was struck by the sheer volume of paper devoted to the patrol of secrecy, detritus of the creaking weight of this vast, unwieldy machine. There were routing sheets tracking the passage of classified materials from one office to another. Multiple memos discussing the best method for sealing envelopes so that they could not be opened and resealed without detection—Scotch tape or sealing wax? And letters listing classified documents that had been lost, misplaced, or improperly released.

So much gestured to all that lay out of sight. Outlines betrayed an absence. Entire folders were filled with cross-reference sheets for documents that were pulled for classification—"This folder contained classified material and has been placed in a separate, classified collection." Or, "Documents were removed from this shipment." Or, "Secret Document Inserted Here." One cross-reference sheet even marked the removal of a memo entitled "Destruction of Classified Documents—1945." What the documents were, why they were destroyed, or why the record of their destruction needed itself to be classified was not indicated.

Shane described the AEC collection like a large mansion you could only view through a keyhole: You glimpse people walking past the entry hall, doorways beckoning, a desk here, part of an armchair there. You hear snippets of conversation. You suspect that what you are looking for is in a closet on the third floor. Casual passersby have alluded to it, oblivious to your greedy eye pressed to the keyhole. You cannot get there. You can only crouch unblinking, hoping for the wildly improbable, putting together the clues, surmising the whole.

Privately, of course, I hoped to find George himself. Were his cracks already beginning to show when the first psychiatrists arrived in town? Not according to the family, and the evidence of his successful career after the war suggested otherwise. But I searched anyway. I searched for anything that might help me find the human breath of him.

From the history of Y-12 compiled by Bill Wilcox, I gathered a list of keywords that might help me find him: the numbers designating the buildings he might have worked in, names of the production processes he was involved with, the elements used in those processes, code names for those processes, code names for the elements. As I scanned each onionskin memo in the reading room, I repeated to myself what sounded like some alchemical incantation—9203, uranium, tuballoy, 9704–4, hafnium-zirconium separation, alloy development program, 9211, lithium, 9204–4.

Perhaps by taking the temperature of the place, I'd touch something of the man who stood like a cutout in the fabric of my history, all edges without center. I chased the ghost of him, my white rabbit, into a shadowy underworld. Here was a file on "human radiation experiments." Here was a handwritten note from an Oak Ridge plant manager—"Did I recently authorize a waste burial ground here?" George lingered at the edge of my vision, then flickered out of sight, came into focus for a moment, blurred again. Shane's mansion seemed a metaphor not only for the difficulties of researching secrets but also for the absurd task I'd set for myself—to try to know a dead man by the debris of his life.

For some time now, I had been trying to track down the photograph of George in front of the nuclear fireball, the one from my childhood. I began casually, poking in closets and drawers during summer weeks at the lake, certain it would soon turn up. After months, a year of this, I polled the family over email, hoping for a lead.

Instead, I received a flurry of uncertain responses:

"I don't remember that one, exactly . . ."

"There was one of a fireball, but none with George in it."

"I remember mushroom clouds."

"Are you sure there was one with George?"

I was shocked, panicked almost. I would have signed sworn testimony to the photograph's existence. Would have described it before a jury, under oath. Now when I was at the lake, I searched with increasing urgency, methodically emptying the contents of each drawer and closet. I removed the backs of framed photographs to ensure no second image was hidden behind the first.

My uncle Paul made fun of me sometimes. "Looking for secrets?" he teased when he caught me one summer poking through old boxes in the storeroom at the lake house. I mumbled and shut the boxes, but he was right. I was always looking. And someone was always telling me there was nothing to find.

The archives, then, for all their holes and ominous omissions, were intoxicating in their tangibility. I was obsessed by the texture of it all. A penciled note in the corner of a memo, a smudged fingerprint, the rusted stain from a paperclip—all promised some human pulse behind the dead skin of bureaucracy. My heart leaped when I found a memo from a building George might have worked in, or even better, the name of someone I knew was a colleague or a friend, a name I recognized from my childhood. I thought if I stayed here long enough, if I gathered enough evidence, I might be able to say one true thing.

In the meantime, it was the thrill of the hunt. Individuals were almost impossible to track, Shane cautioned me. I felt like a silly schoolgirl doing family research while, around me, serious scholars unfolded historical maps, studied draft lists, and asked the archivists specific questions. They moved through a reasonable number of boxes quickly, while I requested an unreasonable number of boxes that I worked through at a snail's pace. They photocopied selectively, while I snapped thousands of digital photographs.

Some days my mother came with me. She packed us lunches so I didn't neglect sustenance—peanut butter and jelly or cheese sandwiches on thick, seedy bread and carrot sticks or apple slices—and we drove down together from my childhood home in Atlanta, where I was staying for this holiday break. Sitting across the table like two spies who'd found their way into the enemy's vault, we called out in excited whispers when we came across one of our keywords, the thrill taut between us. Each relevant document led to more keywords, as we noted down the buildings memos came from, the authors, the addressees. I had ambitious plans of methodically mapping the data, plotting names, dates, buildings, and elements in an ever-widening web of association until I could triangulate George's location, pin him to a moment in time.

Later, over dinner and glasses of red wine, we'd tell my father about our day in the archives, how it felt like we were breathing in history. There was a palpable postwar paranoia in those vaults. Security files marked "ALIEN" in large red capital letters tracked foreign visitors to the plants. In files from the summer of 1945, there was a roster of foreign language classes being held for community members at the Oak Ridge High School; the Russian class roster was annotated with the address and employment of each participant.

My father was amused by our fascination, puzzled by our enthusiasm and the hours we'd spent thumbing through old papers. A child of the secret city, none of it struck him as all that remarkable. And what were we learning, anyway? Where was George in all this?

Not until I was far from the spell of the archives did I realize he was right. Only when I was faced with the task of organizing the thousands of photographs I'd snapped did I perceive how absurd was the task I'd set myself—to build some vast, intersecting lattice onto which I could map George to learn, what? Where he stood at a particular moment in time? Where his office might have been?

I connected with a Y-12 historian, who sent me photographs of some of the buildings George worked in. And I was surprised at how they looked almost cheery, their red tile bright in the overcast day, their purposes suggested only by an external skeleton of pipe-work, obtrusive air ducts, long, windowless exteriors. Their blank faces betrayed nothing of their insides.

I began to see what my father learned growing up—that what went on behind the gates of the plants was protected by more than armed guards and fences and color-coded badges. That information itself might be a facade, an illusion of access protecting all that remained withheld.

I began to understand that this, too, was how my family operated. George's career was never fully hidden but never discussed either. Just as my father brought up his father's drinking, his swings of depression, never by way of announcement or revelation, but as if I already knew, as if there was nothing more to remark on. The family's silence about George's work, understatements, and acceptance of the strange and extreme were a subtler version of what was magnified and institutionalized within the nuclear complex.

After the war, the Atomic Energy Act of 1946 transferred management of nuclear production from the military to the newly created Atomic Energy Commission. The act also created an unprecedented category of secret: Restricted Data included "any document, writing, sketch, photograph, plan, model, instrument, appliance, note or information involving or incorporating" details pertaining to the development, manufacture, and use of nuclear weapons, nuclear materials, and nuclear energy.

The Restricted Data designation sometimes leads to extreme and illogical classifications. It is one of the reasons, Shane explained, that the AEC archive is so full of holes. Restricted Data is "born secret," meaning it falls under the sole jurisdiction of the DOE (formerly the AEC), whether it was created within a government agency or not. Technically, this means that even when civilians with no access to classified information write about nuclear weapons, they are subject to stringent restrictions. Former nuclear scientists have been pressured to remove descriptions of nuclear weapons science from their writings even when all the material they have revealed is publicly available. My uncle Paul, the retired nuclear physicist, cannot draw a certain shape on a napkin without breaking the law.

Unlike other classified information, anything categorized as Restricted Data is not subject to automatic declassification after a certain passage of time but must be reviewed page by page. It is, until review, a permanent secret.

Carrying a secret is a metaphor that suggests a felt reality. In 2012, experimental psychology researchers reviewing the results of four different studies found that people keeping secrets perceive hills as steeper and distances as longer, as if they are struggling under a physical weight. The bigger the secret, the heftier the perceived burden. Another study by two University of Virginia researchers focused on the cognitive strain of secret-keeping. They found that suppressed thoughts become our most prevalent and accessible, blazing brightest just at the moments we push them to the furthest reaches of our minds. The heavier the secret, the larger the audience from which it must be kept, the more taxing the effort. Long-term secret-keeping can lead to health problems and psychological distress that may remain long after a secret has been aired.

Over the course of World War II, the Manhattan Project initiated some half a million people into a stringent code of silence. And that was only the beginning, before the Cold War extended the culture of secrecy throughout the growing nuclear industry. As one son of an Oak Ridge scientist reflected on growing up in Cold War Oak Ridge, "There was still a formal apparatus to prevent the development of public knowledge—loyalty oaths, security clearances, lie-detector tests, badges and so forth—but what was most effective was an almost unconscious conspiracy of silence in which secrets were protected by voluntary non-communication."

I never found the original letter I sought in the archives, but I did finally run across a string of memos about the wartime psychiatric program—the chief psychiatrist's monthly reports to the head medical officer. Reporting a caseload of 165 in March 1945, Dr. Clarke advised: "This is far beyond the capacities of a staff of this size to accomplish good work," and later, "Although the new psychiatric ward, which will give 10 allotted beds to this service, is not completed, it is already apparent that the new space will barely meet our present needs."

Causes for the unanticipated and steadily increasing caseload, Dr. Clarke wrote, included the difficulty of living conditions, the temporary nature of the town, and the strain of secrecy.

A report on social services in Oak Ridge put it this way: "Although many people are able to adjust to these conditions as a necessary sacrifice in helping win the war, others, being human, find themselves not always able to 'take it' as well as it is desired they should."

What does "being human" mean? I want to believe that, deep down, below the stories we tell and the habits we learn and the calluses we grow, we are soft-bodied and soft-hearted, permeable. I want to believe that we feel, whether we allow ourselves to know it or not. I wanted to find George being human.

In July 1945, exactly one month before the bombing, Dr. Clarke reported, "The caseload of the present staff is at saturation point."

Compartmentalization extended even to the therapist's couch. Psychiatric patients with access to classified information had to be treated in isolation, for fear they might spill secrets. In one striking example, a man suffering from a psychotic breakdown was moved from the hospital to a private apartment converted to an isolation ward, with bars on the windows, doors that opened only from the outside, and soundproof barriers. He was raving about his work and threatening to warn the emperor of Japan.

George was not that man.

That man was unusual, both in what he knew and in his sense of responsibility. Purportedly one woman, on hearing the news of the bombing and learning the nature of her husband's work, ran to the hospital where he was recovering and berated him for contributing to the loss of innocent life. A Y-12 calutron girl became so depressed when she learned of the massive casualties that she couldn't sleep for a week. Though she eventually became convinced that the bomb saved lives, she would never like thinking about her role: "It really, really bothered me because I had a part in killing all those people."

Yet those are uncommon stories. After Hiroshima, Dr. Clarke wrote: "When the announcement was made that the project was the origin of the Atomic Bomb and the press was full of its great destructive power and the hazards of manufacture, the staff anticipated a flood of acute anxiety reactions." Instead, he was surprised to find that after the bombing, his patients were most concerned about the security of their jobs.

On August 31, 1946, just over a year after the war's end, the *New Yorker* devoted its entire issue to John Hersey's "Hiroshima," a detailed, chilling account of the aftermath of the bombing through the eyes of six survivors—a young clerk, a doctor, a tailor's widow and mother of three, a German Jesuit priest, a young surgeon at the Red Cross hospital, and a Methodist pastor. The minutiae of their lives in the days and weeks and months after the bombing brought the massive, distant horror into personal, visceral relief for American readers.

In the pages of the *New Yorker*, Americans saw the overwhelming bewilderment of people experiencing devastation beyond comprehension. After rescuing her three children from their collapsed home, the widow, in an automatic if nonsensical gesture of care, dressed them in thick winter clothes despite the sweltering heat of August exacerbated by the hot wind blowing from burning buildings. A woman in a park full of the dead and dying mended a small tear in her kimono. A boy cried out in excitement when he saw a friend. A young mother held the dead, decaying body of her infant daughter for four days.

Into the night, the Methodist pastor ferried the wounded across a river and away from spreading fires. When he grasped a woman's hand to help her into the boat, "her skin slipped off in huge, glovelike pieces." Others he helped had slick and discolored skin, marked by smelly, festering burns. Fighting back sickness, he repeated to himself: "These are human beings."

The German priest was most disturbed by the profound silence of the wounded, dying, and grieving: "The hurt ones were quiet; no one wept, much less screamed in pain; no one complained; none of the many who died did so noisily; not even the children cried; very few people even spoke."

After the acute anguish of those first days, some who had apparently survived developed high fevers, headaches, and nausea. Hair fell out. Gums bled. White blood cell counts fell, wounds grew infected, and burns developed disfiguring keloid tumors. Some people died within days, weeks, or months. Others recovered but feared what future horrors lay in store, writ into their bodies and genes.

"Hiroshima" was reprinted widely and read in its entirety on ABC radio over the course of four nights. One young Manhattan Project scientist wrote to the *New Yorker* of his shame to remember how he and his fellow scientists had celebrated the bombing in a "whoopee spirit." Until "Hiroshima," the tight restrictions on press coverage of the bombings, which had suppressed reporting on radiation and kept images of human suffering at a distance, had largely managed to dampen public unease over the attacks, but Hersey's story ignited a wave of critical articles and public soul-searching that alarmed the military and civilian leaders who had been instrumental in the development and use of the bomb and sent them scrambling to reassert a narrative of necessity.

Some top Manhattan Project scientists had, in fact, expressed concerns about the bomb's use even before the end of the war. Many of the scientists were Jewish refugees from Europe, and they had devoted themselves to building the bomb as deterrence against a possible Nazi bomb. By late 1944, when it became clear that the Germans were nowhere near having an atomic bomb, some of the scientists discussed whether and how their work should continue. Polish Jewish physicist Joseph Rotblat left Los Alamos then, convinced that to persist with the project was immoral.

Hungarian Jewish physicist Leo Szilard had been instrumental in the Manhattan Project's very existence; he'd both conceived of the nuclear chain reaction that made the bomb possible and subsequently persuaded Einstein to write to President Roosevelt of the need to research and develop an atomic bomb before the Nazis could. Yet as Germany's defeat became inevitable, Szilard campaigned hard to stop the atomic bombs from being used; he tried to reach President Roosevelt and then President Truman, worked with his colleagues to draft a report advising that the bomb should first be publicly demonstrated, and circulated petitions among Manhattan Project scientists. The final version of the petition warned: "A nation which sets the precedent of using these newly liberated forces of nature for purposes of destruction may have to bear the responsibility of opening the door to an era of devastation on an unimaginable scale." A total of 155 scientists signed some version of Szilard's petition. Routed through official channels, it did not reach President Truman until after the bombings.

Rotblat and the petition signatories, though, were in the minority. Rotblat reflected that most of those who had moral qualms about their work were swayed by scientific curiosity, convinced by the argument that the bomb would save American lives, or afraid of reprisals on their careers if they took a stance. "The majority," however, wrote Rotblat, "were not bothered by moral scruples; they were quite content to leave it to others to decide how their work would be used."

Robert Jay Lifton and Greg Mitchell, in their book *Hiroshima in America*, chronicling the nation's response to the atomic bombings, argue that the country's refusal to morally reckon with the bomb comes from both a self-preserving "psychic numbing" and from the concerted efforts of the government to promote a more palatable narrative. They document the psychological cost of suppression on even those most publicly committed to the bomb.

When I finally found George in the archives, it was not on a list of psychiatric patients. It was August 1952, and he was doing his job. The memo detailed a meeting with a scientist visiting from the Washington branch of the AEC to learn about the reactor materials work being done at Y-12. George explained the process of producing hafnium-free zirconium, used as cladding for nuclear-powered submarines: "Mr. Strasser pointed out that the production of pure Hafnium might be desirable as the Zirconium yield would thus be increased."

Shane did not seem all that impressed when I told him that I had found my grandfather. I wanted to dart about the quiet room waving the memo around, to announce my victory to all the methodical researchers. *See, he was here!* My eye was pressed to the keyhole, dry, because I dared not blink. George could not sense me there, watching. He walked out of the room, and I could not follow.

I sat with the revelation, and my elation subsided. I had learned nothing I did not know before, caught no glimpse of a George who ever questioned his role after Hiroshima. Instead, he stayed in Oak Ridge, continued to build nuclear weapons, and rose rapidly through the ranks of Y-12.

I had gleaned the basic outline of his career from publicly available Y-12 histories, old plant newsletters, and the memories of his family and colleagues. Between 1943 and 1953, George rose from "Jr. Chemist #2" to building supervisor to manager of a brand-new Development Division. In that role, he oversaw the piloting of production and manufacturing processes. By the end of 1954, he was the assistant plant superintendent. Throughout the fifties and sixties, George was flown to Nevada to witness nuclear tests, to Washington, DC, to study satellite photographs of Soviet nuclear facilities, and to Europe to attend international conferences on nuclear energy.

As I pieced together his career, I saw the unmoved face of a man who posed before a nuclear explosion. According to my family's memory, it was an image that my childhood mind might have conjured up—and yet, the portrait seemed true. Devastatingly so. He was good at his job. He would remain good at his job for a long time. This I knew.

8

# LYING

In the archives, I also unearthed a curious series of memos from the late 1940s detailing a string of petty and accidental thefts of uranium from Y-12. A man found uranium chips in the cuffs of his pants while changing clothes at the end of the day, and "after thinking the situation over," took them home and burned them on the stove in front of his wife. Another carried a chunk of uranium home to show his son, who was interested in chemistry. One admitted to keeping a metal chip as a souvenir. Others recalled that they had returned from work to find bits of uranium in their hair, under their fingernails, or clinging to their socks.

The thefts came to light during routine polygraph, or lie detector, examinations. The original intent of the exams was not to catch workers stealing bits of uranium but to police loyalty and smoke out potential spies in the creeping chill of the early Cold War.

A new trend had begun among Manhattan Project scientists, a trend that unsettled the conservative anticommunists in Washington. Just over a month after the bombings of Hiroshima and Nagasaki, twelve Oak Ridge scientists from the X-10 plant met to draft a statement of intent. Agreeing that it would be impossible for the United States to maintain a monopoly over the bomb and that "future security" depended on international cooperation, the scientists resolved to advocate for international governance of nuclear knowledge and facilities. Or as a parallel group of Oak Ridge engineers at K-25 put it:

1) There is no secret to the atomic bomb.
2) There is no effective defense.
3) Any plan to control the atomic bomb must be based on those facts.

These two groups would soon combine with a group of Y-12 scientists to become the Association of Oak Ridge Engineers and Scientists, committed to having their say about the fate of the terrible weapon they had helped bring into the world.

They were not alone. In Los Alamos and Chicago and Berkeley and New York, scientists held meetings and community forums, published press releases designed to educate the public on the political and military implications of the new weapon, advocated for international governance of atomic energy, and lobbied Congress to transfer nuclear material, knowledge, and production facilities from military to civilian control. They warned of an arms race. They feared worldwide nuclear annihilation.

Central to their message was the conviction that there was now *no longer any meaningful secret* about the science of the bomb. The underlying principle of the atomic bomb—that an atom could be split—was widely understood within international scientific circles, and it was only a matter of time before other nations developed the industrial capabilities to make their own bombs. Secrecy, then, was no longer protective but a barrier to the international cooperation and public knowledge that would be essential to preventing an international arms race or full-blown nuclear war.

It was a moment of openness and possibility, when many of those who'd had a hand in the bomb's creation sought to take responsibility for its future. They did not want their legacy to be the weapon that destroyed all human life.

All this organizing made Washington nervous, especially the House Un-American Activities Committee. The congressional committee, intent on uncovering dissidents among public employees and private citizens, singled out Oak Ridge specifically, suggesting the existence of a Communist spy ring as early as January 1946. A June

1946 report detailed such damning accusations as: the scientists "not only admit communications with persons outside of the United States but in substance say they intend to continue this practice."

A year later, in a *Liberty* magazine article entitled "Reds in Our Atom Bomb Plants," the House Un-American Activities Committee chairman, Congressman J. Parnell Thomas, detailed the threats posed by the politically active scientists: "They have a weakness for attending meetings, signing petitions, sponsoring committees, and joining organizations labeled 'liberal' or 'progressive' but which are actually often Communist fronts."

The Oak Ridge scientists, it seemed, were guilty of talking to foreigners, and to each other. They were, in other words, guilty of talking.

At the first whispers of these traitorous activities, in February 1946, an eager young polygrapher named Leonarde Keeler was sent down to sniff out the subversives. He was given an empty office in which to set up his lie-detecting machine. He turned the chair adjacent to the desk and ran wires through holes drilled in the bare plywood front to a little rectangle of dials and knobs set into the lower left-hand corner of the desk's top. By turns, he would ask each subject to sit in the chair with their back to shades drawn shut against the sunshine, to stretch their arms out on the long armrests, hands resting palms down. *Relax*, he might have cautioned, as he pushed up a sleeve to wrap a cool blood pressure cuff around a bare bicep, stretched a rubber hose tight across a chest until his subject could feel it dig in with every inhalation. *Breathe normally.*

In photographs, Keeler has a dark searching gaze beneath thin eyebrows and something in his look that says, *I'll listen all day.*

The polygraph, or lie detector, as we know it was developed by a Berkeley police officer named John Larson in 1921. Inspired by the work of Harvard psychologist and lawyer William Marston, who had tested the honesty of his classmates by measuring their blood pressure while they told tall tales, Larson designed a device that continuously recorded a subject's blood pressure and depth of breathing while an interrogator asked a series of questions. The physiological responses were transcribed in a squiggling line on a roll of paper. The idea was that a person could be caught in a lie by a quickened pulse or a catch in the breath.

The polygraph relies on the belief that our bodies reveal our feelings. It suggests that it is possible to know the inside of a person by reading the outside. How many hours did I spend staring at photographs of George, searching for evidence of his inner life in the squint of an eye, a tightening of the lips? How I wanted to see him tremble.

Keeler's charge was to suss out, "insofar as possible, the loyalty, integrity, reliability, mental stability, and suitability" of his subjects. It was that word *integrity* that got me. I remember learning that word; from the ceiling of my sixth-grade homeroom classroom hung the words *simplicity, peace, integrity, community, equality,* and *stewardship*, written in glitter glue on construction paper. They were the six Quaker testimonies, or core values. Having attended Quaker school since second grade, I was familiar with most of these. Simplicity was the way we sat together in silence on the floor once a week, inviting but not demanding prayer and reflection. Equality meant we learned protest songs in lieu of the Pledge of Allegiance and studied the civil rights movement every year. Peace was, well, not war, and also why we weren't supposed to keep score during recess games. But I was puzzled by integrity. I asked my homeroom teacher—a nervous but deeply kind man with very straight shoulders and dark, shiny hair. "Integrity," he explained, "means being honest with yourself."

The definition, and the challenge contained within it, struck me profoundly, expressing some true thing I had never before heard articulated. To have integrity, I understood, required a kind of brutal self-examination. It meant you couldn't rely on teachers or friends or religion or the government to tell you what was right. It meant that only the self knew what it meant to be good.

In the first round of testing, Keeler didn't find any spies, but some of the 690 examinees did admit to lying on their job applications, to stealing tools and slivers of uranium, and to neglecting to report radioactive spills. The army signed a contract with one of Keeler's team to continue regular testing of all workers in the uranium separation plants.

Subjects of the exams were rated on the basis of attitude, behavior, and personality. They were then recommended for one of six possible courses, including continued employment, reexamination, and reference to a psychiatrist. Eighty out of 6,058 Oak Ridge workers tested in a six-month period in 1952 were found to have "uninterpretable charts . . . as a result of either a mental or organic disorder at the time of examination."

"Revelation of the mental stability of personnel as it pertains to security risk" was considered one of the "principle advantages" of polygraph use at the Oak Ridge plants.

*Integrity* is from the Latin *integritās* for wholeness, entireness, completeness. It means being undivided and unbroken, true all the way through. Integrity is when there is no fissure between conscience and intention, intention and act.

I suppose I was enamored with the polygraph because of what it promises: that the integrity of a person can be sounded, as the ripeness of a melon, by a hollow thwack. The polygraph promises that truth rings in a heartbeat, that clarity is attainable, that reliability can be measured, loyalty assured. It is the dream that we might know each other.

When the polygraph came to Oak Ridge in 1946, George was just twenty-seven, one of the city's proud founding residents, and his career was on the rise. He was thin, compared to what he would be later, and prematurely bald. He wore round, wire-rimmed glasses and a crooked smile enhanced by ears that stuck out a bit too far on either side. By the time Keeler unpacked his machine in the empty office at Y-12 in February 1946, George was the father of a blue-eyed girl, just three months old, my aunt Karin.

Between 1946 and 1953, eighteen thousand Oak Ridge workers were subjected to some fifty thousand polygraph tests. Having read that questionable polygraph results were forwarded to the

Knoxville FBI office, I submitted a Freedom of Information Act (FOIA) request to the FBI, requesting "all records concerning a deceased individual named George Albert Strasser."

After some months, I received this mysterious response: "Records that may have been responsive to your request were destroyed on June 17, 2004."

I called the FBI's FOIA office for an explanation. "The only thing we do is we type it in the computer, and the computer says that records that may have been responsive were destroyed on that day," the FOIA officer told me, unhelpfully.

I asked what sorts of records were destroyed that day. She told me they didn't know. "All that it says is that records were destroyed on that date." I asked how they knew that the records I wanted might have been destroyed that day and not some other. She told me they had no way of knowing what records were destroyed, because they were destroyed.

I called the Oak Ridge Office of the DOE, and an official told me that personnel polygraph records would have been put into individual security files, which were destroyed five years after termination. The officer told me, however, that I could submit a request for George's personnel and medical files. And so I did.

Some weeks later, I received an envelope in the mail. The discs inside contained scanned images of some 250 pages of personnel files and 150 pages of medical files: barely legible handwritten notes, typewritten letters, charts and memos, medical histories, and career summaries, a bewildering array of detail.

I was startled, almost embarrassed, by the level of intimacy they contained. I could know George's weight, blood pressure, and temperature on a given day. When he had a UTI, a bout of conjunctivitis, a sore throat, a cold sore, a sprained ankle. In November 1952, he needed glasses, caught severe colds, cleared his throat frequently, suffered from indigestion and headaches, smoked more than twenty cigarettes a day, and drank more than six cups of coffee a day.

His files from the wartime days detailed frequent visits to the medical wing: lacerations on his arms and fingers, ether burns on his face and neck, first-degree burns on his right palm from grasping a hot wire, tiny acid burns on his hands. Likely this catalog of injuries reflected the frenzied chaos of the wartime laboratory that put safety concerns second to production, but I also recognized myself and my father in George's clumsiness: our flailing limbs and poor sense of space, the overturned water glasses, hands smacked into walls. On May 25, 1945, two weeks after Germany's unconditional surrender, George sliced his palm open on the sharp edge of a centrifuge. Two months later, and two days before the bombing of Hiroshima would answer the riddle of what he had been working on, George checked into the medical building with a 2.5-inch cut on his forehead where he'd collided with a centrifuge discharge spout.

I found his electrocardiograms, his heartbeat distilled to a repetitive topography, steep peaks and sudden valleys, or tight, low gradients, like the hills that stacked across the landscape he made home.

I arced the images around me until I sat encircled by thirty years of my grandfather's heartbeat doled out in six-second segments. I stared, willing them to meaning. A strange séance, this. But who was haunting whom? The tracings remained silent.

As it turns out, the promise of the polygraph is a false one. The language in Keeler's stated mission, "insofar as possible," nodded to the lie concealed at the heart of the lie detector—that it cannot detect lies. It is now, as it was then, a failed enterprise. The technique has been widely scientifically discredited, dismissed as nothing more than pseudoscience and psychological coercion.

It is not that the lie detector measures nothing, but that what it measures—sweaty palms, increased heartbeat, rapid breathing— does not correspond to deception. The fear of false accusation turns out to be indistinguishable from the fear of detection. One squiggling line, the tracing of a pulse across a page, may indicate nerves, may indicate guilt, or may indicate almost anything at all. Whether a subject passes a polygraph exam depends, instead, on whether the polygrapher believes the subject is telling the truth.

During the Cold War, the US relied on the strategy of nuclear deterrence, the conviction that the threat of retaliation would be enough to prevent an attack. Deterrence is a psychological game, dependent on bluff and belief rather than action, requiring a careful control and release of information. The enemy must know enough to believe the threat is real but not enough to counter an attack. Information withheld will be filled in by the imagination. Our minds draw monsters in the dark.

Cold War deterrence depended on the doctrine of mutually assured destruction, the belief that use of a nuclear weapon against the enemy would ensure an equal and escalating response that could only end in total annihilation. A successful deterrence strategy builds a fully operational nuclear arsenal that is meant never to be used. Mutually assured destruction is shortened to the acronym MAD.

Polygraph historian Ken Alder suggests that the polygraph operates, as the bomb does, by deterrence. It is not the machine itself that enforces honesty but the belief in its validity.

The Oak Ridge workers mostly tested "clean." The interviews found no spies and identified more members of the Ku Klux Klan than of the Communist Party. But regular polygraph testing clamped down on "loose talk," reduced petty theft, depressed union organizing, and discouraged people from speaking out about releases of contaminants into the environment. As Alder writes: "This mass screening was designed not so much to uncover deceit as to enforce a new form of loyalty."

For some of the Oak Ridge workers, the polygraph tests revealed, or perhaps created, an underlying self-doubt, a nagging unease. Many could not be sure whether they were innocent. Of a man who worried he might secretly be a Communist because he supported federally subsidized housing, the polygrapher determined that he had "probably confused his 'isms.'" Another man, who worked in uranium processing, was called in for follow-up questioning when his polygraph registered a response to a question about revealing secret information to an unauthorized person. It turned out that he had only told his wife how hard he worked. A man who went into his exam "visibly nervous and unsure of himself" had spoken in vague terms about his work to friends and family. Investigators determined that neither posed much of a threat.

The gates of Oak Ridge were opened on March 19, 1949, in a ceremony dubbed Operation Open Sesame, attended by thousands. A spark from a uranium chain reaction channeled from the reactor at X-10 ignited a scarlet ribbon, generating a miniature mushroom cloud and symbolically inaugurating a new era of openness for the secret city.

After, some residents missed the fences and the feeling of safety they had provided. So too, some workers reported in a 1951 survey of the Oak Ridge polygraph program that the regular tests made them more trusting of their coworkers and even of themselves. With the strict and evolving parameters of secrecy, it was difficult to know whether one had unconsciously broken the rules. To pass the test was to be declared clear and honest. One physicist commented, "I have a personal satisfaction in passing each test, to have a recalibration so to speak."

The Association of Oak Ridge Engineers and Scientists joined with partner organizations of former Manhattan Project scientists to found the national umbrella organization called the Federation of American Scientists. The members' advocacy was instrumental in the passage of the McMahon Act in 1946, which arranged for nuclear facilities, research, and energy to pass into civilian control under the newly created Atomic Energy Commission. Still, amid rising tensions with the Soviets, opponents of the bill used the specter of nuclear espionage and the threat of "Communist" scientists to curtail the free exchange of information that the scientists had fought so hard for, instead instituting highly restrictive secrecy measures with harsh penalties for infractions. Fed by Cold War fears, the AEC moved far from the peaceful and collaborative civilian mission the activist scientists had envisioned. Local advocacy in Oak Ridge died down by 1950.

The Oak Ridge polygraph program operated until 1953, when the AEC became worried that the unscientific tool was alienating the very scientists they needed to attract and retain. Perhaps, too, the tests were no longer needed; by then, Oak Ridgers were well-trained in a certain kind of carefulness.

The Y-12 *Bulletin*, the weekly newsletter distributed to workers and their families, did not announce the end of the Oak Ridge polygraph program. Instead, it simply noted, in September 1953, that the bulletin and recreation office had moved to "quarters formerly occupied by the Polygraph Office." The same issue congratulated George on the birth of his new son, my father.

Nearly half a century after the end of the Oak Ridge polygraph program, in the wake of a false Chinese espionage scare at Los Alamos, the DOE instituted widespread polygraph screenings of nuclear weapons scientists. The program operated from 1999 until 2006 despite intense criticism from the scientific community, including a damning study by the National Academy of Sciences.

Deterrence is still used to justify our continued possession of nuclear weapons, and the polygraph is still used by many federal agencies, including the CIA, the FBI, and the NSA. Under revised regulations, the DOE uses the polygraph on a more limited basis to test employees under suspicion of sabotage, espionage, terrorism, or the release of classified information.

It was not until I had looked through George's files several times that I noticed a cramped, handwritten note from the winter of 1946: just over a year after Hiroshima and some ten months after the polygraph's arrival in Oak Ridge, George was treated for a bout of insomnia, nausea, and indigestion.

His doctor attributed the episode to nervousness and the "great deal of pressure" he was under. I had no other details of this incident; it was mentioned in his medical files only in passing, in relation to a similar episode two years later. But I could not help but note the timing—on the heels of Hiroshima, at the beginning of a career that would thrive in direct proportion to our proximity to nuclear anni-hilation. Hersey's "Hiroshima" had been published a few months before, but I did not know whether George had read it.

After this discovery, I began to more systematically examine George's health records. I took note of curiously long absences throughout the late forties and early fifties for colds, strep throat, the flu. It seemed unusual for a healthy man in his prime to be out sick for more than a week or two with such common, mild illnesses, especially a man of the restless temperament George's children remembered. I didn't know what to make of it.

I consulted a health physicist who worked at Y-12 under George in the 1970s and an industrial hygienist who specialized in workplace exposures to hazardous substances: both agreed it was possible that workplace chemical exposures could have mimicked flu-like symptoms or compromised George's immune system so that he was susceptible to other infections. But the information about his symptoms and exposures was far too sparse to say anything more definitive.

It took many passes through the files before I noticed a strange discrepancy: the medical files noted that between June and July 1951, George missed work for more than three weeks due to "viral pneumonia," while the insurance claim for the same dates reported his diagnosis not as pneumonia but as "neurasthenia."

Neurasthenia was a vague catchall diagnosis denoting a variety of mental and physical symptoms that could include anxiety, depression, fatigue, insomnia, headaches, and others associated with a body and mind under great strain. During World War I, the diagnosis was used to treat soldiers suffering from shell shock. It described a person crumbling under overwork, stress, or overstimulation but without the same degree of stigma that came with other mental health diagnoses.

What did it all mean? Did George's physical symptoms present as pneumonia? Did he ask his doctor to lie? Or did the doctor misrepresent George's ailment of his own initiative? Would a diagnosis of a mental disorder have flagged George as a security concern, threaten his employment? Or were plant officials protecting the institution itself, upholding the image of a workforce healthy and robust in mind and body?

Even the diagnosis of neurasthenia seemed suspect—by 1951, neurasthenia was already decades out of vogue, largely medically debunked as doctors and psychologists found more precise ways to explain and differentiate the many divergent symptoms the diagnosis encompassed. Had the doctor, confronted with a patient desperate to maintain an image of mental fitness, reached for an older, more palatable diagnosis and then later thought even that could be too suggestive?

And what about the other absences, the weeks he was purportedly sick with the common cold? Had those diagnoses, too, been cover-ups for more emotional ills? How long did George hide what hurt before it became unhideable?

How was I to read the evidence of the body?

In November 1952, a year and a half after George's episode of "neurasthenia," he filled out a detailed health questionnaire that included not just physical symptoms but also a psychological evaluation. George circled "no" in response to the questions: Do you sweat or tremble a lot during examinations or questioning? Do you get nervous or shaky when approached by a superior? Do you feel alone and sad at a party? Do you often cry? Do you often wish you were dead and away from it all? Were you ever a patient in a *mental* hospital (for your nerves)?

He circled "yes" in response to: Is it always hard for you to make up your mind? Does worrying continually get you down? Does nervousness run in your family? Did anyone in your family ever have a nervous breakdown? Was anyone in your family ever a patient in a *mental* hospital (for their nerves)? Are your feelings easily hurt?

I was surprised by the wash of sympathy that came over me. I'd been looking for the human face of the scientist posed unflinching before a nuclear explosion. I'd been searching for his vulnerability, and here he was, admitting that his feelings were hurt easily. But what brought a sort of prickling familiarity was that the human face I saw was my own.

*Is it always hard for you to make up your mind?* I am inde-cisive to a painful degree, to the point that I often mistrust my own emotions. I can see the thing from every angle and long for someone to tell me what is right. Strap me into a polygraph and tell me I am true.

Some days, I wish I didn't care about George. I wish I could condemn him and walk away. But there are moments when I feel so close to him it aches.

*Does nervousness run in your family?* Yes. I know. I come from this family.

The quarterly report for the Oak Ridge psychiatric services from July to September 1945, the months spanning the bombings of Hiroshima and Nagasaki and the end of the war, records fifty-nine admissions in August; at one time, there were twenty-six occupying the psychiatric ward of the hospital with a capacity for just fourteen. George was not one of those admissions, as far as I know.

In the same report, Dr. Clarke expressed frustration at the resis-tance toward psychiatric services exhibited by management at the nuclear plants: "The prevalent level of thought is that psychiatrists deal only with the grossly psychotic and that association with the psychiatric service is consequently embarrassing or disgraceful." The stigma, he explained, meant that cases did not reach psychiatric services until "after the symptoms had persisted so long and were so pronounced that rehabilitation and return to work was difficult" or impossible. Y-12 workers pretended health until they couldn't.

# 9

# Practicing for Doomsday

### The Wait

It is May 5, 1955. The bomb sits heavy atop a five-hundred-foot steel tower above Yucca Flat, a large arid basin ringed by mountains. The white light of the nearly full moon illuminates the houses of Doom Town below, brick and wood and cinder block arrayed on a handful of streets complete with power lines and parked cars, a slim skeleton stitched across a large dry landscape.

The houses are furnished with couches, beds, desks, lamps, radios, TVs, ovens, water heaters, and coffee tables, all the trappings of a middle-class, suburban American life. Framed art hangs on the walls, pictures of birds, fruit, or dancers. Patterned curtains adorn windows. Pantries are stocked with Quaker Oats, dry milk, Lipton Tea, beef stew, canned corn; fridges are filled with root beer, bread, and mayonnaise.

It must be morning, because kitchen tables are set for breakfast, coffee cups for Mom and Dad, juice glasses for the kids. Mother is smart in a pencil skirt, patent leather pumps, and blouse, or she is relaxed in a satin kimono-style robe. Father is ready for work in a dark suit, or he's on the couch in striped pajamas, playing with his little boy, who is wearing jeans and a T-shirt. A girl in pigtails and shorts leans into her father's knee. All are clad in brand-new J. C. Penney clothes, donated especially for the occasion.

In one kitchen, two women gesture toward each other with elbows crooked at exactly the same angle while a kid finishes breakfast. A toddler lies alone on a bare mattress, limbs eerily frozen in midair. A child and father take cover in a basement shelter, but most seem unaware of the nuclear bomb glinting in the moonlight above their breakfast tables. The bright expressions painted on their pale plastic faces remain fixed.

Outside, dead-eyed mannequins stand in a long row, some strange first line of defense, a breeze lifting their starched collars and skirt hems.

It is 5:00 a.m., and the sky is cloudless. On a hill above the town, George waits in the predawn chill for the countdown.

On June 23, 2014, I sat in an air-conditioned hotel room in Las Vegas thinking about what it must have been like to wait for a nuclear bomb to explode. What it must have been like to wait for a nuclear bomb to explode if you had helped make that bomb, if you knew exactly what it did. What it must have been like to wait for a nuclear bomb to explode if you were George and it was May 5, 1955.

Outside, the hotel grounds were a maze of lush green lawns, glowing, kidney-shaped pools, the soft white twinkle lights of a wedding chapel. The night was still hot, and with the pools and palm trees, without the view of low brown hills hunching in the distance, it felt tropical, easy to forget this was the desert. But I was thinking of the desert.

I hadn't found the photograph, but tucked into the frame of a different portrait of George that now hung where the bomb photo used to hang, I found a security badge for the Nevada Test Site. Yellow and laminated, it read: "Atomic Energy Commission. Nevada Proving Grounds. 5 May 55. Strasser, George A. Oak Ridge. Insert No. W 8293." His ID photo was washed out, ghostly.

For so long, the photograph of George before the nuclear explosion dwelled in my memory as something mythic, untethered to time and place. But now, a circumstance. So this was how it was. Nevada. It was a nuclear test in the desert of Nevada. It was boots on dry ground, nighttime rent by atomic blaze.

Or at least, it might have been. And now I had become obsessed with filling in the picture beyond the dark edges and blinding flash of my memory. If the photograph existed, how? Why did George pose in front of a nuclear explosion? Who clicked the shutter? What were all the little pieces that led up to the moment when he turned his back to a rising nuclear fireball and met the camera lens with a steady gaze?

On May 5, 1955, the United States government set off an atomic bomb above a model American neighborhood in the Nevada desert to see what would happen. Now, sitting in a cool hotel room in a false tropical paradise in the middle of the desert, I couldn't sleep because I was thinking of fake houses populated with mannequin families awaiting a nuclear bombing.

The Federal Civil Defense Administration (FCDA) wanted to know how a "typical" American town would weather a nuclear bombing. They wanted to know how a brick-and-cinder-block house would fare in comparison to a wooden frame house. Whether a basement shelter would stand even as the house crumpled around it. Whether phone lines and electricity could withstand the blast. Whether the beer would be drinkable. What would happen to bomb-fried bacon.

While public acceptance of the bomb project required turning away from the real horrors of Hiroshima and Nagasaki, it simultaneously relied on cultivating the fear that those very horrors would be visited upon Americans; specifically, the white suburban nuclear family, the model for those blank-faced mannequins frozen in scenes of apparent domestic harmony. As Patrick Sharp writes of both apocalyptic science fiction novels and government propaganda of the time, "author after author colonized the lived experience of the Japanese *hibakusha* to imagine what would happen to the white middle class in the event of a nuclear Pearl Harbor." A 1948 version of Hersey's *Hiroshima* even featured an illustration of a bedraggled white couple fleeing a nuclear attack.

The Apple II nuclear test was designed to conjure this specter of attack, to impress the American public with the seriousness of atomic warfare, to convince them of the necessity and safety of nuclear testing, and to instill the project of civil defense with a spirit of patriotism and industrious optimism. To that end, media observers, congressmen, civil defense volunteers, and representatives of AEC nuclear facilities were invited to witness the spectacle.

"It was a very public event," the attendant in the archives reading room told me, "not like some of the other tests, where they couldn't bring cameras or anything. So, maybe. Maybe your grandfather could have taken a picture then."

I'd spent days now in the Nuclear Testing Archive, reading through the reports documenting the Apple II test and scouring old newspaper articles until my eyes blurred. Finally, I stumbled across the street in the oven-hot air to Jack in the Box for a too-sweet iced coffee. Everything I was finding was fascinating and disturbing, but I'd gotten no leads on the photograph; I grasped the archivist's small concession with outsize hope.

In a few days, I would get to see the bombed desert itself. The Nevada National Security Site, still commonly called the Nevada Test Site, is thirteen hundred square miles spanning the transition between the Mojave and Great Basin Deserts, just sixty-five miles northwest of Las Vegas. Then known as the Nevada Proving Grounds, it was established in 1950 as the continental testing site for nuclear weapons; the AEC had been testing bombs in the Pacific Marshall Islands since 1946 but decided they could save time and money by testing some weapons in the continental United States. Between 1951 and 1992, when the US government adopted a moratorium on all US testing, this square of desert felt the reverberations of a hundred open-air detonations and more than nine hundred below ground. Now, the site offers public tours once a month—they're so popular they fill up six months in advance. I'd signed up. In the meantime, I spent my days in the archives.

The Nuclear Testing Archive shares a building with the National Atomic Testing Museum, just over a mile and a half from the Las Vegas Strip. It was nearly one hundred degrees by the time I set out in the morning on the twenty-minute walk from my hotel. I stopped at a giant CVS, half-filled by a liquor store, to buy an apple and a sandwich. The clerk who checked me out first had to soothe an agitated drunk. It was 9:30 in the morning. "You have a blessed day," she told him with genuine kindness, and I, already drooping in the heat, anticipating another futile day of research, felt oddly comforted.

In the reading room, I watched videos of houses crumpling in a flash followed by a wave of dust. I squinted to compare grainy before and after photos of the bomb-scorched J. C. Penney clothes. After, some of the mannequins were missing heads or limbs; some, gone entirely, were replaced by black rectangles. When I needed a break, I talked to my new friend, Dick Mingus.

Dick was one of the museum security guards. I met him a few days before. I'd been in the gift shop at closing time—you could buy a snow globe with a mushroom cloud in it, alien sunglasses, or an oven mitt decorated with the radioactive symbol in rhinestones. The gift shop attendant was chatty. "I just can't get enough of this history," she said, shaking her head. When I told her what I was researching, she looked up Apple II in what she called the "shot book," a DOE publication that lists the date, time, size, location, and method of detonation for each of the 1,149 nuclear bombs set off by the United States between 1945 and 1992. There were bombs shot off from hot air balloons, towers, even a cannon, and later, in tunnels dug deep underground. Apple II was part of the Operation Teapot series, she reported; it exploded with a force of twenty-nine kilotons, nearly twice the yield of the Hiroshima bomb but small for its day.

"My sister's an artist," she told me. "She doesn't get it. She's always saying to me—'What do you do, sell bomb stuff all day?'"

I guess she decided I was someone who "got it," because she leaned over the counter and asked me, "Have you met Dick Mingus yet?" I told her I hadn't. "Oh, you have to meet Dick. He worked out there, on the test site for, I don't know, twenty, thirty years? He'll tell you stories . . . He'll be here tomorrow. Be sure to talk to him."

When Dick found me the next morning, he was full of questions. Who was my grandfather? What was his job? What tests did he see? Dick became my personal guide.

He was in his mid-eighties and worked just a few days a week. Sometimes he stood at the ticket booth; sometimes he walked through the exhibits, walkie-talkie occasionally crackling on his shoulder; but he could also sit and talk to me for hours. He was interested in the photograph. And he thought that if he could see it, he could tell me where George was standing just by the barest hint of landscape. "You know, I seen 'em so many times I know what those ol' mountains look like . . . Like an old house, you remember everything about it." Dick recalled his days on the test site with aching nostalgia. He knew the landscape, I thought, like I knew the lake. But despite his willingness to help me, he said he'd never seen anything like my photograph—one person posing in front of a fireball. And because he seemed to know everything about the test site, this troubled me.

As the possibility of finding the photograph receded, I clung to the notion of finding an official record, beyond his security badge, of George's presence at the test. As if the whole history might dissipate like a strange dream gone by lunchtime. As if I might call home one day and my father would say, "What do you mean, nuclear bombs? My dad was an insurance salesman."

In the reading room, I wasn't making much headway. The attendants kept giving me DOE pamphlets and fact sheets on various tests. I sensed that I was asking the wrong questions. "Surely there is some record," I persisted. "Didn't they keep lists of security badges? Readings from dosimeters?"

The attendant seemed wearied by my questions. She directed me to a DOE archive search tool online, showed me where to find historical test videos on the Nevada National Security Site website, and told me they didn't keep records of everything. I couldn't help but suspect that I was being sidestepped, distracted with publicly available materials. Yet at the same time, I suspected myself—of paranoia, an overzealous search.

I was tempted to go back to CVS, buy a mini bottle of something fruity, and be blessed by the kind clerk for my wayward humanity. But I made myself try once more. "Please," I asked. "There has to be something." Finally, the woman went upstairs and returned with another woman—chin-length white hair, wire-rimmed glasses, and prominent salt-and-pepper eyebrows—the archivist herself, apparently. I didn't know why she hadn't appeared before, but I didn't want to push my luck so I said nothing. I explained what I was looking for, and without a word, she disappeared. Ten minutes later, she returned with a single sheet of paper.

It was a copy rather than the original document, the paper bright white. There was George's name on a passenger list of "official observers" for the upcoming "Open Shot."

"He was there," she said. The eighteen observers were due to fly on a US Air Force plane from National Airport in DC to Indian Springs Air Force Base, adjacent to the test site, at 8:00 a.m. on April 22, 1955. Official observers would be bunked at the Air Force base to await "shot day."

My eyes rested on George's name, unbelieving for a moment, before I took in the rest—above and below, the other names were blacked out in thick marker.

"Privacy," explained the archivist. Since names that suggested a person's presence at a nuclear test might indicate radiation exposure, she explained, the DOE treated them as medical information.

Though none of George's kids remembered the photograph, they did remember him flying out to see the tests. Kurt remembered his father telling him that most of witnessing a nuclear test was time spent waiting. With his position in the plant—by 1955, George was assistant plant superintendent—he was invited more than once to witness the proof of his efforts burst in the desert sky. But not every trip resulted in his actually seeing a test. Weather conditions were delicate, and tests were frequently delayed. The wind had to be just right. Sometimes George flew out to Nevada, spent a few days, a week or so, and then flew home without having seen a thing.

Sometimes tests were not canceled until the last minute, when everything was set—the mannequins dressed and arranged, the observers bused out to wooden bleachers. Apple II was delayed ten days. Three times the observers—civil defense workers, media representatives, political officials, nuclear workers, soldiers, photographers, and security guards—were called from their sleep. Three times they stood vigil, and three times the test was pulled at the last minute because of unfavorable weather. After days of waiting, many went home. Of thirteen hundred media and official observers originally registered, just five hundred remained by May 5, 1955.

Perhaps it was during those mornings, when George was pulled from bed and then sent back again, the quiet undisturbed, that he went walking. That was the thing, Kurt said, his father liked most about nuclear tests—not the awesome power of the explosions, the lights of Las Vegas, or schmoozing with nuclear big wigs, but early morning walks in the desert.

We call the desert wasteland or holy land; we go there to die or to be reborn. This desert, deemed expendable by those who decided it could be bombed one thousand times over, is the ancestral home and unceded land of the Western Shoshone, beloved and claimed by them still, despite nuclear waste and armed guards and bomb craters, despite the usual story of broken treaties. To the boy who'd grown up in the gentle, rolling greens of Tennessee farmland, it must have seemed a desolate landscape, but he learned to see its stark beauty, the low slanting light catching the leaves of ground-hugging shrubs, revealing the golds and greens and violets that would be scorched away by the midday sun.

The walks and the waiting—that's all Kurt remembered his father saying about the tests. It must have been a luxury, this time away from the deafening industrial churn of the plant, away from a small house full of children and an overburdened wife. Time for quiet. Time to match his steps to his thoughts.

On May 5, 1955, there was no early morning walk because, at last, the wind was right. Everything was ready. Boxes of baby food lay in shallow trenches in the dry earth. A mannequin child stood obediently beneath a lean-to shelter. Filing cabinets and bank safes were set out on the desert floor, cars parked outside houses, radio towers constructed, power lines strung up.

George would have probably stood on News Nob, an elevated observation point eight miles south of the shot tower, along with the media, officials, civil defense volunteers, and industry representatives who had not gone home. Observers of the test could purchase coffee and doughnuts while they waited.

Below, one thousand troops of Task Force Razor—human troops, not mannequins—in eighty-nine armored vehicles were arrayed in a wedge formation from 1.76 to 4 miles south-southwest of the shot tower, awaiting orders to move into ground zero just after the detonation. The troops were meant to demonstrate the capability of American soldiers to operate in a nuclear war zone. Just a mile and a half from the shot tower, ten volunteer observers, including one civilian, crouched unprotected in a trench. Hundreds of others, including troops, media observers, FCDA volunteers, and foreign NATO observers, waited in trenches at various distances from the bomb.

Finally, the hour arrived. At 5:09 a.m., a loudspeaker announced, "H minus one minute. Put on your goggles. Observers without goggles must face away from the blast."

George kneels to set his coffee and half-eaten doughnut on a nearby rock. He turns his back to the shot tower and hands his camera to, who is it? A friend, perhaps? Another Oak Ridge scientist? Perhaps they plan to take turns posing. George places his feet, smooths the wrinkles on his shirt.

### The Flash

Zero. Dawn is shattered by a white-hot light many times brighter than the sun. Like an overexposed photograph, the shadows are stripped and the desert subtleties of lavender and gray, rose and sage, are bleached to bone. See it all, the rocks, grasses, and mountains, the shadowed crevasses, the gnarled Joshua tree, see it flash fatal, flash flat, no longer the landscape George had learned to love, but an X-ray of it, a memento mori.

The world's first nuclear explosion was not the bomb exploding over Hiroshima but the Trinity test, detonated twenty-one days before on July 16, 1945, in the Alamogordo Bombing Range in New Mexico. Some of the Los Alamos scientists witnessing the test joked about whether the blast would ignite the atmosphere; they even set up a betting pool. They had calculated that possibility as being extremely unlikely, probably impossible, and yet how many, for one icy moment as the fireball surged into the predawn sky, feared they had made a mistake?

Apple II was not the world's first nuclear test but the nation's sixty-second one. Imagine sixty-two nuclear bombs. Repeated sixty-two times, perhaps anything can become unremarkable. Perhaps the observers of the sixty-second explosion could see the bomb's flash as an impressive firework or as a single, brief, blinding stage light.

But Apple II was not George's sixty-second explosion. As far as I could find, it was his first. The first time he saw with his own eyes what he had been building. Surely this sight trembled the soul, if only for one forgetful moment.

An official pamphlet distributed to test observers in 1955 described the flash like this: "Within thousandths of a second after the detonation the heat, light, and instantaneous radiations sweep the target area and a 'fireball' appears as the air is heated to incandescence by temperatures approaching a million degrees centigrade." Within a second, the fireball swells to a radius of several hundred feet and "begins to rise like a gas balloon." Ten seconds later, the light is nearly gone, leaving behind the thick smudge of the mushroom cloud against the sky.

In my memory of the photograph, the mushroom shape behind George still glowed orange. If this was so, the photograph had to have been taken within ten seconds after detonation. One Mississippi. White all the way to the edges. The end, perhaps, or the beginning. Two Mississippi. Fire roiling, billowing, expanding. Perhaps it will keep on growing, consume the Doom Town houses, the troops of Task Force Razor, the Joshua trees, melt the sand to glass, race up the hill to where George is standing, burn up dough-nuts in brief round flares, and keep on going. Perhaps it will never stop. Three Mississippi. He turns his back to the fire, shuffles his feet on the dry ground. Four Mississippi. Regards the lens. Five Mississippi. He doesn't smile.

After a day in the archives reading room, I walked the Strip in the somewhat cooled evening air. Everything was so mammoth that my sense of scale was thrown off the way it is in the mountains—I could see where I was going but seemed to make no progress. A cartoonish castle loomed like a Playmobil set on steroids. The angled arms of one hulk of a casino rose in stripes of lit green windows, glittering like Oz. A golden Eiffel tower glowed invitingly. A fake volcano belched real fire, and around it, little flame-shooters threw fireballs into the air. They emerged in mushroom shapes, blue at the bottom, then orange, then gone. I shivered despite the heat and walked on.

This party capital of the world was once the gateway to the training ground for doomsday. When they couldn't be accommo-dated in Mercury, the strange little frontier town built at the edge of the test site to house test workers, participants, and witnesses, or the nearby Indian Springs Air Force Base, test observers stayed at Las Vegas casino hotels.

I passed women in sequined dresses and feathered headpieces posing for photos with chunky bros in baseball caps, bachelorette partyers teetering drunkenly on high heels, dusty-faced young cou-ples propping cardboard signs with pleas for money against their knees. I wondered how many of them knew that this city was once illuminated by the flashes of one hundred atomic bombs. Shots detonated during the day could be seen from Las Vegas, while shots detonated before dawn were visible as far as six hundred miles away. The boom was both literal and figurative in the 1950s, shattering downtown shop windows and bringing not only jobs and government investment but also a craze of atomic tourism. The chamber of commerce printed a calendar listing scheduled tests and prime viewing spots. Casinos hosted rooftop viewing parties, inviting guests to sip atomic-themed cocktails from midnight until detonation in the early morning. Showgirls wore mushroom cloud headdresses, and beauty queens paraded for the honor of being named Miss Atomic Bomb. Within ten years of the first Nevada test, the population of Las Vegas had doubled.

Now, Las Vegas feels like a place devoid of history, seasons, even the normal cycle of day and night. There is always a brighter light, a newer casino, a bigger win to erase all previous mistakes. The excitement of gambling is the chance that starts anew with every pull of the lever. Get richer, get drunker, get poorer. Don't add up the losses, the shots downed, the hours passed, and you'll never know how much they cost. Las Vegas was the perfect city to absorb, and then forget, the atomic craze.

Finally, exhausted, I nearly collapsed into a table on the upper level of an Italian restaurant. I'd chosen this spot for the view— through a colonnaded archway, I overlooked a "Venetian" canal under an arched ceiling painted a perfect sky blue, dotted with wispy clouds. I was the wrong audience for this whimsy, because all I could think of was how, on shot day, May 5, 1955, the sky was called "clear with an unlimited ceiling."

I took out the passenger list from the archives and pored over it again, searching for something more to latch onto, but there were just the thick black stripes of the marked-out names, uneven because they had been drawn by hand. George and all his ghost companions, there to watch the dress rehearsal for doomsday. There to pose with the star of the show?

I had about a week in Las Vegas. Plenty of time to go cross-eyed in the reading room, to spend hours talking to Dick, and to wander through the museum reading every plaque, taking copious notes in some futile attempt to fill the gaps of everything I couldn't know with everything I could.

The museum displayed walls of security badges just like George's, timelines of nuclear testing, and kitschy atomic-themed toys and household items from the 1950s and '60s—dinner plates decorated with zooming atoms, comic books, KIX cereal boxes advertising an atomic bomb ring for fifteen cents plus a cereal box top. In one corner, there was a diorama of a Doom Town living room, like those bombed during the Apple II test—mannequin mama in a blue dress, sitting with folded hands; boy in overalls at her knees; papa turned outward with clenched fists, as if he meant to personally face down the nuclear explosion.

In the Ground Zero theater, I sat on a wooden bench and watched a large-screen video of a test shot as if I were actually an observer—the countdown, a brilliant flash, and then the floor rumbled and a burst of air filled the theater. A couple of kids screamed.

Dick accompanied me through the museum, enlivening each display with his personal stories. His eyes crinkled as he described eating lunch beside one of the bombs, perched on the shot tower hundreds of feet above the desert. It was nice—a spectacular view, a bit of a breeze, no dust. If another guard was up there, they'd make paper airplanes and bet a penny on whose plane could fly farthest.

He told me how, while setting up the houses for one of the civil effects tests, some of the guys arranged the mannequins in compromising positions. He winked, and I knew what he meant. They figured the blast would scatter the figurines, but when the test was delayed, some officials toured the model neighborhood and were treated to an eyeful. Dick swore he wasn't involved in this particular episode.

These were the same guys who exposed themselves to radiation in order to evacuate contaminated areas of personnel when an atmospheric test detonated with a higher-than-expected yield, or an underground shot vented. I liked Dick—he was gentle and proud of his work. He hated that live animals were used to test the effects of radiation. He believed nuclear testing was necessary for deterrence but was angry about the times officials screwed up and put test participants and the public in needless danger.

"I've lost a lot of my old buddies to cancer," he told me in a low voice.

In the museum, the darker sides of nuclear testing were touched on and dismissed in a few cursory displays. Fallout was addressed in terms of the "international outrage" and "public pressure" that eventually led to the 1963 Limited Test Ban Treaty, which put a stop to atmospheric testing. The reason fallout was the subject of outrage was not elaborated on.

Some of the site workers and scientists interviewed in the videos expressed disappointment, even anger, that the government ceased testing. The panel on subcritical testing, a way of evaluating the soundness of aging weapons without actually blowing them up, read, "As long as nuclear testing is not allowed, these experiments are needed to determine the physical and chemical degradation . . . of weapons materials and components." *As long as nuclear testing is not allowed . . .*

As the official site literature emphasized, the National Nuclear Security Administration is tasked with maintaining readiness for a resumption of underground testing within two to three years of a presidential order. I got the unnerving sense that the museum's curators saw their role as not only documenting history but also preserving knowledge until it is needed again.

Dick, however, did not seem to believe that nuclear testing had a future. Some of his former coworkers, the few who were still alive, worked as tour guides out at the site. But he didn't want to see what the place had become, empty, deserted, stripped of purpose despite what the promotional videos said of its still-vital role in our national security. "If I could go back like we were in the fifties or sixties, I'd do it in a heartbeat," he said, "but now, it's kinda like a ghost town. It would be like going back home and your house had burned down."

### The Blast

Light moves faster than sound. We know this. Or at least, we have been told. Yet most everything we've seen has taught us otherwise.

In movies, the flash, the fire, and the boom of the explosion come simultaneously. The hero runs toward us, silhouetted by flames. He is the lone survivor of an apocalyptic attack, or he has lit the fuse and this end is the beginning of a world born in the destruction of evil, a world free of tyranny. The music soars; a single flower quivers in the breeze.

Most of the videos you see of nuclear tests confirm this expectation because most publicly released nuclear testing footage has been dubbed, sound added afterward to coincide with the flash. Imagine, then, the disorientation of the observers on News Nob, eight miles from ground zero, when the flash occurred in silence and they waited, watching the fireball balloon and fade to gray, for nearly half a minute before the sound and the force of the blast reached them.

Observers of the Apple II test were encouraged to bring maps of their hometowns, along with compasses for transferring circles of destruction from the Nevada desert to the real inhabited Main Streets of suburban America. They were invited to picture their families and friends waiting docile in houses below an armed nuclear bomb.

I imagine George would have resisted such an obvious ploy of emotional manipulation—yet as he watched the fireball expand in silence over that fake town, how could he help but think of the little L-shaped house back in Tennessee with the lawn that sloped down to a quiet, winding street? The house that held his wife and three children, the youngest, my father, not yet two.

That house looked just like all of the other wartime prefabs in Oak Ridge, erected in a matter of hours to serve the needs of the moment without a thought to longevity. In 1945, defense had meant hurry. Defense had meant sacrifice. Defense had meant rationed food, victory gardens, nylon stockings gone to parachutes. Defense had meant live small, make do.

But in 1955, defense meant building fallout shelters, stockpiling food, and testing the latest fashions against nuclear fire. Which colors, dyes, and fabrics offered more protection against heat and radiation? Which melted, disappeared, or burst into flame? How should we shop for the nuclear apocalypse?

In addition to J. C. Penney, more than two hundred other companies participated in the Apple II test, supplying the model houses with refrigerators, ranges, water heaters, clothes dryers, curtains, couches, tables, light fixtures, and all the other commodities of a middle-class American life. The list of participating industries included La-Z-Boy Chair Co., Brandt Furniture Co., Lullaby Furniture Corp., General Electric, Motorola, the American Meat Institute, Society of the Plastics Industry, and the Venetian Blind Association of America. L.A. Darling supplied the mannequins, the same type used in shop windows across the nation. How will our stuff survive nuclear annihilation? It was the test of American consumerism against Soviet Communism.

This glut of stuff was meant to be representative of the contents of a typical American home. "Typical" meant white, suburban, middle-class, idealized nuclear families framed as both victims and heroes in this absurd pageant. Because while government propaganda celebrated preparedness as an all-American virtue, the kind of preparations modeled in these civil defense exercises were designed for a white suburban lifestyle, even though those most likely to be victims of a nuclear attack—low-income people, people of color, and especially Black people living in dense urban housing—lacked the space and means to build and stock shelters and even cars to evacuate a destroyed or threatened city.

Plans for more collective preparations such as public shelters were deemphasized amid the increasing impossibility that cities could be saved at all; at the same time, planners feared that racial violence would erupt if authorities were unable to enforce racial hierarchies in integrated shelters and evacuation centers.

In Oak Ridge, nuclear fear and frenzy funded new development. The 260,000-square-foot Downtown Shopping Center, anchored by J. C. Penney and dwarfed by parking spaces for more than one thousand cars, would open before the end of 1955. George himself had gone from being junior chemist #2 making $180 a month in 1943 to assistant plant superintendent making $1,130 a month in 1955. An accident of geography and education had landed a soil chemist in the nuclear weapons business, and he had thrived. His was a story of the upward mobility possible for hardworking middle-class white Americans. He must have been proud of what he had achieved, how far he'd come—an American dream. Perhaps he wanted a souvenir, a photograph to say, *See this thing I built*.

My mother was the only member of my family to confirm my memory of the photograph: "It is emblazoned in my memory—a glow of a mushroom cloud and George in front, kinda smiling, with sunglasses. The blast takes up the whole background. It always seemed really close to me. I always thought it was odd that it existed, like the pictures I have of my dad, you know, standing in front of a waterfall, some natural phenomenon you would want to photograph and show everyone you were there."

The fireball cools from white to yellow to orange to gray and rises, trailing a radioactive column of smoke and dust in a zigzagging tail. When you've stopped expecting it, the sound of the bomb comes like a shotgun followed by rushing air, cresting, rumbling, fading. The accompanying shock wave, warned an observer handbook, might knock a person to their knees.

If the sight of the silently rising nuclear fireball was unnerving to the observers on May 5, 1955, the events that followed would soon repackage the experience into a more familiar Hollywood war story. Within five minutes of the Apple II detonation, the commander of Task Force Razor ordered attack; eighty-nine armored vehicles advanced north toward ground zero through the thick dust stirred up by the explosion to claim a target northwest of the shot tower.

Observers watched from bleachers while a military commentator narrated the event. The troops fired blanks, threw smoke grenades, and even used napalm to enhance the realism of the spectacle.

In the official video released by the FCDA, the silence after the flash is filled by an orchestral soundtrack in minor chords against a montage of destruction; the desert floor rises as a wooden house buckles, then crumples inward; power lines swing back like a slingshot; a transmission tower shudders but remains standing; the windows of a two-story brick house billow with smoke before the whole structure collapses backward as if by the force of some invisible tidal wave.

The screen goes dark, then opens on blue sky. The music shifts into a major key, and the reassuring voice of the narrator steps in to review the findings of the test. The unreinforced masonry is totally destroyed, while a squat, reinforced cinderblock house remains standing. A bathroom shelter stands intact beneath the ruins of the house collapsed around it.

The bomb that exploded in the Nevada desert on May 5, 1955, was twice as powerful as the bomb dropped on Hiroshima. Yet, as the FCDA video reminds its viewers, the Apple II bomb was tiny by the standards of the day, many times less powerful than the hydrogen bombs being churned out by America's nuclear weapons plants. "It must be borne in mind," the narrator intones, "that multimegaton weapons would result in much greater damage over a larger area. All these factors must be considered as we plan for the survival of our homes, our families, and our nation in the nuclear age."

I asked Dick Mingus to describe what the nuclear blasts looked like. He groped to convey the sheer brightness of the flash. Like the aching white of arc welding, he said.

"Each shot, each explosion, is a little bit different. I watched a shot where I was at a higher elevation than where the bomb was. I was like on a mountainside looking down upon it, and when the shot went off, of course there's like that real sharp arc bright, and then in a matter of, I don't know what it would be, not so much as seconds, but real quick, it was like a brilliant purple. And it was huge, like a big bulb, like purple or dark blue, and then on top of this it looked like an ice cap. And you know, I'm thinking to myself—something wrong with my eyes, you know . . .

"So you see pictures of nothing but that ball of fire, but now, I'm not a photographer—that's someone else's business here. But we used celluloid film at that time. Could that bright have destroyed enough of that film that they couldn't pick that up? I don't know. I don't know. But this is the truth, so help me, of what I've seen from looking down."

Snap a photo, scribble a journal entry, record a memory—in the effort to capture reality, we alter the observed, congeal a partial truth. What is lost in the rendering? Daytime photographs of nuclear blasts appear as if they were taken at night, the sunlight rendered dark beside the bomb's flash.

That my mother remembered the photograph did not reassure me much. Memory can work by suggestion. And my mother is a storyteller, her memory loyal to the best story, subject perhaps, to some subconscious sense for pacing and narrative detail that lets what is extraneous fall away. Sometimes her description of a book or movie is better than the original. She remembered the photograph as I did, but was it possible that the story I told, the one I believed, simply subsumed what was there before?

After some time, my uncle Paul told me that he *did*, in fact, remember the photograph. He told me this as if he had never told me he didn't remember it. Now I wasn't sure I believed him. I was no longer even sure I believed myself.

The night before my scheduled tour, I studied the list of prohibited items sent to me weeks before. Some were what you would expect— no weapons, incendiary devices, or alcohol. And I knew when I signed up that I would not be allowed a camera or voice recorder, but reading through the list, I was struck by the extensive pains to which the DOE had gone to ensure that no part of the public tour could be documented. In addition to cameras, camcorders, and recording devices, the list of prohibited devices included cell phones, Bluetooth-enabled devices, portable data-storage devices, computers, binoculars, optical instruments, and GPSs.

I felt almost panicked. As it began to seem less and less likely that I would find that photograph, as I began to doubt what I knew I knew, it seemed imperative that I record, permanently and irrefutably, as much as possible. How could I trust my eyes, my memory?

But there was nothing for it—feeling rather stripped down, I arrived in the parking lot of the National Atomic Testing Museum the morning of the tour.

By now, I knew the DOE employees who circulated through the reading room, taking turns attending to curious visitors who wandered over from the museum; leafed through the informational pamphlets; gazed wide-eyed at the thick, ominous volumes that lined the shelves; and then, quickly bored, departed. They also got people who came in raving about aliens and volcanoes packed with radioactive materials, fevered for proof of the mad world they lived inside.

"You going on the tour?" the woman at the desk asked me. "My father used to work out at the site," she said. "He was a cement technician—poured cement for underground tests. My husband was a pipe-fitter. The site," she continued, "it used to have a whole town there—bowling alley, theater, bunny farm . . ."

"Bunny farm?" I asked.

She leaned across the desk. "Prostitutes," she said, in a low voice.

In the lobby, I exchanged my driver's license for a temporary badge. This one wasn't like George's—just a yellow rectangle with a number, no name or photograph.

On the bus, a man in front leaned toward the guide, holding up his badge, Temp 285, hung on a red lanyard around his neck. "This isn't a radiation badge, is it?"

Our guide, a wrinkled, white-haired man in a Korea Vet trucker's hat, laughed. "No, you don't have to worry about that any."

### Fallout

The force of the explosion sucks debris and soil, anything in its path, up into the rising fireball. The closer to the ground the bomb explodes, the more debris is lifted and irradiated in the blast. As the cloud rises and cools, drifts in the wind, it begins to drop the radioactive particles, the largest pieces first, as large as several millimeters in diameter, and then smaller and smaller ones, finer than dust; the tiniest, microscopic particles might not fall for months or years. This is what we know as fallout.

At some ten seconds past 5:10 a.m. on the morning of May 5, 1955, the Apple II cloud rose to fifty-one thousand feet and began drifting north. In the wind, the plume split into three parts, and three different airplanes tracked their progress northeast into Utah and north toward Ely and Eureka, Nevada. The cloud spread, dissipated, and after a few hours, the planes returned to their bases. A routine mission.

A public education program before and during the Operation Teapot test series, of which Apple II was a part, included area film screenings about nuclear testing and the distribution of fifty thousand copies of the official illustrated booklet *Atomic Test Effects in the Nevada Test Site Region*, published by the Joint Test Organization (JTO). One of the missions of the educational activities was to "allay unfounded fear of damage or injury that may arise from public misunderstanding of test operations."

*Atomic Test Effects in the Nevada Test Site Region* took a practical and reassuring tone: "So, radiation is not new to our lives. In this atomic age we are living on a more familiar basis with it. It is important that we try to understand it, accept it, and use it. It is also important that we respect its powers, so that we will be guided by knowledge and not be blinded by fear of the unknown."

Don't worry if your Geiger counters go crazy. Geiger counters are just too sensitive, the JTO maintained.

Test officials walked a fine line between cultivating the fear necessary for the public to accept nuclear testing and normalizing the hazards to assuage concerns about safety. Exposure to radiation was compared to a sunburn: "The sun will give you a pleasant suntan, but if you are overexposed it can burn the skin and make you quite sick." The booklet recounted a case in which livestock grazing outside the test site received radiation burns but assured readers that the cows could still be bred and eaten without fear. The JTO even went so far as to claim that many who were harmed by radiation from the bombings in Japan "apparently made good recoveries."

A few hours after detonation, the mushroom cloud is no longer visible, the booklet explained, but still traceable by its widening trail of radiation, stretching to hundreds of miles wide and eventually "distributed uniformly over the earth's surface."

On May 9, four days after the Apple II test, radiation monitors in Oak Ridge, some 1,700 miles away, picked up elevated levels of radioactivity. The amount doubled normal background levels but was nevertheless considered "very minor" and "almost too small to measure."

"[The atomic cloud] does not constitute a serious hazard to any living thing outside the test site," the JTO claimed.

About fifty of us doomsday tourists rode the bus northwest out of Las Vegas toward violet-lit sandstone peaks. Behind us, the casino lights were washed out against the morning sun. Our guide, Ernie Williams, introduced himself. In 1952, during the Korean War, Ernie was in uniform guarding, assembling, and disassembling nuclear weapons at an Air Force base in England. That expertise got him a job at the test site a year after he returned. He worked out at the Pacific site too. Altogether, he told us, he'd seen eighty atmospheric shots and four hundred underground. "I'm a little hard of hearing. I've been involved with too many atmospheric shots," he told us, and his whole face wrinkled up as he grinned.

My uncle Paul, Karin's husband, who followed his father-in-law into the weapons business, was with me on the tour. During his time at Y-12 and later at the DOE headquarters in Washington, DC, Paul frequently traveled to the Nevada Test Site. He never saw an open-air test—by the time he came along, the 1963 Limited Test Ban Treaty prohibited atmospheric explosions—but he was sent into shafts hundreds or thousands of feet underground to troubleshoot finicky bombs. His eyes went a little wild when he described the feeling of being deep in the earth, staring down an armed nuclear bomb and hoping like hell the guy in the control room wouldn't sneeze.

When Paul had learned I'd be going on this tour, he offered to join me as an insider expert. He flew into Vegas a few days after I did, and he kept the hotel room stocked with limes and rum, for which I'd been grateful. This morning, though, he was too talkative for my taste—I was journaling furiously, anxious not to miss a thing, while he warmed to his role as expert. "Did I ever tell you about the time I saw a classified weapons part pulled out of a pile of unclassified waste?" he prompted. I responded to his asides with grudging *hmmms*.

"That's Creech Air Force Base," Ernie told us as we passed a large fenced complex, just some long, low, white warehouses visible past the guardhouses and the desert stretching brown behind. "Home of the unmanned aircraft!" Drones, that is. He scanned the sky. "If we're lucky, we'll get to see one." Everyone leaned toward the windows, looking up. Ernie passed out a laminated photograph—a drone called a Reaper. It looked ungainly, front heavy, all its lines smooth and round, like something you might get if you crossed a manatee with a fighter jet. "We're not gonna see one today," the bus driver said, disappointed.

As we approached the gate to the test site, I noticed the holding pens first: two squares of desert, each about the size of a basketball court, surrounded by chain-link fence topped with barbed wire, empty but for a porta-potty in each. They sat just beyond a white line painted across the road; peace protesters who crossed the line would be handcuffed and held in the pen until they were sent on to jail or cited and released. A hot wind blew through the fence.

As we approached the gates, we passed a red sign directing trucks carrying radioactive waste. We stopped, and an armed guard boarded. "We don't have any paperwork for you guys for some reason," he told Ernie. Ernie got off with him, then boarded again.

"He tells me they're gonna do a search," Ernie told the bus driver.

"Nah," said the driver.

We sat for a few minutes. On our right was a short, beige building—the badge office. Patches of sagebrush were lit yellow in the sun, and gnarled Joshua trees broke the monotony of flat desert, which gave way, finally, to reddish-brown mountains, stark and bare in the distance.

Ernie radioed, "Bird dog, bird dog, this is Ernie. I'm here at the gate with a tour group." He learned that Frenchman's Flat, one of the two primary shot areas, was closed for the day for a hazardous spill test.

The old nuclear proving ground is now the world's largest site for open-air testing of hazardous materials. For a fee, public and private entities can spew or spill or explode chemicals, biological simulants, or radioactive materials into the desert basin to test technologies that require or might lead to toxic or radiological releases, and train employees and first responders in monitoring, detection, and accident response.

"I had no idea about all this," Paul said. "When I came out here, we only saw the one area. Seems like they're trying to make sure the site remains relevant."

There was no search, after all. Paperwork apparently sorted out, we drove through the gate, passing the dosimetry building, a track where security guards trained, and some squat cinder block housing facilities left over from the heyday of the 1950s. The bowling alley, swimming pool, and movie theater were gone, but there was still a cafeteria and post office. The streets of this town, just a slight grid sketched over the desert, were named after test series— Ranger, Knothole, Buster, Hardtack.

"There used to be a facility for little animals," Ernie said. In one 1957 shot, more than seven hundred pigs were placed in foxholes or in the open air at various distances from the bomb, which exploded from a balloon seven hundred feet above the desert floor. The pigs were used because their flesh most closely resembled human flesh and they could be placed closer to the bomb than human volunteers. Some of the pigs were dressed in military uniforms to test the protectiveness of soldiers' fatigues.

I pulled on a sweater against the air-conditioning and looked out the window, searching for something living. We passed flat stretches of earth marked by small yellow signs. "Caution—Underground Radioactive Material." Ernie assured us that we could walk 98 percent of the site without danger. Still, I was suspicious of the official explanation for why pregnant women were discouraged from attending the tour: "the long bus ride and uneven terrain." In any case, we were shepherded through most of the tour from the confines of the bus.

The land was pocked with craters. Open-air shots detonated close to the ground might form a shallow crater, but most of the craters came from the underground tests, Ernie explained. When bombs are shot off underground, they vaporize earth and melt rock; minutes or hours later, the land subsides into the empty space. On films, the yellow desert earth suddenly dimples and goes dark, then clouds of dust rise in a perfect circle. From satellite pictures, the test site looks like some giant and perplexing long-abandoned game board.

I felt my search had become diffuse, spread out like a mushroom cloud until it no longer had shape or name. I was far beyond the frame. I knew I would not find George out here, downwind. And yet, fallout teaches us that nothing will be contained, that we cannot pluck at one thread without shivering the whole web.

American civil defense exercises enacted a grand fantasy—the triumph of whiteness, domesticity, capitalism, and American self-reliance against nuclear apocalypse. Some civil defense propaganda and apocalyptic science fiction novels of the time explicitly linked the scene of nuclear apocalypse to the frontier, the image of the brave and hardy white families to the celebrated colonists of the previous century, those instruments and soldiers of the government's genocidal policies. There was even a yearning in the worst of these narratives—that nuclear war might wipe out racially diverse cities, cleanse the country of the blight of urban decay, and return the nation to the independent spirit of the idealized pioneers.

Despite these racist fantasies, the idea that anyone could survive a direct nuclear attack became an increasingly dubious prospect with the development of more and more powerful bombs. But while the government staged elaborate games of make-believe, spinning out a narrative of white victimhood and survival on Native land, people were actually being harmed.

The prevailing winds through the Nevada Test Site carried fallout away from densely populated Las Vegas and Los Angeles, north and east toward more sparsely populated parts of Nevada, southern Utah, northern Arizona. This was thought to be ideal, of course; wind patterns that would expose fewer people were a factor in choosing the location of the test site. But where there is an upwind, there is a downwind.

Downwind, particles irradiated by the bomb's explosion drifted like invisible snow, dusted cars, rooftops, gardens, and schoolyards. Sometimes families would rise before dawn to watch the blush of the explosions over the mountains, feel the earth tremble beneath them, or take picnics out to sit under the towering mushroom clouds. Later, some would remember noticing reddened skin or strange sores, hair falling out, dead or sickened animals. Caught outside, ranchers might brace themselves against a cloud of dust and, after, feel their hair and skin gritty. Some said the dust left them racked with chills and vomiting.

Among the most heavily exposed were Mormon communities and Southern Paiute and Western Shoshone people living on tribal lands. Due to a diet that included hunted game, foraged wild plants, and milk from cows grazing on contaminated grass, Native communities were particularly vulnerable, though major studies of radiation exposures to downwinders have failed to take these unique factors into account. "The pine trees we use for food and heating were exposed, the plants we use for food and medicine were exposed, the animals we use for food were exposed. We were exposed," Ian Zabarte, the principal man of the Western Shoshone, wrote for *Al Jazeera* in 2020. Native activists and community leaders who have seen many relatives and neighbors die of cancers and other conditions they suspect were caused by radiation exposure are still fighting for funding to support health research and monitoring.

With the passage of the Radiation Exposure Compensation Act (RECA) in 1990, the US Congress took one step toward acknowledging that the US government, in the name of national security, exposed the very people it promised to protect to dangerous levels of radiation from nuclear testing and uranium mining. RECA has awarded more than two and a half billion dollars to more than thirty-nine thousand claimants or their survivors who contracted certain covered cancers or other diseases—downwinders in certain counties of Utah, Nevada, and Arizona; test site workers and participants; and uranium miners, millers, and transporters. Another thirteen thousand claims have been denied.

Despite playing a leading role in advocating for the compensation program, Indigenous communities, particularly Navajo miners, who sometimes do not have the official proofs of residence or medical records required to prove eligibility, are compensated at lower rates than other populations. And though county lines do not prevent the drift of fallout, downwinders who did not live in the right county during the testing years or who did not get sick in the right way are not eligible. RECA is due to sunset in June of 2024; activists continue to fight for its expansion.

In fact, fallout from the Nevada tests reached the entire continental United States, increasing cancer risks nationwide. One of the most widespread effects was elevated incidence of thyroid cancers from drinking milk contaminated by iodine-131; female children who drank lots of milk from backyard livestock bore the highest risk. Cancers may not show up for decades after exposure, but scientists estimate that Nevada testing will eventually cause some forty-nine thousand cases of thyroid cancer among those who were milk-drinking children in the 1950s.

As it turns out, everyone, everywhere on Earth, was exposed to radiation from nuclear testing. Aware of the hazards of fallout while publicly downplaying the danger, the AEC saved its largest tests for the Marshall Islands of the Pacific. The US "protectorate," writes historian Robert Jacobs, was "treated . . . as a colony to be used for military experimentation." There, bombs a thousand times more powerful than the bombs that devastated Hiroshima and Nagasaki swallowed islands whole, rendered others uninhabitable, spewed massive amounts of fallout on displaced and neighboring islanders, and carried radioactive particles way up into the atmosphere where they lingered for months or years before falling across the entire Earth.

The fingerprints of atmospheric testing, called the bomb pulse, can be found in tree rings from France to Nagasaki, in the eye lenses of sharks, even in human hearts. Our stratosphere is still stitched in radioactive particles.

Our first stop on the tour was the Radioactive Waste Management Complex, a facility for storing low-level radioactive waste. An energetic man boarded the bus and explained that "low-level" included contaminated rags, tools, soil, and building debris from retired nuclear complexes; contaminated personal protective equipment; and anything that fit an "approved waste profile."

Where to store high-level and transuranic waste such as spent fuel rods from nuclear reactors and highly radioactive by-products of nuclear weapons production, stuff that stays dangerous for tens of thousands of years, far more than the amount of time we can imagine protecting anything, has been the subject of decades of scientific and political debate. "Put it in New Jersey!" someone on the bus recommended.

"What's wrong with New Jersey?" asked our low-level expert. "How about Washington? There's a big white building they're not using for anything." He was a government employee. Obama was in the White House. Paul and I raised our eyebrows at each other.

"I used to be out at Oak Ridge," Paul said, leaning into the aisle. "You got anything from out there?"

"Oh yeah," said the man, pointing out a pile of massive gray bags. "Those are converters from K-25." Demolition of K-25, the massive gaseous diffusion uranium enrichment plant where my grandmother spent her wartime days as a secretary, was completed in 2013.

We drove through long stretches of bomb-pocked desert. Finally, we were allowed to get out of the bus to stand on an elevated wooden platform at the lip of the Sedan Crater. The hot dry air was a relief on my chilled skin. The crater was round, massive, and smooth-sided, a startling absence of earth. This place felt absolutely lifeless.

Sedan, Ernie told us, was created on July 6, 1962, by a 104-kiloton nuclear explosion buried 635 feet below the desert floor. It was part of Project Plowshare, an attempt to find peaceful uses for nuclear weapons by exploiting their force to dig dams, canals, mines, and tunnels. The Sedan explosion, the equivalent of about seven Hiroshima bombs, lifted twelve million tons of earth and plumed into a radioactive cloud that ballooned to a width of forty miles over Ely, Nevada, before disappearing and drifting into southern Minnesota and eastern Tennessee, spreading fallout farther, perhaps, than any other nuclear test conducted in the continental United States.

"The fireball went up eleven thousand feet!" Ernie marveled. At the bottom of the crater lay several rubber tires. I asked Ernie about them. "Probably the construction guys rolled them down," he said, "to see whose would get to the bottom first."

We loaded back onto the bus.

I once asked Paul whether he felt at all guilty for his work building nuclear weapons. "Absolutely not," he replied in a booming voice. He believed in mutually assured destruction, he explained, and thought that each weapon he touched helped shore up against nuclear annihilation. But he understands the insanity of such a doctrine; one of his favorite movies is *Dr. Strangelove*, Stanley Kubrick's 1964 satirical black comedy following the events triggered when a rogue American general launches a first strike against the Soviet Union, leading to irreversible nuclear annihilation of all life on earth.

Paul carries his weight in a taut beer belly, lets his whitening hair grow unruly, smokes cigars, and flirts outrageously with women not his wife, but there is also a deep kindness in him. I love my uncle. He is loud and irreverent, sometimes obnoxiously so, but he is also uncannily perceptive. And he has always heard my quiet voice at the end of the dinner table, straining to edge in amid the louder voices of the rest of the family.

How was I to make sense of these men of my family? Paul, with his loud humor and emotional intelligence. George, who walked at dawn in the desert and who watched that desert blaze white-hot with nuclear fire.

The Apple II site was the last stop on the tour. By now, Paul had shown his hand to the rest of the bus, and they plied him with questions: *How much does a nuclear bomb cost to make? How long does it take? How deep do they dig the tunnels? What's it like to be down there?* He held court, relishing the attention. And I was left to my thoughts.

I could see one of the houses that survived, glittering dimly in the heat. Its dark wood planks looked scorched. The windows gaped, glassless. As we circled the house, I pressed my nose to the window of the bus. I guessed that the wood smelled hot and dry, like the cracking planks of the dock at the lake house baking on an August afternoon. As we rounded the corner, I looked through two angled windows to a square of perfect blue sky. The house was completely empty.

Apple II's ground zero was strewn with mangled trucks, derailed train cars, overturned trailers, and emergency vehicles. A Delta plane, broken in three, looked like an oversized toy, a casualty of some giant child's tantrum. This spot is now used as a training ground for counterterrorism. First responders practice using radiation detectors on the still-radioactive remains of the five-hundred-foot steel tower that held the Apple II bomb.

The sun was high above now, the shadows almost gone, the desert bleached, overexposed.

The photograph did not turn up in the Nuclear Testing Archive or in a closet at the lake house. It did not turn up at the Oak Ridge Library, at the American Museum of Science and Energy, or in the files of the current DOE photographer at Y-12. I asked historians, scholars, and former test site workers; no one had ever seen a similar photograph.

Then, digging through boxes in her daughter's attic in Middle Tennessee, my aunt Karin found a box of photographs that were displaced from the lake. Inside, there was a photograph of a test blast.

Though the image is faded, the center of the fireball is searingly bright. The stem of the blast extends to the ground, fading from luminous yellow to a thick gray, ending in angry swirls of smoke and dust at the desert floor, the perfect mushroom shape. There is no man in this photograph. No sign of life at all.

Was it possible, then, that a photograph of George was tucked into the frame of this atomic blast, and my memory smoothed the edges between them? Perhaps this was the way I had made sense of these two things I barely knew—grandfather and bomb. Perhaps. Memory bled into dream, receding into some gray distance until I had to remind myself of what I was looking for in the first place.

When I allowed myself to admit this possibility, I began to doubt all the rest too. By now, I had spent years chasing the ghost of George in hints and fragments, myths and contradicted memories.

I had tried to make sense of George as a way of making sense of myself, my world. To unravel his contradiction would be a kind of evidence for a belief I stubbornly held onto in the face of so many indications to the contrary: that people, at their most essential core, are good. And that the harm we do to others, in an individual and a global sense, comes from our brokenness and feeds our brokenness. Perhaps then I could hold the pain and love and guilt as a whole story, the story of my home.

One summer afternoon as we were driving into Oak Ridge from the lake house to pick up dessert from Secret City Pies, Nellie said to me, "I don't think my dad was ever the same after Hiroshima."

I did not ask her what she meant, because I knew. Nellie didn't know her father before Hiroshima, but she knew him after as a deeply depressed, unstable, alcoholic, and verbally abusive man. As the youngest child, and the last one left at home when George was at his worst, she knew him this way more than her siblings did. And in Nellie's story of her life, her father's guilt over Hiroshima was part of how he became a man who was alternately gentle and cruel, caring and violent. Hiroshima helped explain her father.

I agreed. I wanted to believe her. But on another day, I would suspect that we were both clinging to a self-serving narrative, no better than the polygraphers reading what they liked into the symptoms of a body under stress. For Nellie, belief in her father's prior woundedness might allow her to forgive him for the darkness he cast over her young life. For me, it allowed me to think of him as a man of conscience. A man unable to have a hand, however indirectly, in the death and brutal suffering of hundreds of thousands without deep remorse.

I wanted to make George speak. I tried to make him and his pain play a role in my own personal mythos. But at the end of the day, the dead remain their own, no matter how much we yearn for their voices. I would never be able to speak the truth of George's inner life. I would never be able to say what it meant.

I was nagged by the thought that what I was really after was my own innocence. As if, by circling backward, I could unspool this heritage. I wanted to live pure, unguilty, unencumbered.

I wanted George to be culpable, and I wanted to redeem him. But he was like any middle-class white American, both exquisitely unique and overwhelmingly ordinary in his midlevel talent, his desire to secure a certain level of American comfort and prosperity, his acceptance of a narrative that assured him of his and his country's superiority, his ability to turn from the harm he was complicit in. To expect anything else—was it to cleave to a rigid and unrealistic idealism?

So George posed for a photograph. Or he didn't. Who cared? I was jousting at windmills.

# 10

# FUSION

One summer afternoon at the lake house, I gathered my aunts and uncle upstairs and asked them to tell me about their happiest memories of George. I realized I had never before asked such a question, never really invited happiness into the story even though, for me, this story began with happiness.

We sat on faded couches that smelled of sun and dust. Karin, Kurt, and Nellie looked a little startled, dreamy.

Karin chimed in first. As the eldest, she had more happy memories of her dad than the others. He worked hard, sure, but he still showed up—to school plays, father-daughter dinners, even to a party she hosted for her classmates after a high school football game. He was charming, funny, easy with her friends. Once, before a high school dance, Doris was out for the evening, and so George stepped into the role of overseeing Karin's hair and makeup preparations with great gusto.

Kurt remembered fishing with his father. How they'd rise before dawn, venture out in a little johnboat, the water still and shining beneath an inky sky. They were partners then, teammates at this magic, silent hour. They'd watch the sun rise over the water and bring home buckets of striped bass and crappie. It wasn't until Kurt was an adult that he realized one couldn't always depend on catching a boatload of fish, that his father was an uncommonly good fisherman. He laughed at this, eyes blurry behind the thick lenses that were a George inheritance.

Nellie remembered a game she played with her father. When she was three or four, she'd wait in taut excitement for him to arrive home from work. Hearing his car pull in, his footsteps on the driveway, she'd fly to her room to don a stiff old lady's hat and a blouse with shoulder pads that hung to her elbows. Then, she'd creep out the back door and wobble in her mother's heels around to the front to ring the doorbell.

"Oh, Mrs. Brown, come in!" George would exclaim, leaning down to regard her earnestly. "How nice to see you! Do come in for some tea."

Sitting at the kitchen table, Nellie dangling her small legs, George exhausted from a long day at the plant, father and daughter would share a snack prepared by Doris, and then "Mrs. Brown" would excuse herself in a breathless giggle. "Goodbye! See you tomorrow!"

"I really thought I had one over on my dad," she laughed.

I blinked rapidly, surprised by a sudden wave of tenderness. For what he could have been. For what he sometimes was.

George had not had a happy childhood. His father, Joseph Henry Strasser, had been strict to the point of coldness. Karin, the only child old enough to remember her grandfather, had been afraid of the severe man. George did not speak of his mother.

Among his siblings, George was odd, a bit of a loner—short, awkward, and a bit too book-smart for his own good. He taught himself to read at a young age and excelled in school. But study took him from farm work, and so he was selfish, lazy in his father's eyes. Of the six Strasser children, George was the only one to finish a four-year degree and the only one to move more than a few miles from home.

In Oak Ridge, George bloomed, easily straddling the divide between the highly educated city and its rural surrounds. The city had, and still has, an elitist reputation in the area, but George respected everyone and was counted a friend by farmers and scientists alike. My father remembers how George loved to spend long hours on the porches of local farmers, discussing soil, weather, and farming techniques in granular detail. Dragged along on these interminable afternoons, my father squirmed in unbearable boredom.

Oak Ridge itself fostered an unusual closeness. Far from their families and bound by their peculiar work, George's colleagues at the plant bonded deeply. The widow of one of George's best friends and coworkers, and my grandmother's friend, Mary Jane Hibbs, told me, "None of us had any families there. We all became each other's families. We helped each other; if someone needed emergency help, we were there to help. We didn't have parents that could kind of guide us along, so we tried to help each other."

Before the lake house, George and Doris owned a little place on a steep lot on the Little Emory River, an old railroad car converted to a cottage where the children slept on the screened-in porch. But at the end of 1959, they pooled their money with a group of his coworkers and their wives to buy a small peninsula on a wide segment of Watts Bar Lake, twenty miles outside of Oak Ridge. They called it Pirate Cove, divided lots, built docks and then houses, and caravanned their families out for weekends and summers.

Here, my father and his siblings spent weeks running ragged and barefoot between lots without fences. They paired off by age with the closest Hibbs kid or Googin girl. The Jasnys and the Eberts and the Wilkinsons—all the families had kids around the same age, and it was a sort of paradise. They pulled off daring waterskiing stunts, took snacks from whichever kitchen was closest, and slept where they found a pillow. Mrs. Hibbs would sometimes wake to find my father reading comics on her front porch, and Doris would find that Mrs. Hibbs's daughter Joanne had stayed the night with Nellie. George bought a horse called Big Red, a magnificent creature; he could hold five kids on his back at once. He would wade into the water to cool his belly and soak the kids' calves. Or did he belong to one of the neighbors? No one could remember for sure now. It didn't matter, really.

This was the land that would become the lake house, my lake, where on a summer afternoon Karin, Kurt, Nellie, and I sat around remembering the best things.

It seemed an ideal improbability, what one said among a group of friends after a satisfying homemade meal and a couple of bottles of wine—"Let's buy a farm! A peninsula! An island!" The dream of being able to choose one's family, to extend a moment of feeling good and whole and part of something into a lifetime.

In Oak Ridge, such a miracle was possible. Here, odd men, misfits, could find each other, could thrive, could relieve the pressure of their strange and stressful jobs among people who understood them. Every house on the peninsula had an extra refrigerator for storing a keg of beer; one had two spares, and another served hard liquor, both legal spirits and local moonshine.

There were peculiarities among this cohort: a raft built on big Styrofoam blocks from the plant, leftover packing material for some kind of chemical; precisely spherical grills made of a thick, heavy metal that never rusted no matter how long it stayed in the rain, parts from spare fuel capsules for hydrogen bombs, so the story went.

None of this was remarkable, though. Here, there was ease. During the week, the men worked together. On the weekends, they fished and swam together. The kids romped wild together. The wives played bridge together. The men drank together. Drank too much together? But what did it matter? This was home.

This spirit of carefree community echoed down to my generation. Though the land was no longer held in common, we still spilled over into the Jasnys' and the Wilkinsons'—both still owned by the children of George's colleagues—when there were not enough beds for a family reunion. And when I met the children and grandchildren of the men who built these houses, we introduced ourselves as "the originals."

I had few memories of the men behind those names. By the time I traversed their lots, they were white-haired and boring or already gone. But now I recognized their names from the Y-12 newsletters and plant histories. They were the men promoted alongside George, working above him, or reporting directly to him. This place was the playground of Y-12's up-and-coming.

Now I knew that George and his friends bought this land, built this little paradise, with bomb money.

In October 1949, the General Advisory Committee to the AEC met to discuss whether the country should pursue development of a hydrogen bomb. A hydrogen bomb is a nuclear bomb fueled not by fission, the splitting of atoms, but by fusion, the joining of them; it had the potential to be hundreds or thousands of times more powerful than the bombs dropped on Hiroshima and Nagasaki. It was then speculated that it would be possible to build a single hydrogen bomb powerful enough to wipe out the entire human population.

The committee was chaired by J. Robert Oppenheimer, wartime director of Los Alamos, known as the father of the atomic bomb, and included seven other top scientists and engineers, many of whom had played fundamental roles in the Manhattan Project. The majority opinion, written by Oppenheimer, advised against prioritizing the development of a fusion weapon, cautioning technical challenges beside moral objections: "If super bombs will work at all, there is no inherent limit in the destructive power that may be attained with them. Therefore, a super bomb might become a weapon of genocide. . . . In determining not to proceed to develop the super bomb, we see a unique opportunity of providing by example some limitations on the totality of war and thus of limiting the fear and arousing the hope of mankind."

The minority opinion opposed the development even more adamantly, stating, "It is necessarily an evil thing considered in any light."

The Soviet Union had conducted its first nuclear test, of a fission bomb, just two months before that meeting. Despite the objections of the General Advisory Committee, Truman announced on January 31, 1950: "I have directed the Atomic Energy Commission to continue its work on all forms of atomic weapons, including the so-called hydrogen or superbomb."

The weapons business of Oak Ridge would have continued without the superbomb. Y-12 would have continued to churn out parts for smaller and more powerful fission bombs, which were devastating enough. But the superbomb injected the plant with new funding, new priorities, and renewed urgency. Y-12 did not design the superbomb—that work was done at Los Alamos—but was tasked with manufacturing an essential fuel component for the bomb by separating isotopes of lithium.

Lithium isotope separation would be Y-12's top priority for more than a decade. It would require incredible industrial output and a total commitment from its workers. The fate of the nation might depend on the success of their efforts, so they were told.

George reached the pinnacle of his career overseeing Y-12's lithium isotope separation efforts. The Manhattan Project was just the warm-up act; he came of age as a scientist, as a father, as a man, building bombs that were worse than the worst bombs ever used.

The gap between what George might have been, what he sometimes could be, and what he was yawned wide. Sitting with my aunts and uncle that summer afternoon, upstairs in the house that George built, our conversation turned eventually, as it must.

He was interested in his children and warm. But he was absent more often than not. He worked a tremendous number of hours, and when he wasn't at the plant, he filled his spare time with strenuous self-imposed tasks. He seemed possessed of inexhaustible energy. My father remembered coming home from school one afternoon to find his father, home with a fever, in the front yard wearing a tattered, blue terry-cloth bathrobe, seeding the lawn.

It was difficult to sort out where the eccentricities of personality stopped and mental illness began. Children build their understanding of the world around the patterns of their homes. "At the time, I just thought Dad starts a lot of projects and then drifts off into something else, and then, you know, when you're a kid, however your parents are, you just think that's how people are," reflected Kurt. My father grew up believing that all fathers were scientists, that it was normal to never see their offices or hear about their work. And Nellie thought that all grills were like the heavy spherical one that never rusted. All the other houses on the peninsula had them.

Because George never took time off work, he'd wind up with lots of unused vacation he had to use up at the end of the year, around the holidays. And that was a problem, Karin said. Downtime was stressful; he'd attack the empty hours with sudden, involved projects. One year, two or three days before Christmas, he decided to repanel the dining room. "Mother just went berserk," Karin laughed, remembering. "Really, she didn't want to deal with repaneling the dining room two or three days before Christmas!"

Despite having escaped a grueling childhood on the farm, George bought land up the road from the lake house and spent free hours planting crops, running cattle, and raising horses. Kurt, as an adult, swore off farming, even simple gardening, for all the Saturdays he'd been forced to act as his father's farmhand. Where George's father had run a strictly ordered operation, George farmed with experimental exuberance. He had big dreams and boundless energy but no patience for the tedious labor required to keep a farm in working order. Some days, he would wake before dawn, on fire to plant half an acre of strawberries or hundreds of fruit trees. He loved to buy and test the latest tools. But no sooner was a tool mastered than it was abandoned in the rusted chaos of his toolshed. My father and his siblings laughed to remember their mother's distress that all of the forks and butter knives would become nicked and twisted from being drafted into service as makeshift tools.

For a while, George's energy served him well in the feverish pace of Cold War weapons production. "He would get manic," recalled Nellie, who knew what manic felt like, "and when you get manic, you feel really good, and you feel like you can do everything. You can, you know, accomplish the world. And that combined with an incredible amount of energy is why he did so well." But *manic* is a word applied in retrospect. George was just like that.

Over beer and pizza, I asked my uncle Paul to explain how fusion bombs work. "First," he said, "you get a bunch of deuterium and tritium. That's hydrogen with two and three protons. Then you set off a fission bomb that brings the two parts together." He moved his hands close to each other, cupped loosely as if holding two halves of a grapefruit, intertwined his fingers. Stopped.

"And then what happens?"

"You make a sun."

The sun was burning in fusion long before we ever called it so. Bombs are not the only application for harnessing this celestial energy.

We already know the fate of fission energy, the process that currently powers all viable nuclear reactors. Fission reactors produce clean, abundant energy, yet they leave behind nasty radioactive waste that we still have no good way of dealing with. And then there's the risk of meltdown: if a plant malfunctions and the fuel rods become overheated, they can melt through their containment vessels and release massive amounts of radiation into the environment.

But what if we could build a star on earth?

Unlike fission, which requires dangerous radioactive fuels such as uranium or plutonium, fusion can theoretically be produced using small, innocuous elements such as deuterium, an isotope of hydrogen (thus, the hydrogen bomb). The necessary components can be extracted from seawater. And while fission reactors leave behind spent fuel rods that are dangerously radioactive for thousands of years, fusion leaves behind only helium. A fusion reactor cannot melt down. It promises energy that might cost nearly nothing.

If the fusion bomb threatened genocidal destruction, the worst of what humanity could do to itself, fusion energy promised salvation, endless clean energy, a utopian future.

In the spring of 1951, the AEC set up Project Matterhorn at Princeton University with a twin mission—to perform the calculations necessary for the design of the first hydrogen bomb and to explore the feasibility of controlled fusion energy. Princeton astronomy professor Lyman Spitzer conceived of fuel confined in a figure-eight-shaped tube, controlled by a magnetic field. The device was called the stellarator. It would harness the energy of the stars.

Detonated on November 1, 1952, the first fusion bomb, code-named Mike, exploded with a force of 10.4 megatons, nearly seven hundred times the power of the Hiroshima bomb, vaporizing a small Pacific island and leaving a crater more than a mile wide and two hundred feet deep in its place. Observers on ships thirty miles away could feel the heat pressing against their skin. The mushroom cloud surged twenty-seven miles high and more than one hundred miles wide, dropping fallout on research vessels, Navy ships, and neighboring islands. Islanders displaced from their homes on nearby islands for ongoing tests would not be able to return for decades, or ever, due to high levels of radioactive contamination.

The difference between nuclear reactors and nuclear bombs, that is, between energy that can be used to sustain life and that which can only destroy it, is speed. Nuclear reactors use the energy of fission like bombs do but require material with a much lower concentration of radioactive atoms and release the energy more slowly. To sustain controlled fission, neutron-absorbing rods are inserted into the nuclear reactor to catch the extra excited particles and ensure a steady release of energy; too quick and the reactor can melt down. The fissioning atoms generate heat, which boils water and creates steam, which turns turbines to produce electricity. It's all just a rather high-tech waterwheel.

"A ton of explosive energy is about the same as a million food calories, enough to keep a human going for about 500 days," writes Los Alamos physicist Kenneth Ford in his memoir *Building the H Bomb*. "A kiloton would 'feed' a thousand people for 500 days. A megaton, spread over that same period of time, would nourish a million people. But that same megaton, released in a fraction of a second in the right place could slaughter a million people."

Fusion, however, is far more difficult to produce and control than fission. While large, unstable atoms like uranium periodically split, for fusion to occur, atoms must overcome the mutual repulsion of their positively charged nuclei; it is easier to break something apart than to put something together. Fusion happens only under extreme conditions of heat and pressure: inside the sun, inside a nuclear bomb.

And once you reach the incredible temperatures needed to generate a fusion reaction, it becomes nearly impossible to contain the fuel and sustain the reaction. Matter at such temperatures goes wild; electrons are stripped from their atoms and zoom about chaotically. This is called plasma, the fourth state of matter.

On the bookshelves at the lake house, I found a booklet from a 1958 international conference on controlled fusion that George attended. The "natural tendency" of plasma, the booklet says, "is to writhe convulsively out of its magnetic confinement."

For weeks, George barely slept. He knocked at D. H.'s door at dawn, uncombed and wild-eyed. "He wanted to go walking in the woods," D. H. said. "He just needed to move, to burn off that excess energy." He bought land, bought cattle, bought horses. On the farm, he could offload his spare hours, tire his muscles, play out fevered ambitions. Was there a little boy there, still hoping to show his father he could be everything? Diligent farmhand and scientist? Bookish but not useless? He'd arrive at the plant in muddy overalls after a morning's work on the land.

Still he thrived. Eccentric but effective. "He was on the fast track, George was," Mary Jane, Roger Hibbs's widow, told me; the Hibbses and the Strassers were the first couples to propose going in together on the peninsula. "George was Roger's boss. And he, George, was on the fast track to become, at that point, superintendent of Y-12. Roger felt like George's boss was pushing him too fast. He thought maybe that brought on some of the mental problems . . . Roger thought George was his best friend. And he didn't want to see him—what is it? Pushed beyond the level of your acuity."

Kay Redfield Jamison, a professor of psychiatry who knows bipolar disorder both as a professional expert and as a patient herself, writes in her memoir *An Unquiet Mind* that for many years she had difficulty recognizing that her extreme cycles of mania and depression were not simply expressions of the passionate moods she'd experienced all her life. Even when diagnosed, she resisted—the depression she could explain circumstantially, and she didn't want to give up the exquisite euphoria of being manic: "When you're high it's tremendous. The ideas and feelings are fast and frequent like shooting stars, and you follow them until you find better and brighter ones. Shyness goes, the right words and gestures are suddenly there, the power to captivate others a felt certainty. . . . Feelings of ease, intensity, power, well-being, financial omnipotence, and euphoria pervade one's marrow."

When she was manic, Jamison wrote research papers in a day, floated through cocktail parties assured of her own irresistible charm, took on ambitious research projects in a wide range of interests, devoured poetry, and perceived the world with "a marvelous kind of cosmic relatedness."

"I think," Nellie reflected of her father, "there were many years when he was manic more than depressive. And they were fine with him working twenty-four seven. Because they were literally working him to death. I mean he worked incredible hours." When she ate over at friends' houses, she was shocked to see their fathers home for dinner.

When George crashed, though, he crashed hard. Doris was irritated by his restlessness, how he'd tear up the house and promise to put it back together, how he'd shuffle in with muddy boots just as guests were arriving for a dinner party. But it was worse when he drank. He ceased to shower and spent days in bed. Day after day, Doris called his secretary, Ruby, to say he wouldn't be coming in. They had an understanding, Karin recalled. Ruby helped cover for George as much as she could.

When George sank into depression, his beloved long-haired collie, named Princess, stopped eating and began to lose hair in tufts. She'd curl beside him in bed, unwell dog beside unwell man.

Maybe only she could reach him then. When Princess was hit by a car one morning, George left work early to be with her when she was put down. "It was one of the few times I saw him cry," remembered Nellie.

During George's depressions, spurts of energy manifested as anger rather than the urge to work. By third grade, Nellie stopped inviting people over to her house; she never knew what kind of father she would come home to. Sometimes George would curse her mother out then storm from the house. Doris would sit tense at the kitchen table, listening to the door shudder behind him, his heavy, stumbling steps crunch on the driveway, his old green Chrysler or English Ford sputter to life.

There were accidents—his lungs punctured in three places, a near spin off a bridge stopped only by a fortunately placed post, a collision on the highway in broad daylight. Doris sat at the table and cried, but she wouldn't phone the police to stop him—to do so might have threatened his security clearance. Work was everything to him. Perhaps she thought he'd die without it.

When Kurt went to stay at a college friend's house, he was surprised that his friend's father did not get drunk and abusive around the dinner table. That was what fathers did, he thought.

"When he was sober and himself, he was an engaging, positive person that everybody liked," Karin said. "But then, I've also thought, who was himself? Was he Dr. Jekyll or Mr. Hyde?"

On Karin's recommendation, I spent several afternoons with Lester and Frankie Hulett. From the mid-sixties to the mid-seventies, the Strassers and the Huletts—Lester; his wife, Frankie; and their two daughters—were next-door neighbors on hilly lots tucked back on a wooded lane on the western edge of Oak Ridge. The houses were like extensions of each other as the kids moved fluidly between them and the families shared holiday meals, carpooling, and babysitting.

Lester was a scientist too, but he spent his career at Oak Ridge National Laboratory (ORNL), or the Lab for short. Though ORNL had begun as X-10, a wartime nuclear weapons laboratory, in the postwar years, as Y-12 remained firmly ensconced in the secrecy of classified weapons work, ORNL developed a research-driven mission to include work on nuclear medicine, renewable energy, neutron science, and more. I spent hours with Lester, hoping to gain insight into George's character, but he spent most of the time giving me a history lesson on the Lab.

Lester and Frankie still lived in the house next door to the last Oak Ridge house my grandparents lived in before they retired full-time to the lake. George had designed and built the Strasser home, with its blonde brick and unfinished cedar siding, its modern, clean lines, with the help of an engineer from Y-12. It was a solid, spacious thing compared to all the little wartime prefabs they'd lived in until then. It was here that my father, as an adolescent, discovered a secret stash of *Playboy*s hidden by some older boys in the culvert in the gully, here that he and his younger sister, Nellie, presided over a city-famous sledding hill, and here that he learned, after accompanying an unlucky sledder to the emergency room after a bad sledding accident, that he would be moving to Brazil for his last year of high school as an exchange student with the American Field Service.

It was also in this house that George's drinking became a constant. Most saw only the facade. Sober George was delightful, hardworking, and funny. But the Huletts were too close not to see more. Karin had hinted as much—that Lester and Frankie were among the trusted few her mother would call when she needed help. Karin and Kurt had left for college by the time the family moved next door to the Huletts; even they didn't see most of how it was at home. But the Huletts couldn't help but see.

It took a couple of meetings and hours of dutifully tracking Lester's history of the scientific developments at the Lab before I worked up the courage to ask about the bad times.

I interrupted one of Lester's monologues—this one on the nuclear-powered submarine—to ask him to tell me more about his memories of George and Doris.

"Of who?" asked Lester.

"Of George and Doris."

"Of George and Doris," he said as if coming out of a dream.

When I brought up George's drinking, the air in the room shifted subtly, as if I had turned a knob to tighten the tuning, and we all sat a bit straighter. Lester and Frankie didn't seem surprised, exactly, just quiet and serious.

"George would amble when he'd get bored. When things were not too good, he'd amble down here a lot," said Frankie.

"He was always a gentleman, even when he was not quite sober," Lester added, his loyalty unflagging. Once, George called Lester up to say he was going to get some whiskey. Lester could tell George was already drunk and shouldn't be driving, so he said he wanted some whiskey too; Lester drove them out to the farm, where they sat in a field drinking, cows nosing around curiously.

"I do remember," interjected Frankie, "a few times, when Lester spent about half his life out at that lab, and sometimes he would leave me with George. And that was fine. I mean, George was a perfect gentleman and all that—but, you know, he was talking about stuff that just didn't concern me or just kind of rambling, you know, and I'd think, 'When is this man going to get out of my house?'" She bit off the memory with a laugh, but I sensed that it was more alarming than funny to have a drunk, manic George rambling in her kitchen, that she never would say so to her husband, who adored George, or to my grandmother, who was a dear friend.

Some nights, the Huletts would open the door to find a tear-streaked Nellie, and they let her in without questions. They lost track of how many nights she stayed over with their daughters.

Lester got glum, and Frankie got teary. Frankie took over most of the talking. "With us, he was never this way, but I think that within the nuclear family from time to time he might have—not exactly been violent—but have been really loud, you know."

"Did my grandmother ever talk to you about what was going on?" I asked.

"A little," Frankie said. "One time I asked her, I said, 'Doris, I don't know how you keep your sanity and live with all this, you know, when it gets bad.' But she said, 'Well,' she said, 'Frankie, you know, I think about divorce or other things but I've got four children, and you know, what would I do?' And then one time she said, 'I also think from time to time that people who have the disease that he has don't usually live too long.'"

The sentence hung in the air. No one asked or clarified which "disease" my grandmother meant—bipolar disorder or alcoholism or something else. The implication was clear and devastating: my grandmother believed only George's death could free her.

"Where your grandparents were concerned," Frankie said, choking up, "just remember one thing, and that was, there was a lot more good in them than evil."

By the time I left the Huletts, dusk had fallen. Before I drove away, I stood at the end of what had been the Strasser driveway and peered down at the wide brick house. There was a basketball hoop, a large carport, and a pumpkin on the railing of a wooden deck. It was December, and the eaves of the roof were lined in a fringe of icicle Christmas lights. The carport was empty and the lights were out, but from the evidence, I guessed the house belonged to a family. I wasn't sure what I hoped to see or sense—some glimpse of the years the Strassers were there, some imprint left in the soil, a whiff in the air—but there was nothing.

I thought of what Frankie told me. That Doris had considered divorce but then rejected the possibility, deciding it was impossible. I thought of her saying (hoping? fearing?) that George might not live very long.

I thought of how she was once a young woman who fell for a boy who was brilliant and funny and kind. She worked the cafeteria counter at the University of Tennessee to help pay her way through college, and George flirted with her for extra helpings—that's how the family story went. She was a home ec major, but she signed up for every chemistry class he took. They'd go on Sunday drives to Gatlinburg, a town on the edge of the Smoky Mountains, eyes tracing the blue layered peaks in the distance, dreaming of the future they might build together. They were married on May 21, 1943. Doris wore a white silk jersey dress and a corsage of orchids. She was twenty-three years old; he, twenty-four.

I wondered if, even then, my grandmother sensed moods she could not touch, noticed the way he leaned into his drink, lost himself a little. I wondered if her hope felt fragile with the things she could not quite allow herself to see. Did she learn to keep secrets from herself even before she signed Oak Ridge's oath of secrecy?

At the end of July 1958, George and Doris boarded a chartered Swissair plane from New York to Geneva, along with fifty-five other Oak Ridge scientists and their spouses, to attend the second international Atoms for Peace conference. The conference was a gathering of sixty-seven nations to celebrate and share advances on the peaceful uses of nuclear energy, including fusion. "Geneva-bound Ridgers Take Off into Big Full Moon," reported the *Oak Ridger*, and there they all were, lined up on the tarmac, ascending stairs into the plane's belly, waving farewells as if from the bow of a ship bound for a promising new land.

As Karin remembered it, her father went in more of a ceremonial than an official capacity. Nuclear energy was not his expertise, and he was bemused to be invited at all. In any case, George and Doris had the time to make a vacation of the trip, knocking around Geneva with their Oak Ridge friends, taking a weekend in the Italian Alps, a tour through the Netherlands, a few days in London.

In family memory, George was still doing okay in 1958, the year of the conference. He was still the average overworked father, distracted, at work more than at home. His children did not yet fear his moods.

And yet—vacations were difficult. George had never learned leisure. In his childhood, it was the farm, and his exacting father, that demanded all his hours. Then, barely an adult, he'd signed his life away to a more powerful, more exacting taskmaster, whose emergencies—The Nazis! The Soviets! Nuclear annihilation!—would always command, or justify, more hours.

Far from home, without the always-urgent demands of a Cold War weapons plant, the days must have fallen slack. Without the din of machines and the whir of fans venting production rooms, there was just the buzzing in his ears, his own heartbeat.

Fourteen years later, a psychiatrist at the Regional Mental Health Center of Oak Ridge would write in George's discharge summary: "Has had psychological problems that go back for fifteen or twenty years. . . . He has been treated for this in 1958 while in Europe."

While George had likely experienced earlier episodes—the neurasthenia/pneumonia cover-up of 1951, for instance—this was the earliest record I could find of George explicitly receiving mental health treatment. And though he would remain working at the highest clearance level for fourteen more years after this, in 1962, a career ascent that until then had been described by his bosses as "quite rapid" came abruptly to a halt when he did not receive an expected promotion to plant superintendent. George would never regain the momentum of his early career, would linger as a department head as his friends rose through the ranks.

My father told me he always had the impression that George's friends and colleagues protected him, kept him on long after a man with fewer loyal allies would have been let go. What the 1958 episode suggested was that they protected him far longer than his kids even knew. That George, with his drinking and unpredictable mental health, was a liability at the plant through a period of Cold War paranoia for fifteen or twenty years before he finally retired.

When I told another writer, someone immersed in researching a story of Cold War intrigue, about George's breakdown in Europe, he said what I'd been thinking: "A nuclear scientist of his position has a psychiatric breakdown while in Europe, surrounded by international scientists, including Soviets? At that time? The CIA is all over him."

My FOIA requests to the State Department, the National Archives (where most historical State Department records wind up), and the FBI turned up nothing. The CIA responded that it could "neither confirm nor deny the existence or nonexistence of records responsive to your request." In a mystifyingly circular telephone conversation with a CIA FOIA official, I pressed until she finally snapped, "We don't have access to everything in the absolute universe!" My appeal was "denied in full."

This episode seemed to have sunk like a stone in a lake, the water smoothed poker-faced above it.

Controlled thermonuclear fusion was first achieved momentarily in 1958 at Los Alamos on a machine called Scylla.

In *The Odyssey*, Scylla and Charybdis are monsters on opposite shores of the narrow Strait of Messina, terrorizing sailors traversing it. Odysseus, on Circe's advice, hugs Scylla's shore; she devours six of his men, but he avoids the certain total loss of life and ship that would have come from entering Charybdis's whirlpool. To be between Scylla and Charybdis is an idiom for having to choose between undesirable options. To have no way out but through.

Since 1958, we have learned to design fusion bombs both smaller and more powerful than the first hydrogen bomb, yet despite decades of research and international collaboration, we have not yet been able to master controlled fusion. So far, we can only blow things up, again and again and again.

"You may have noticed," my father said to me once, "that I have this habit of keeping empty pill bottles. It's because Mom wouldn't throw away Dad's. You know that cedar chest upstairs at the lake, the one that holds all the blankets? That shallow upper tray was full of empty pill bottles. Dozens of them."

We speculated about why. Doris kept family mementos, but she was not a hoarder. Did she fear exposing such evidence of her husband's mental illness to whomever might glance in the family trash?

"Your dad doesn't keep his old pill bottles," my mom corrected. "But he carefully removes all the labels before he throws them out. He soaks them off, runs them through the dishwasher. It's a secrecy thing."

He was defensive. "Well, I'm permitted a few neuroses." I told him I did the same thing, peeled off the labels before recycling my pill bottles. I never knew that was unusual. My mother laughed at us both—who cared what medicine she was taking? And who would bother to look in the trash anyway?

"I think," my dad said, "Mom saw it as her burden to bear."

In 1978, a psychiatrist at the Oak Ridge Mental Health Center described George's fear of intimacy. "His wish is to fuse with the nurturing person (typically his wife)," wrote the doctor. And yet he feared "his own engulfing dependency needs."

After George's death, Doris processed her grief and loneliness in a journal. "I am heartbroken," she wrote, "that I couldn't make him happy."

## 11

# PHANTOM

Karin, Kurt, and I were sitting around the picnic table, snacking on grapes and hummus, my bathing suit drying in the sun after a swim.

I asked them about George's childhood. What came before Oak Ridge, before Doris? They told me stories I already knew. About George's strict father. The tedium of farm work. His closeness with his younger sister Edna, who was intelligent, biting, and also an alcoholic.

I asked about his mother. She was warmer than her husband, Joseph Henry, they said. Gentle. But George didn't talk about her. And then they said as if I already knew, "Well of course you know his mother . . ."

His mother what?

"Oh, well. She killed herself," said Karin.

But I didn't know. No one ever told me.

"She hung herself, that's what I heard, and Uncle Adam found her there," Kurt was saying as I nodded, riveted but detached, processing slowly as if from underwater. The revelation felt both shocking and inevitable, as if I had known it all along, somewhere below articulable thought.

So this was the hurt that came before all the others. Here inside George, and here for me to uncover. No wonder he ran from the farm, as far as he could go to a brand-new city, to a career that not only gave him permission not to speak but demanded it. To find a place to land—what it must have meant to George, careening from a home that would always gape open as a fresh wound.

"He never talked about her. Never."

How, I asked, did they know then?

Kurt remembered the way he stumbled into knowing. It was summer, and he was spending some weeks on Uncle Adam's farm outside of Nashville, not far from the old family farm. The mood had been lighthearted, long-limbed cousins joking as they loaded hay bales onto a trailer. The air was hot and oppressively humid, like something you could almost swim through, and the boys chewed tobacco to moisten their mouths against the dry, dusty work. They teased each other and spat, pretending to be men. Then Kurt made a joke about his klutz of a cousin—"Give him enough rope, and he'll hang himself." And the air went quiet. Later, his oldest cousin took him aside. "Don't say that," he said. "Don't say that around Uncle Adam. He's the one who cut her down."

It was Kurt who told Karin, or at least confirmed what she'd already somehow sensed was embedded in her father's absolute silence about his mother.

When I asked them, Karin, Kurt, my father, and Nellie remembered the visceral thing—she hung herself in the barn—but were unsure of the basic facts. He was a child, no, in college. George found her. No, it was his older brother Adam or his sister Mary.

These details were thin, collected memory worn bare. I wanted to move closer to the fact of the thing, to turn the focus until the blurred lines resolved into crisp edges. I wanted to know what I knew and how I knew it.

On my request, my father emailed a few of the Nashville cousins—that's how I knew them, as part of a vague mass that used to turn up at the yearly family reunions my grandmother dutifully continued to organize after George's death. A few months later, we were in Nolensville, twenty miles south of Nashville, eating corn light bread and deviled eggs in a church gymnasium, speaking over kids bouncing basketballs.

"Now I don't believe I've met this young lady."

I told them who I was.

"So that would make you my second cousin?"

I wasn't even sure.

The family had pulled together old photographs and hand-written family trees, all laid out on one long folding table opposite the food, tin foil platters full of baked beans, potato salad, and soft buttered rolls. We huddled in small groups, balancing plates of food, talking over each other, trading family myth and memory.

"How did they meet, Nannie and Grandad Strasser?"

"Johnny thinks he's got that figured out. Granddaddy was a truck farmer, and her daddy was a huckster."

"What's a huckster?"

"They would be the one that sell it."

"They hawked the wares. And so he thinks that—Johnny, tell us how you think Nannie met Granddaddy."

"Her daddy was a huckster in Woodbine, you done told them all that part? And Granddad Strasser's family raised vegetables and sold them on the market, and it's just a guess, but I think they met—through vegetables."

Joseph Henry Strasser married Nannie Barnes on December 26, 1905.

He was from a large German Catholic family, outsiders in the mostly Protestant farming community of rural Middle Tennessee.

"You didn't necessarily want to be German."

By marrying into the family, Nannie subjected herself to the scrutiny of the small community. Anti-German sentiment would only increase during World War I.

"They were afraid of the Klan during the First World War, is what I've always heard." At the time, the Klan was both racist and xenophobic, their hatred extended to include, in addition to Black Americans, Catholics, immigrants, Jews, and others who threatened their insular white Protestant vision of the nation.

Joseph Henry, though, was stoic. Despite the prejudice, he continued to call his children by German nicknames. Outwardly at least, he was not concerned with the judgment of others.

"He was blunt. He took prisoners, and he didn't take no names."

"If they would bring straight As home from school, he would say, 'Why aren't these A-pluses?'"

"Mother was terrified of him."

"He was just so gruff. I think that was a lot of the trouble—"

"It was during the Depression."

"He was hateful—"

"I guess he was under a lot of pressure."

"All those kids."

By all accounts, Joseph Henry was a harsh and uncompromising disciplinarian by nature, but then the market crashed in 1929, just after he had expanded the farm. The price of tomatoes fell, and the next summer, George and his siblings were slopping the most beautiful, unblemished tomatoes to the hogs. Joseph would be paying off the debt for the rest of his life. He would give himself and his family no respite.

"Hard work covered a multitude of sins. If you worked, he liked you. If you didn't work, he had no use for you."

None of George's siblings were still living, and only one of my father's cousins was old enough to remember their grandmother, George's mother, Nannie. "Sweetest woman you ever could imagine." The others remembered the way their parents described her—soft-spoken, submissive. "A gentle soul."

They showed me a photograph. A high-collared white blouse covered thin, steep shoulders. Dark hair was twisted and pinned back, revealing high cheekbones and a steady, dark-eyed gaze. She didn't look submissive or sweet, exactly, but serious and determined.

Between raising their six children—Mary, Joe, Adam, George, Edna, and Elizabeth—and the relentless work of the farm, Nannie never rested. "Mother said she never remembered seeing Grandmother sit down during the daytime but one time during the summer. It was about a hundred like this, and she had the flu, and it was so hot that she laid on the floor in the living room just to rest a little. But she never sat down. She said, 'I never saw her sit down ever.' Ever."

The children barely played. They would rise before dawn to help with farm work before going to school and return to work well into the evening. It was a cheerless home.

"Do you remember seeing Granddaddy smile?" the cousins asked each other.

I asked about Nannie's death. We sat around a table draped in a red plastic tablecloth and leaned close to be heard over the shouts of the kids.

"That was a taboo subject. You did not discuss her. You didn't ask any questions about her."

"I used to ride the horse up there by the potato cellar . . . I'd climb up the tree and hitch the horse, and I'd eat my lunch up there. And Grandad caught me there one time, and he absolutely came unglued. And I didn't understand why, you know. And Mama didn't tell me why. And I didn't know till I was grown that I guess they thought I had the same propensity . . ."

"We all asked. They just said, 'She died.'"

"We didn't know about it until we were in high school."

"How did it come up?"

"I don't know."

"They never talked about it. Never mentioned it."

The cousins came and went, refilling paper plates with fruit salad and handfuls of chips. They said, "Mama always said, Mama this, Mama that . . .," and I couldn't keep track of whose mama was whose. The confusion was compounded by family nicknames; George was Tid, because he liked to play tiddlywinks, and Elizabeth, the youngest, was Tookie, after the family mule, Took Eye. Poor thing. "She hated that name."

"What I heard was, Nannie, her blood pressure got up extremely high, and in those days, the doctors didn't know what to do. They just put her to bed. She couldn't get up, and she'd never known anything but work, and Mother said she just got more and more depressed. It's about all I know about it."

I pushed cold macaroni and cheese around my plate. Crunched a potato chip. My father and I listened.

In the summer of 1938, George, not yet twenty, was at home after his first year of college. Tookie, Elizabeth, was eighteen, charged with watching her mother.

"They knew she was depressed." No one said so exactly, but I thought this must have meant that there were other incidents or previous bouts of despair so long and deep that anyone could guess what Nannie might do.

The doctor's orders could not keep Nannie entirely from her chores. "She went out at the same time every afternoon to feed the chickens, and she took the little tin thing with chicken feed out, but she never came back. And they found—she fed the chickens—they found the bucket there. So, I guess that's why Aunt Tookie didn't look for her immediately."

A child screamed, and a basketball narrowly missed the buffet table.

"You're eighteen, and it's your job to watch someone, and you've let them out of your sight."

"It was just about as devastating as you could imagine."

Adam cut her down, they said. Adam, the second oldest, would have been out in the fields, I thought. How long did Tookie stand frozen while the chickens pecked the ground before running to find him? Nannie was living, barely, when Adam arrived. From the field above, Joe Jr., Nannie's first grandchild, watched the ambulance pull out of the driveway.

"They buried their mother, everyone went back to work, and they never mentioned it, not one time. That's what was wrong with all of them."

"My mama was not open at all," Tookie's son said. "She would have died. They could have put her on the rack, and she wouldn't have divulged a bit of family information."

Tookie would struggle with deep depression all her life. She would not speak of her mother until she was in her eighties.

Hungarian-born French psychoanalysts Maria Torok and Nicolas Abraham theorized the notion of "the crypt" to explain how people preserve but hide unspeakable trauma: the experience is "entombed" in a deep, inaccessible part of the psyche, simultaneously sealed outside of language and unconsciously transmitted through what is spoken and unspoken.

Crypts often result, they write, from an experience of unresolved mourning for the loss of a beloved subject, a loss made unbearable by guilt or shame or overwhelming trauma that threatens to undo us.

A crypt that remains hidden, Abraham and Torok insist, can be passed down unconsciously by parents to their children through elision, distortion, linguistic devices such as metaphor and homonym, and wordless, somatic signals. The child feels the absence but does not understand the context and so becomes an unwitting carrier of the shameful secret. An inherited crypt becomes a "phantom," driving the obsessions and neurosis of the child and ultimately leading to transgenerational haunting.

George's sister Edna believed that her nephew Stanley, an infant when Nannie died, stuttered as a young boy as a result of the unspoken trauma of her suicide.

I thought of how, curiously, my father's generation, all of his siblings and cousins, knew of Nannie's death though their parents never spoke of it. Now, when I scrutinized my own memory, I became certain that I must have known too before that conversation with Kurt and Karin. I could feel the knowing in my body. I could feel it in my parents' watchfulness. My aunts and uncles saying, "There's family history here. Don't wait to ask for help. There's no shame." I'd never been suicidal, but I'd felt the family's fear of sadness and an unarticulated shame. I could feel it in my own irrational fear of asking about George, the uneasy sense that I would find something I didn't want to know.

Had my father told me, when I called to check D. H.'s memory of George's suicide, years before? Had he suggested George's mother's suicide as the possible origin for D. H.'s mistake? But that couldn't have been the first I'd heard of it, or the revelation would have made a certain impression. The more I tried to pin the moment, the further it slipped from me, until all I held was an uncanny feeling of simultaneous surprise and recognition, each moment of discovery also a remembrance.

The phantom is a *nescience*, an "unknown knowledge." Writes Esther Rashkin, a scholar of Abraham and Torok: "The psychological effect of something seeming familiar and strange at the same time can be explained through the specific configuration in which something is unknown (*unheimlich*) to the subject in one generation and secretly 'known' or 'within the family or house' (literally *heimlich*) in the preceding one."

George was mostly absent from the story of that day as remembered by the children of his brothers and sisters. Even as a child, he was always a bit out of step with his family. Book smart, odd. "I can remember Mother saying that when Uncle Tid was little, long before he went to school, that when the paper would come on Sunday, he'd get the funny papers—and he'd just laugh and giggle. They thought he was just playing, but he was reading that early!"

Once during a state exam, his teacher scolded him for doodling on his papers; George had finished an hour early. "Uncle Tid was one of the smartest people I ever dealt with."

But that kind of intelligence had no currency on the farm, and George had no patience for farm work. He looked for shortcuts, and then snuck away to read a book behind a hay bale or up in the barn loft. Of Joseph and Nannie's six children, only two went to college. Mary completed a two-year teaching degree; George was the only one to earn a bachelor's degree and the only one to move away.

He started at the University of Tennessee Junior College in Martin, on the western edge of the state, then transferred to UT Knoxville, holding jobs throughout. He hitchhiked his way to and from school using an old suitcase on which he'd painted "Knoxville" and "Nashville" on opposite sides. After graduating in 1941, he went on to Virginia Polytechnic Institute to pursue his master's degree and from there to work for a chemical company until, hearing of scientists needed for necessary war work outside of Knoxville, George left for Oak Ridge.

Oak Ridge was only 160 miles from his home, but it might have been on the other side of the country, this city thick with PhD physicists, chemists, and engineers from the cities and college towns of the Northeast, the universities of the Midwest and West Coast, tucked into a rural corner of East Tennessee.

While Adam took over his father's farm as the primary means of supporting the family, George farmed sporadically, manically. "Well, George," said Adam, inspecting a haphazard cattle fence his little brother had constructed, "it might scare the cows."

The Nashville cousins felt the difference between themselves and their city cousins.

"Them intellectual boys in Oak Ridge didn't like us little country boys up there."

"I went to Oak Ridge every summer. Of course, we were country kids, and I had never seen streetlights. I mean, I'd seen 'em but not in the neighborhood. And I remember at night it would shine in the blinds, and it would keep me awake 'cause I was used to total darkness."

Two generations later, the children of George's siblings lived outside of Nashville within miles of a road called Strasser Drive that ran through the land where the old family farm used to be. George's children, my aunts and uncles, were scattered throughout the country like thumbtacks holding a map in place. The deep Tennessee accent that once embarrassed my father when, as a high schooler passing through New York City on his way to Brazil, he met fellow exchange students from around the country, now slipped only occasionally around the edges of his words; but the Nashville cousins spoke with long dipping vowels and soft consonants. My father's name, Dale, became two definitive syllables in their mouths.

Because Joseph Henry would allow no idle hands in his household, college be damned, George must have been in the fields with Adam when Tookie came running. Yet nowhere was he present in the inherited memory of that day as told by his nieces and nephews. Perhaps George's course had been set when he learned to read before attending school or perhaps when he painted "Knoxville" onto his suitcase. By the summer of 1938, George had left home; he would always, after that, be something of an outsider in his own family, no matter that his suitcase had "Nashville" painted on the other side.

I pictured the brothers in the fields together, teasing each other as they picked tomatoes, the heat of the day already dampening their brows. Their sister running toward them, her words indiscernible at first. When they finally understood her, they must have stood for a moment, putting the words together again. Adam, who was stronger from long days on the farm, would have run faster than his studious brother. Perhaps he was already pulling out the ladder by the time George arrived in the barn doorway. Or perhaps he had stopped still, and George, halting breathless behind him, first glimpsed his mother over his brother's broad shoulder.

I did not expect to be able to learn more than the family could tell me of Nannie. She had to exist now only in paling memory. When it finally occurred to me to look, I was stunned to find her death certificate almost immediately, on Ancestry.com.

Out of what felt like myth came the breathtaking specificity of recorded fact.

In loose cursive, the principal cause of death was named: "strangulation." Contributory cause: "melancholia."

I stared at the words. The old-fashioned elegance of "melancholia" beside the brutal "strangulation." The blunt facts—how closely they hewed to the family's memory. How irrefutably they recorded the moment we thought unspeakable.

In the adjacent column, labeled "date of onset," the doctor scribbled "sudden" beside "strangulation," "2 yrs" beside "melancholia."

It was the pairing of "sudden" and "2 yrs" that blew me porous and tender. The acuteness of her tragedy clarified in those two phrases; "sudden" implied chance, as if, catching a glint of sunlight through the barn window, Nannie might have picked up the empty feed bucket and walked back to the house, while "2 yrs" betrayed a long-fought struggle, as if it were only a matter of time before Nannie self-inflicted some "sudden" violence to end her life.

I felt soft with sudden grief. For my great-grandmother, for her desperate life and death, for the way she was entombed even afterward, her memory unspeakable, unthinkable, ungrievable by those who knew and loved her.

She died on July 27, 1938. 2:35 p.m.

George, unlike Meemaw, kept few mementos from his childhood, kept few mementos at all. So I was surprised when, sifting idly through piles of Meemaw's papers upstairs at the lake house, I found his fifth-grade report card from Tusculum Elementary School, the years 1929–1930. I didn't know how many times I'd overlooked it.

It was postcard-sized, spotted by age, the grades filling a neat, printed grid in irregular felt-tipped markings. He was, as I'd been told, a smart kid; the grid was marked almost entirely with A-pluses. He excelled only slightly less in "Deportment," receiving A-pluses only four months out of nine. Just a few scattered minuses marred the record.

On the flip side in faint pencil across the lines for a parent's signature, almost illegible in the shadowed room: Mrs. J. H. Strasser. It took me a moment to see what I was seeing—I thought of her by her maiden name, Barnes. I traced the letters with my fingertip. It was the careful handwriting of a woman who'd learned cursive in school yet had no cause to develop the messy ease of a signature. The last three months were signed "J. H. Strasser," no "Mrs.," but the handwriting was the same.

She is sitting for a rare moment at the rough-hewn kitchen table. Her boy, who shares her deep-set brow and angled nose, leans against her, his mop of curly hair mussed from the day. By fifth grade, he has learned not to show his report card to his father, who will see only the few minuses. Nannie is the only one who will praise her too-bright boy. His siblings are outside, and for a few minutes, it is just the two of them.

Does she run a hand through his curls as she scans the line of A's? Does he watch her dark eyes for a glimmer of pride, the corner of her mouth for the turn of a smile? Can she see that this report card is her son's ticket off the farm? And when he comes home in the seventh month of his fifth-grade year and tells his mother that his teacher wants to see his father's signature, does she give him a little smile, pull him close, and sign "J. H. Strasser"?

There was a faint darkened ring from where a glass of water must have been set on the paper, and it was creased down the center where it must have been folded into a back pocket to and from school. Seven years later, Nannie would bid her son farewell when he left for college. He was the only one of her children who ever left home.

She would never know that he would not only complete his bachelor's degree but would go on to get a master's. And she wouldn't smile to learn that the boy who'd left for college so he wouldn't have to spend his days digging in the dirt chose to specialize in soil chemistry. Nor would she know that at the right time in the right place, the gates of the secret city would open for the clever son of a farmer. That he would excel in the business of bomb-building.

The card rested lightly on the carpet, half-illuminated by a stray sunbeam.

## 12

# TALKING

After learning about Nannie's death, I began to think again, uneasily, about the conversation I'd had with D. H., the one in which he insisted that George had committed suicide. At that time, I took my father's reassurance that George had died of a heart attack, and that D. H. was losing his memory, as permission to leave it be. But having learned about Nannie's death, I now knew how entire families could fall silent, could swallow the thing that could not be said.

By now, D. H. was further into Alzheimer's. He knew who I was, sometimes, and remembered George, but when I sat with him, he repeated the same stories twice, three times, within twenty minutes.

I needed something more definitive. I needed to know how my grandfather died because I needed to know when I'd hit bottom— not the despair kind of bottom, but the solid ground kind. I needed to know what I was walking on.

Though I was queasy about it, I went looking. I could not call up George's death certificate on Ancestry.com, the way I did for Nannie, because he died too recently. The Tennessee Office of Vital Records retains death certificates for fifty years before releasing them for public access. Before this time, the office will verify information contained in their records, *excluding cause of death*, to any requestor. The significance of this detail would not previously have occurred to me: fifty years is the amount of time the government is willing to protect a dead man's secrets.

Before the passage of fifty years, only immediate family members, or affiliated attorneys, can obtain information on cause of death. Which was all to say, I couldn't just peek into the matter on my own and tuck it away again.

I tried not to think too much about what it meant for me to ask my father for his help. He did not seem surprised or worried. Maybe it was the doctor in him; he valued science, a disinterested process of inquiry, the need for evidence. He requested a copy of George's death certificate. When it arrived at my childhood home in Atlanta, he scanned it and emailed me. He must have read it, but he did not tell me what he found.

It took me moments of scanning down, past the perfunctory details, neatly typed—George Albert Strasser; died January 9, 1984; age 65; white; American; male—until finally, at the bottom of the document in a box with the tiny words "death was caused by," I found in loopy cursive the words "cardiopulmonary arrest."

I had avoided calling Nellie for a long time. As George's youngest, left at home after her siblings had gone to college, she was the witness, the Tookie of the next generation. She had battled her own demons. If inheritance includes biology and circumstance, Nellie bore the brunt of both. By the time I became interested in George, she'd been sober for years, but during my childhood, it wasn't always so. I'd learned a certain carefulness, a fear of upsetting the balance. And I wondered whether it was my right to pry into such a painful past.

When I finally did call her though, she was frank and open, preparing a salad on the other end of the line. Her voice didn't shake when she said of her father, "He tried to kill himself many times. He wanted to die. He was a tortured soul."

She was the first person to tell me so definitively, to use those words. Her frankness was jarring after the clinical distance I'd learned since childhood. *We're wired that way.* All the talk of medication and brain chemistry. No one else had told me it was so bad.

Nellie remembered the incident D. H. misremembered as the end, when George drank wood alcohol. Her mother called her at college—"Dad is really ill. You need to come home." Pulling into the Oak Ridge hospital parking lot, Nellie saw a hearse. *That hearse is for Dad*, she thought, and the thought was the obvious conclusion to everything.

But then she walked into the hospital and found his room by following his barrage of obscenities. "He was a mean drunk."

Nellie was the only one who ever heard her father speak of his mother. "He found his mother swinging from the rafters," she told me. "When he got drunk, he would describe it in detail, walking into the barn and seeing her swinging from the rafters."

Once, when she was six or seven, Nellie came home from school to hear her father sobbing in the basement. She stood at the top of the stairs listening to his great choking gasps.

I asked if George was ever abusive to his family. He was verbally abusive, she said, mostly toward her mother. He never hurt the children, but one night, when Nellie was eight or nine, she heard yelling coming from her parents' bedroom. She tried the door, but it was locked. "I heard Mom screaming, like a weird scream, like a scared scream." She never found out what happened that night, but after that, on bad nights, Doris would slip into her daughter's room and curl beside her in bed. George would leave her alone there.

"If things were real bad, we would go over to Karin's—Karin only lived a mile away—and spend the night there. And then of course he'd call. He wouldn't leave us alone."

Nellie was frustrated with, and angered by, her mother's refusal to take a heavier hand with George—to leave him for good, to call the police, to take him to a hospital when he needed it. Despite the hell he put her through, Doris was committed to maintaining an appearance of normalcy and decorum no matter the cost.

"Her motto was denial with a capital *D* and go to church three times a week," Nellie said.

When she left for college, Nellie told her mother she wasn't coming home anymore. This was the time to find her independence, and she declared she wouldn't wait around for her father to kill himself while her mother denied the severity of his problems. But she did come home when her mother called. She came home again and again.

George was smarter than his doctors, Nellie said, to his detriment. "The head psychiatrist said, 'This is the smartest man that's walked in here, and that's including all the shrinks,'" she remembered. He could appear well when he was anything but. Once, on a Friday afternoon, one of many Friday afternoons when Nellie should have been getting ready for a night out with her friends, she looked into her father's dull eyes in the lobby of the mental health center and told the nurse he could not come home.

The nurse shook her head. "He has to admit himself." Since Nellie was just seventeen, she did not have the legal authority to commit him against his will.

"I know my dad," she insisted, through tears. "I know my dad, and he's suicidal. I can see it. He doesn't need to be home," she pleaded. When her distress began to draw attention, the nurse pulled them into a back room.

He's promised not to kill himself, the nurse insisted. George, the scientist, composed amid the hysteria, maintained, "I'm good enough to go home."

Nellie pulled in a shaking breath, drew herself up, all five feet of her, and looking straight at the nurse, said, "If he kills himself, it's gonna be on you."

The next morning, she found him passed out and liquor-soaked, a dead weight on the couch. So the men wrestled him into a straitjacket and drove him back to the hospital.

We spoke for over an hour. I was practically tingling with the relief of speaking so openly. Some deep part of me, sealed up, stale, and scared, was breathing. So we could say the true things after all. So we could survive the telling.

Nellie hunted around for a top to match her Tupperware. "I don't know that I've ever talked to your dad about Dad, really," she mused.

---

Closest in age, Nellie and my dad should have had plenty to discuss about their father. Karin and Kurt were gone by then, but the two youngest siblings saw, and survived, the worst of his moods together. What caution or code, what unspoken understanding, kept them from this conversation?

But I, too, had been careful with my father. My gentle, hard-working, anxious, goofy dad. We are wired the same way. We have broad shoulders, but we slump. We are irritable and withdrawn in the mornings. We keep busy, even in our free time. We've had to learn leisure. We'll never unlearn fidgeting, to my mother's distress. There's a trace of George, I think, in our restless edges, our inability to be still.

I don't know how George experienced anxiety, but for my father and me, our anxiety snags on a little thing and swirls out to become all things, then dips, sometimes, into depression. We are introverted and private, and sometimes that means we don't know how to talk to each other. The last thing I wanted to do was upset my father.

But we have our ways of talking. When I was in elementary school, he liked to help me with my science fair projects. We tracked the growth of bean sprouts in various lighting conditions, compared the volume and weight of ice and water, measured the lumens of a candle flame reflected in a mirror. And so we'd approached George as a shared task. A homework assignment. I had needed my father's memories, and he had given them to me. I had needed his signature, and he had signed. Quietly, tentatively, we backed into the conversation anyway.

When I got ahold of George's files from the Oak Ridge Mental Health Center, my father read through them. Ever a doctor, he made a list: "GAS MH Admits" for George Albert Strasser, Mental Health Admissions. The list included twenty entries, with columns for admit date, discharge date, number of days, and notes. The number of days ranged from 6 to 63 to 173 for "partial hosp (outpt day prog)." The notes included "first admission depressed 4–5 weeks, psychiatric problems 15–20 yrs," "severely depressed, no drinking; ECT (shock therapy) X 24," "Had flu and heavy drinking over Holidays, admitted thru police," and "Took unkn # of sleeping pills, drank perfume."

When he couldn't get liquor, George drank rubbing alcohol. He broke his elbow in a car accident—slick ice—and drank as he recovered. He drank because there was a long weekend, because his psychiatrist left town, because Nellie left for college, because his wife left town, because Nellie got married, because the "cows were a problem."

This was his "umpteenth hospital admission," wrote his doctor.

His daughters found him hallucinating. He was picked up by the police when he threatened Doris. He took Valium. He was admitted to the psychiatric ward when he talked of suicide. He was admitted when he attempted suicide, drank wood alcohol behind the barn.

His doctor wrote, "The long-term prognosis for psychotherapy is poor."

They put him on Tofranil, an antidepressant that was later found to heighten symptoms of mania. They put him on sedatives. They put him on laxatives. Sometimes they put him on five medications at a time. They tried electroshock therapy. They tried group therapy.

They always checked "condition improved" on discharge. He always came back.

"It's sobering to see how much pain he was in," my father said.

My father remembered the months his father spent in daycare at the mental health center making wooden crafts, soup-can footstools. George learned folk songs from the other patients that he liked to sing off-key while driving, tapping out the beat on the steering wheel.

I asked him how he'd felt when I'd asked him to get George's death certificate. Whether he was worried. "I never thought he committed suicide," he told me. "I knew how things were with D. H."

By then, D. H. had moved into an assisted living facility for people with Alzheimer's. The one-time nuclear weapons scientist spent his days dismantling the lamp, the mini-fridge, the nightstand in his room. He flooded his bathroom when he took apart the sink. After they'd removed everything that he could deconstruct from his room, nurses found him in the dining hall unscrewing the legs of a table.

I couldn't help but wonder at the significance of what stayed when everything else had gone. The muscle memory. The stories that got stuck in rotation. It seemed that George did not kill himself, yet one of his best friends would die believing he had. This, too, was a kind of truth.

Was it upsetting, though, I pushed my father. "Maybe I'm too clinical about this," he said.

Another time, he would tell me he had learned a lot about his father through my research. I knew he was more moved than he would say.

My father didn't know the details of the wood alcohol incident because he'd returned to Brazil the year after college to teach English. He'd fallen in love with the country during his senior year of high school as an exchange student, when he'd lived with a host family, begun to dream in Portuguese, learned to wear his jeans tailored like a glove and dance samba. He remembered when the American Field Service representatives came for the home visit part of the application process. He'd been anxious for weeks that his father would be drunk. But George showered and shaved, sobered up for the occasion, and charmed the representatives. My dad had forgotten his father could be like that, so intelligent and charismatic. He insists, though, that he didn't go abroad to get away from home. His siblings all think otherwise.

From Brazil, my dad wrote his father careful letters on his mother's urging. He reported on his grades, told George he liked physics more than chemistry and that Brazilians "seem to enjoy life more than Americans." "I hope you're enjoying your stay in Virginia," he wrote, referring obliquely to the psychiatric hospital where George was treated for months at a time when he'd exhausted the local facilities. "I hope you find it productive." In another letter, he commented on the merits of tennis—it's cheap to play, and you don't need many players—one of the recreational activities available to George at the hospital.

When I asked my dad about George's suicide attempts, he remembered an incident long before the wood alcohol. He was ten or twelve when his father stormed from the house in a drunken rage, carrying a pistol, threatening to shoot himself. There was the smack of the wooden screen door behind him, his heavy footsteps on the gravel, and the dull glint of the gun in the moonlight.

When my dad heard the shot, his first feeling was of relief, followed immediately by fear. "The closest I ever came to praying was then," my dad told me. "But I wasn't sure what I wanted." This admission was perhaps the most emotional statement I had ever heard from my dad about George. My heart broke for the little boy he was, the boy who didn't know if it would be worse if his violent, unstable father killed himself or if he didn't.

When my dad returned from his year as an exchange student in Brazil, he majored in psychology. He said that choice didn't have anything to do with his father either. "It was an easy major," he explained, shrugging. The humanities and social sciences, he thought, could speak to human truths and moral quandaries, while science seemed amoral, if not immoral. Science was napalm and atomic bombs. Science was his father, but he did not say that.

He went back to Brazil after college, and when he returned home, he planned to become a psychiatrist. He took premed classes and got a job as an aide at a psychiatric hospital in Knoxville; George had been hospitalized there for an extended stay just two years before.

Frequently, it was my dad's job to sit with patients on suicide watch. Those he met, what he saw, what he felt, shook him. My dad does not speak of his father in relation to this time of his life, this choice, these experiences. This is the story of his life, not mine; I cannot say what it meant.

He doesn't exactly say it was too much for him, but after med school, my father decided to go into rehabilitation medicine instead. He helped people get back on their feet after traumatic injuries, adjust to lives with permanently altered abilities. Healing in this field, he explained to me, is holistic. In the aftermath of strokes, head trauma, spinal cord injuries, surgery, patients need pain medicine and physical therapy, but they also need counseling, antidepressants, and compassion. "It's important," he said, "that I take time to listen to my patients."

My mother remembered waking in my father's Chicago apartment to Paul's middle-of-the-night phone call to say George had died. She said she'd never seen my father cry like he did on that January night. She held him as he sobbed like a little boy.

# 13

# Half-Life

The effect of the phantom, write Abraham and Torok, "can persist through several generations and determine the fate of an entire family line."

No one told me to uncover this story, to write it. Yet I have spent years of my adult life looking backward at the traumas and moral failings of my grandfather. Abraham and Torok might say that my obsessive circling comes from a compulsion to resolve the unfinished business of my ancestors. I hope there is some healing in the telling, the decrypting. At least, there is relief in feeling the air in the once-sealed spaces.

And yet the greater haunting is not George's pain or his mother's, but what George did with that pain, through that pain, because of or in spite of that pain. There is always, still, the beginning: my grandfather posing placidly in front of an exploding nuclear bomb. Lost artifact or child's imagination, there is some truth in the vision.

When I spoke to Colleen Black, old friend of Dot and my grandmother and early Oak Ridger, she kept marveling at her own ignorance during the war. "We didn't know," she said. "We were told what to do, and we did it. Isn't that strange? I find that strange now."

Colleen was proud of her history. She'd given countless interviews to historians; in the apartment of her assisted living home, decked out in leopard and zebra prints, one large wall was dedicated to Oak Ridge memorabilia—the photographs, newspaper clippings, and ticket stubs she'd collected over a lifetime as a proud resident, a giant scrapbook shellacked in place.

Decades after the war, Colleen and her daughter toured local schools with a slideshow about wartime Oak Ridge.

"Why did you drop that bomb? Oh, that was awful of you," the children said with a directness most adults shy away from.

Colleen tried to explain: "You gotta remember the time it was. We were at war. They were killing us."

The children didn't understand. "Why would you want to bomb and destroy the whole city?" they persisted.

"I didn't want to do it. And, I mean, we didn't know that's what we were doing. And why didn't I have a clue? I don't know." Faced with these most relentless of critics, she held up ignorance like a shield. "I didn't want to know," she admitted.

The children, we might say, misunderstood responsibility—of course Colleen did not drop that bomb, did not choose to destroy a whole city, did not even know what she was doing. She was blameless.

But also, the children understood responsibility with a terrifying and naked clarity.

As a child, I felt acutely the injustices my life touched. When I passed a man sleeping on the street, I felt sad for his suffering, and I knew that there was something unfair in my comfort alongside his deprivation. I did not need to understand the complexities of capitalism, addiction, structural racism, or my country's failure to treat its mentally ill veterans to know that my warm bed and plentiful food were bound up in the same system that left a man sleeping on a flattened cardboard box on a winter's night.

As children we are taught to share. We are taught equality. We are taught respect. And we know there is a kind of responsibility, however diffuse, in our participation in a nation that inflicts violence and upholds injustice. As adults, we learn to unknow what is too painful to hold. We soothe ourselves with ignorance and helplessness.

That day in Colleen's living room, I asked about George's drinking. She lowered her voice and met my gaze sideways. "You know, he had such an important job, and maybe that was the reason. I think a lot of men at that time had problems . . . maybe the stress of the work and knowing what they were doing. It happened to a lot of the men in the higher positions."

Scholar Gabriele Schwab, a child of postwar Germany, argues that Abraham and Torok's concept of the crypt can illuminate not just the transmission of trauma in individual families but also the repression of memory around collective historical trauma, repression that occurs both in victims and in perpetrators of violence. She finds the crypt particularly salient in understanding the silence around Nazi atrocities and the stunted mourning of Germany's wartime losses. Germans, she argues, could neither face their own guilt nor mourn their own dead in light of that guilt and thus buried both personal losses and collective guilt: their conflicted feelings "were repressed, split off, and pushed into the cultural unconscious."

While most trauma discourse appropriately centers on the experience of the victims, Schwab, the child of perpetrators, argues for the importance of recognizing that both victims and perpetrators experience "the psychic deformations of violent histories." Understanding this can help to reveal the mechanisms by which trauma in both groups is internalized, repressed, and reenacted. She writes: "The collective or communal silencing of violent histories leads to the transgenerational transmission of trauma and the specter of an involuntary repetition of cycles of violence." Nazism itself, she argues, drawing on Hannah Arendt and others, was the result of the unresolved phantoms of colonial and imperial violence returned to Europe.

The perpetrators' unmourned phantoms might include a loss of ideals, a loss of a certain sense of self, or a loss of a particular understanding of the world. Germans after World War II, Schwab suggests, may have encrypted their unprocessed grief over their own war dead, their complicity in the mass murder of the Jewish people, their adulation of Hitler, and their own humanity.

We might call the nuclear bomb one of the United States' many collective phantoms. Along the lines of Schwab's argument, we might say the bomb was the result of the unresolved phantoms of a nation founded on stolen land, genocide, and slavery, a history of denying the humanity of others.

It is no accident that in the wake of the bombings of Hiroshima and Nagasaki, many Black American intellectuals, activists, artists, and religious leaders, including Zora Neale Hurston, W. E. B. Du Bois, and Paul Robeson, understood the threat of nuclear weapons as inextricably intertwined with the global fight against racism and colonialism. The first of these terrible new weapons had been made from uranium mined in the Congo under Belgian colonial rule and had been used against nonwhite people in Japan. And as global nuclear arsenals grew, colonizer nations including the United States, England, France, the Soviet Union, and China would test their weapons in colonized lands, exposing Native Americans, Marshallese Islanders, Indigenous people in Australia, Algerians, Tahitians, Indigenous people in the Russian Arctic, Uyghurs, and others to fallout.

For those who have had a stake in the myth of America, Hiroshima and the continued production of nuclear weapons threaten the belief in the nation as a force for moral good. "It has never been easy to reconcile dropping the bomb with a sense of ourselves as a decent people," write Robert Jay Lifton and Greg Mitchell in their book *Hiroshima in America*, a study of the ways the story of Hiroshima has been sanitized to avoid a national moral reckoning. "Hiroshima remains a raw nerve."

When India tested its first hydrogen bomb in May 1998, the Indian writer and activist Arundhati Roy penned a heartbroken, enraged essay in response. "If only, if only, nuclear war was just another kind of war," she lamented. But no, if it comes to nuclear war, "our foe will be the earth herself. The very elements—the sky, the air, the land, the wind and water—will all turn against us. Their wrath will be terrible."

This moment was not all that remarkable in the history of nuclear weapons proliferation. India had already had the atomic bomb for more than two decades, and the US had tested a hydrogen bomb more than four decades before. "There's nothing new or original left to be said about nuclear weapons," Roy admitted wearily. Still, she advocated outraged protest at this nonhistoric moment: "Let's pick up our parts, put on these discarded costumes and speak our secondhand lines in this sad secondhand play. . . . Our fatigue and our shame could mean the end of us."

Rage and fear among those who live closest to the bomb, in both physical proximity and knowledge, are regarded as the irrational hysteria of the uninformed. In Oak Ridge, and among others with a stake in this industry, I have seen a certain protective distance when it comes to nuclear weapons. I have been told to contextualize the horror of Hiroshima in relation to the Rape of Nanjing, the bombing of Dresden, and any number of other historical atrocities, as if the existence of other atrocities mitigates the severity of this one. I have been reminded that the apocalyptic predictions of a single bomb capable of destroying all life on earth have not (yet) come to pass, as if the continued existence of nuclear weapons do not still pose an existential threat. I have been told to keep my feelings out if it, as if the nation's suppressed feelings about the bomb were not the result of a concerted political effort.

Nuclear bombs become jokes. In a presentation at Y-12's history center, a communications representative jovially described the mechanism of the Hiroshima bomb like this: "You jam two pieces of uranium together, they go boom."

Often, writes Schwab, the silence around phantoms is not complete, but certain kinds of telling—those that are primarily informational or defensive, those that dissociate from emotion—can actually serve to further encrypt.

I've inherited the fatigue and shame of this sad, secondhand play. I have been ashamed of my anger. I have been told I am too sensitive to the world's injustices. Therapists have said I take on too much responsibility, when I have done quite little. They say I carry too much guilt for what is beyond my control. They suggest upping my antidepressants. They look for reasons in my childhood.

I am stunned and roused by Roy's utter, unabashed rage. "Thank you for altering the very meaning of life." Practically spitting with sarcasm, she addresses "The Men who made it happen. The Masters of the Universe. Ladies and gentlemen, the United States of America!" She might as well have been addressing George. "From now on it is not dying we must fear, but living."

Of course there are reasons, and of course I feel guilty. The comfort of my life is founded on the nuclear weapons industry. My grandfather, the child who left the farm to go to college, landed a high-powered career building nuclear weapons, a career that afforded his family a vacation home and elite educations for his children, who would go on to be doctors and lawyers and scientists with vacation homes of their own. My very pursuit of this story has been made easier by my expensive education, my supportive teachers, my freedom to take on the tenuous career of a writer. And that is only one way that my comfort and success are bound up in violence and oppression.

"You take on too much," I'm told. "Don't worry so much. Don't take everything so personally."

This story is and isn't personal. What I see in my childhood, in my family, is just a magnification of what I see in Oak Ridge, in the nation at large. George is not remarkable. My family is not remarkable.

Take your pills. Swallow the bomb.

"The bomb isn't in your backyard. It's in your body," insists Roy. "Take it very personally."

When burying radioactive nuclear waste from energy or weapons production, the major concern is half-life. Half-life describes the amount of time it takes for half of a given quantity of an unstable, radioactive element to decay into another element. Some elements must first decay into a series of other radioactive elements before reaching a stable, harmless state.

Half-lives can range from seconds to billions of years; the hazardous life of radioactive waste is generally considered to be around ten half-lives, though that number depends on the amount and type of waste. The relevant question in disposing of radioactive waste is: How long does it have to stay buried before it can't hurt us any longer?

What is the half-life of a secret?

Certain kinds of radioactive waste remain dangerously radioactive for hundreds of thousands, even a million, years. The Waste Isolation Pilot Plant, carved into ancient salt beds twenty-six miles from Carlsbad, New Mexico, is the nation's only permanent disposal site for transuranic waste—plutonium-contaminated clothing, soil, rags, tools, and other radioactive by-products of nuclear weapons manufacturing. The site promises to keep the waste isolated for at least ten thousand years.

Whether it is possible to contain the waste for that long—to seal it against corrosion and groundwater and earthquakes and climate change—is the subject of contentious debate among activists, environmentalists, nuclear waste experts, and those who hope to keep producing such waste.

Yet even if we manage to successfully isolate the waste for that long, how do we warn humans of the future not to go digging? In the 1980s and 1990s, in a rare consideration for the distant future, the DOE convened panels of anthropologists, archeologists, artists, philosophers, materials scientists, linguists, and other experts to answer this very question. The trouble is—we have no idea what human culture will look like in ten thousand years, what language we'll speak, what symbols we'll understand. *The Canterbury Tales*, written just over six hundred years ago, may be alright for leisurely parsing in a high school English class, but we wouldn't want our emergency evacuation procedures to be written in Chaucer's English. Humans have only had written language for fifty-five hundred years, just over half the time the DOE promises to keep the waste contained. And even ten thousand years is an arbitrary number, just a fraction of the time these lethal leftovers will remain dangerous; ten thousand was chosen because a higher number was too absurd to contemplate.

The panelists tried to predict what human society might look like in ten thousand years, what would endure three hundred generations into the future. They came up with proposals that ranged from hiding the burial site under a menacing thicket of enormous thorns, to creating an "atomic priesthood" responsible for disseminating legends and performing rituals to ensure cultural memory of the site's danger, to genetically modifying cats to change color in the presence of radiation. One group would cover the site with basalt or painted concrete to create an ominous "black hole"; the dark material would absorb and radiate the sun's oppressive heat, emanating a physical and emotional sense of danger.

Initially, there was some debate about whether it would be safer to, in fact, leave the site unmarked—and thus not invite attention and curiosity—but it was feared that the waste could be forgotten and later accidentally discovered. And so, writes Peter van Wyck, scholar of communication, semiotics, and nuclear history, the secret of the desert "must be kept and always disclosed—simultaneously."

Months after my trip to Las Vegas, after I had nearly resigned myself to the possibility that the photograph of George with the nuclear blast was a fabrication of my memory, someone mentioned that one of George's cousins remembered it. I called her at her home outside of Nashville. She didn't remember where she saw it—in an album, or at his funeral, but her memory was as confident as mine used to be. George, unmoved before the consuming blaze of nuclear fire.

"It does exist," she promised. We speculated that George's children had become so accustomed to everything nuclear that the photograph would have made no impression on them. Overexposure, I supposed, could inure one to anything. It took the cousins visiting from Nashville to see it, the in-laws, the granddaughter.

"I always thought," she offered unprompted, "that George had the whole picture. I don't know. I always felt like all of that maybe influenced his later problems in life."

I called my father to tell him that Mary Beth remembered the photograph. "Now remind me," he said, "what photograph is that?"

## 14

# MERCURY

Though its name comes from the Greek *lithos*, for stone, lithium is the lightest solid element, a metal so light you can cut it with a butter knife and float it on water. Lithium is silvery but grays when exposed to air. It is so reactive to its environment that it never occurs in pure form; it must be laboriously extracted, often at high environmental cost, from mines, seawater, salt flats, brine pools, and hot springs from Australia to Zimbabwe, Chile to Tibet. Lithium burns crimson at first, and then brightest white.

Most of the Earth's lithium comes from exploding stars, but tiny amounts were produced millions of years before the first stars, at the very beginning. Formed in the big bang along with hydrogen, helium, and beryllium, lithium is one of the first four bits of our universe.

To make a hydrogen bomb, smash hydrogen together with a lithium hydrogen compound and heat it all to many times the temperature of the sun. For a moment, these primordial elements return to their origins, blazing bright as a small star.

Is there irony, natural law, or some dark magic in the fact that the first elements of our universe are also the ones capable of undoing life on this earth? Does the beginning always contain the end?

The first person to tell me about George's involvement with Y-12's lithium work was Bill Wilcox, the chemist who labored beside

George in the 9203 chemistry building in the earliest days of the war. Before I met Bill, he told me over email, "I knew both your grandparents, George very well. We worked together all through that first winter and spring. . . . I'm so glad to be able to help you know the neat guy he was!"

In retirement, Bill devoted himself to Oak Ridge history, giving speeches at historical events, visiting schools, and compiling a detailed chronicle of Y-12. To prepare for my visit, he'd marked all the places George is mentioned in the chronicle. He read those passages aloud to me in his Oak Ridge living room, voice booming like a movie announcer. "July 15, 1952: George Strasser will assume complete charge of the ELEX development program." ELEX, Bill explained, stood for electrical exchange and was the first of several processes used to separate lithium isotopes. He called lithium isotope separation Y-12's "Second Manhattan Project."

"It was a huge plant that cost millions of dollars to build. And it was all super secret and very, very fast. George was put in complete charge of the operations there. I mean, this would have been hundreds of people working on every shift . . . His star was really climbing." Within a few years, George was one of the men overseeing all lithium development work. He was promoted to assistant plant superintendent in 1958.

Despite his nearly ninety years, Bill carried a boyish exuberance. He loved his city, loved his work, loved to tell people about it. And he wanted me to be proud of George, proud of this heritage.

He showed me a photograph of plant management from 1959: twelve men in suits and ties grouped haphazardly around a Buick, a couple of large white papers unrolled on the trunk. George in the center, much shorter than the others, looked off to the side. Behind them rose imposing smokestacks, giant metal cylinders, rows of barrels on their sides, all the ominous shapes and angles of a Cold War weapons plant. In addition to George's, I recognized five other names from the caption—the ones who would, in the year or so after the picture was taken, become tenants in common of a pretty jut of land on the Emory River.

George's promotions stopped after this 1959 photograph. Three years later, Roger Hibbs, also pictured, would be promoted to plant manager instead of George.

I told Bill I knew about George's problems. I asked, gently, whether he knew anything about them. He nodded as if my question was not a surprise but answered that he'd moved to K-25 by then and didn't return to Y-12 until 1970. "So I missed that whole . . . I just really didn't get in on any of his problem years. My memories of him were just unclouded."

In nature, lithium occurs in two isotopes, lithium-6 and lithium-7. Lithium-6 was called "aspen" in Y-12 code: a sunlit grove atop a rocky ridge, all the leaves shimmering in the breeze. Lithium-7, on the other hand, was called "marble": the hard unblinking eyes of a statue, blank, with no pupils in them. Lithium-7 is the slower sister, steady and calming; unlikely to react, she's used as a coolant or pH stabilizer in nuclear reactors. The bomb-makers, of course, needed the volatile one.

Lithium-6 makes up only 7.5 percent of naturally occurring lithium. To separate lithium-6 from lithium-7, Y-12 chemists and engineers relied on an essential property of lithium-6—that it dissolves more readily in mercury than does lithium-7.

Lithium may be one of the oldest elements, but mercury is the stuff of ancient human magic. Liquid at room temperature, mercury was called quicksilver by Aristotle, who thought it the essence of all metals. In China and Europe, alchemists studied the strange substance for the secrets to immortality and endless wealth. Archeologists have found mercury in Egyptian and Mayan tombs and painted on prehistoric skulls in Turkey and Italy. At Y-12, faced with a mythic task—to sort this scarce tiny thing from an abundance of another thing, like Cinderella sifting lentils from ash or Psyche sorting grains—the chemists turned to old magic, the stuff of life and death.

The scientists tried several processes that relied on mercury before settling on the COLEX (column exchange) process. Two of the Y-12 buildings housing the Alpha II calutrons that had been used to separate uranium during World War II were stripped of their old equipment, replaced with fifty-foot-high steel columns, pumps, and miles of piping. The process went something like this: the chemists prepared two solutions—one an amalgam of lithium dissolved in mercury, and the other, a solution of lithium hydroxide. They pumped the two in counterflow against one another through a cascade of upright columns, and the lithium-6 gradually concentrated in the mercury amalgam, while the lithium-7 migrated to the hydroxide.

Once the process went live in January of 1955, it operated continuously twenty-four hours a day, seven days a week.

In the 1950s and '60s, some Oak Ridge schoolchildren wore dog tags. Stamped with names, addresses, and telephone numbers, they were to serve a dual purpose—to reunite children with their parents in the event of evacuation or to identify bodies after a nuclear attack.

One little girl, who worried that her family did not have a bomb shelter like many of her friends' families, had frequent nightmares about fighting the Soviets; in the dreams, it was hand-to-hand combat in the streets, like in some World War I scene in a French village. She could taste the fear, even if she couldn't grasp the nature of the threat.

Teachers led their classes in evacuation drills out to the playground, into the woods, or down steep winding routes snaking from the ridge and out of the city. Told their city was "number one on the hit list," kids were tight with anxiety, imagining being separated from their parents. Or else they ran and laughed in the fresh air beneath the trees, delighted by the break from school. "One kid tripped on a root and broke his leg," Karin remembered.

The shift change whistle from the plants went off every evening at five o'clock, functioning as a convenient dinner bell, calling the children home from play. Some children mistook the whistles for air-raid sirens, which were also tested regularly. If the sirens went off outside of a scheduled test, families were supposed to leave by the closest evacuation route within five minutes. "But what if the Soviets attack at exactly five o'clock?" the children joked.

The fathers who worked at the plants might not make it home for dinner. Or they came home and went back to work again afterward. Not an hour to lose.

My father was born just one month after the Soviets' first test of a hydrogen bomb. He and his friends laughed at the anticommunist propaganda films they were shown in school, rolled their eyes at the righteous injunction to "kill a Commie for Christ." He remembered the civil defense drills of his elementary school years as routine, almost a joke. He crouched beneath his desk, pointing his ruler like a machine gun at his friends. *Poppoppoppoppoppoppop.*

"Do you think your dad was ever afraid?" I asked him.

"Hmm." He paused. "I think in Oak Ridge there was a bell curve of fear, with paranoid people on the one end, and on the other, the 'hyperrational,' those who knew if it came, there wasn't anything you could do about it."

Mercury was the swiftest among the gods, messenger of the winged sandals, protector of both traders and thieves. Guardian of the open road. He slipped between the realms of the living and the dead, played tricks on other gods, talked his way out of trouble. The planet that zips fastest around the sun is named for him, so is the metal that runs liquid at room temperature, the element that won't stay put.

The scientists were wary of using mercury. They knew how difficult it was to contain. They knew it posed toxic dangers. They tried other methods, but only mercury would do. The nation demanded hydrogen bombs, and hydrogen bombs needed lithium, and lithium required mercury.

Between 1950 and 1963, Y-12 lithium separation processes used more than twenty-four million pounds of mercury, enough to fill eleven billion thermometers. The process worked the way it was supposed to. Over thirteen years, Y-12 enriched all the lithium the bomb-builders needed and more. But the mercury also behaved true to its name. The heavy liquid metal strained pumps and valves, burst through pipes, pooled on the floor, sunk through cracks and seams into the dirt below, and collected in storm sewers and drain lines. Workers remember wading through rooms flooded with the strange silver substance, liquid metal lapping at their boots. If the process was epic, so was the mess it made.

As management, George would have spent most of his days in an office rather than on the plant floor. But George was a hands-on kind of boss. A man who worked under him years after the lithium program was completed told me that George was not the type to sit in his office while something was going on. If there was a leak, this man said, George would be charging in to see what was wrong. He must have been in the fray. He must have seen silver streaming from a split pipe, beading down a concrete wall, spiraling into a drain. He must have seen himself reflected in a pool of liquid metal at his feet.

Bill Wilcox wanted me to be proud of George. I suppose George had the makings of a good hero—the youngest son who left the farm to seek his fortune in the world and found his home with a sacred brotherhood in care of secret knowledge. But in the old stories, the heroes and gods are not always, and sometimes not even a little, good.

Mercury is a shapeshifter, a traveler between worlds. Vaporized mercury wafted from air vents, through fences, over lawns, playgrounds, cars, rooftops. Mercury from wastewater and spills ran out through storm drains into the East Fork Poplar Creek originating at a spring below the plant. As early as 1955, scientists at the K-25 gaseous diffusion plant measured increased levels of mercury where East Fork Poplar Creek empties into Poplar Creek, and further downstream, into the Clinch River. K-25 scientists suspected, but did not know, that the mercury was coming from Y-12. The process was classified even from the other plants.

In nature, mercury occurs in three forms—elemental, organic compounds, and inorganic compounds. The Y-12 processes used elemental mercury, the pure, silver kind found in thermometers. This is mercury unbound to other elements.

Swallow elemental mercury from a thermometer, and very little of it will be absorbed into your stomach and intestines. But elemental mercury at room temperature is prone to evaporation. Airborne, it becomes a colorless, odorless vapor that will sneak into your bloodstream and ride to your brain and kidneys. Exposure to high levels of elemental mercury can harm the nervous system, cause permanent brain damage, and lead to tremors, a constriction of vision, hearing loss, memory loss, personality changes, and other symptoms.

Though children of the fifties still played with the mercury spilled from broken thermometers, the dangers of mercury exposure at high levels were well-known by then, and the scientists were concerned with worker safety. They tracked airflow in the process buildings, regularly measured the concentration of mercury vapor, and monitored worker exposure with urine tests.

When I requested documents from Y-12 containing George's name, I received, after they had been reviewed and cleared for public release, memos reporting on worker urinalysis and on monthly air sampling data. Frequent "irregular" high readings of mercury concentration were explained due to leaks and spills. There was a letter to George from December 1955 documenting a phone call to a chemical company, looking for advice on mitigating worker exposure to mercury. The call was made by a member of George's division, apparently on George's request. So he was aware of the problems and hazards, and concerned, at least, for the safety of the workers. The memos were also peppered with other names I recognized—Hibbs, Googin, Ebert, Jasny: the lake brethren.

Huge exhaust fans installed to lower mercury concentrations inside the process buildings droned day and night, pulling mercury-thick air out to disperse under a southern sky.

Once outside the metal pipes and concrete walls of a lab, elemental mercury combines with other elements—such as chlorine or sulfur or oxygen—to form mercury salts, crystals, white powders, or bright-red mercuric sulfide. Inorganic mercury compounds are absorbed more easily through the intestines than elemental mercury, and small amounts can pass through the skin. In a body, inorganic mercury compounds travel the bloodstream to various tissues, where they can damage the kidney, stomach, and intestines.

In the soil and water, microbes can combine mercury with carbon to form an organic compound, most commonly in the form of methylmercury. Methylmercury bioaccumulates as it climbs the food chain, from microorganisms to insects to ducks, bats, fish, humans. Easily absorbed by the digestive system and able to travel freely through the body and pass through the blood-brain barrier, methylmercury is the form most toxic to humans.

Large doses of methylmercury can cause nausea, vomiting, kidney damage, slurring of speech, memory loss, and brain damage. Growing evidence also suggests a link between methylmercury exposure and heart disease.

All three forms of mercury, once in the body, can change form again and exit in feces or urine or vapor on the breath. They can seep from a mother's milk to a child's mouth or from her womb into the unborn baby's body.

A seventeenth-century British alchemist described the difficulty of defining the true nature of mercury due to its great transmutability: "Having looked up and down for him . . . we quickly discovered him, and then we found he was everywhere."

Sometimes fathers brought metallic mercury home to show their children. What fun! How educational! "Kids would bring it to school, and we'd play with it on our desks. We would shoot mercury balls across the desk to each other with our fingers," recalled one former resident.

The fans in the process buildings blew and blew, pushing mercury-saturated air out into the valley, where it drifted downwind to settle on small farms and pastures. Pine Ridge, which ran like a spine along the plant's northern boundary, limited airflow between Y-12 and the neighborhood of Scarboro, the historically

Black community less than half a mile from the plant, established in 1950 as housing for Black residents to replace the shoddy World War II hutments. It was not a perfect boundary, though, and some air escaped over the tree-lined ridge to fall on homes and gardens.

East Fork Poplar Creek exited Y-12 and ran beyond the northeastern edge of Scarboro; one longtime resident of the neighborhood recalled kids bringing home bottles filled with metallic beads of mercury.

The creek wound through the center of town, nudged up against the Oak Ridge Turnpike, and ran parallel to the major thruway. It passed a softball field; kids splashed through the shallows and launched leaf rafts. It slipped a finger across the turnpike through a culvert; kids would use the tunnel to cross the busy street, their own secret passageway, the cool gray concrete arching above them. It snaked by a tennis complex, where kids waiting for their fathers built little dams of sticks and mud, caught tadpoles, squatted ankle-deep to study the aquatic world.

Robertsville Junior High sat adjacent to the creek, and its schoolyard occasionally flooded when heavy rains swelled the stream; an April 1956 storm saw the end zone of the football field a foot under water. My father attended Robertsville. He remembers when his eighth-grade science class ventured to the creek to search for salamanders. He watched his classmates gingerly step on rocks and submerged branches to cross. *Oh, this will be easy*, he thought. *I can just jump over.* So he backed up about ten feet and started running, but a foot from the creek's edge, his foot sank into soft ground, and he toppled face-first into the water. He emerged laughing, streaming, skin and clothes plastered in mud.

Near the western edge of the city, East Fork Poplar Creek flowed into Poplar Creek, which wound into the Clinch River, which emptied, finally, into Watts Bar Lake, the lake on which my father and his siblings would spend amphibious childhood summers.

Fish consumption is one of the most common pathways of human exposure to methylmercury. The Oak Ridge newspaper and plant newsletters regularly reported on fishing conditions in the local waterways and printed pictures of proud residents with their catches. How many photographs had I seen of George clutching heavy bundles of fish like slippery, upside-down bouquets?

George's first admission to the Oak Ridge Mental Health Center was in 1972, after he had missed six days of work. The psychiatrist's note says he was urged to admit himself by a colleague. He stayed six days.

He'd be admitted five more times in the next two years, treated as an inpatient for up to sixty-three days at a time.

George was first diagnosed with depression, but by the time of his second admission, in February of 1973, his diagnosis had been changed to "manic depressive disease." By 1980, he had been diagnosed with bipolar disorder.

Today, psychiatrists distinguish between several types of bipolar disorders, including the classic bipolar I and its milder cousin, bipolar II. The manic episodes of bipolar I may be characterized by hyperactivity, euphoria, grandiose ambition, outsize self-confidence, excessive spending, substance abuse, a decreased need for sleep, and in some cases, delusions and psychosis. The similar but less intense hypomanic symptoms of bipolar II are sometimes overlooked as high energy, productivity, and achievement. "Mania is having five grand pianos delivered to your house; trying to buy the Sears company; sleeping with the local baseball team," writes Linda Logan for the *New York Times*. "Hypomania is mania with a tether, and, while it might avert some of the financial and interpersonal disasters that unchecked mania may engender, it can still feel like a runaway train."

Logan was diagnosed with bipolar II in her midthirties. Her hypomanic symptoms—sleeping two hours a night, eating very little, and studying for the MCATs with no relevant academic experience—sound very much like George's. I imagine that today, George would likely be diagnosed as bipolar II. He fluctuated wildly between weights, shaved irregularly, then let his beard grow long. He had two speeds—lightning and dead halt. Karin reflected: "My father did everything too much. He worked too hard; he would get depressed; he went down too hard. He drank too much; he smoked too much. He was sort of all or nothing."

To be mercurial means to be "volatile," to have "sudden and unpredictable changes of mood or mind."

By the time I obtained a copy of George's Y-12 personnel file, Bill Wilcox had passed away, at age ninety. When I found his name, on a memo dated June 21, 1971, I froze. I blinked away the trick of the eyes, but the name remained.

On June 21, 1971, George had just returned from an extended stay at the St. Albans psychiatric hospital in Radford, Virginia.

Bill wrote: "[George] talked freely about his experiences at Radford and seems to me to be in excellent physical health and is eager to go back to work. I told him I was delighted to have him back. . . . George says it is clear to him that he was not doing a satisfactory job; but that is over, and he wants a chance to show what he can do."

Hardly believing what I'd just read, I looked around the room, as if for someone to verify it.

"My memories of him were just unclouded," he'd assured me.

When I met him, Bill did not appear to have the slightest memory problem. He recited precise numbers—dates, quantities of uranium—and names from memory with the confidence of a historian. In 1971, Bill was the technical director of both Y-12 and K-25. Judging by the memo, he had some sort of supervisory role over George. I could not imagine he did not remember George's unraveling.

It was too late to ask him why he'd told me otherwise.

I read on.

On March 30, 1972, George sent a letter to Bill from the same hospital in Virginia, his second stay there. "Dear Bill," he wrote. "I am pleased to report that I am feeling much better. I am sleeping better than in years and my appetite for breakfast is excellent."

On August 31, 1972, Bill wrote: "I talked to George for about one-half hour after lunch about his health and job performance. I told him I was displeased by his failure to come to work on Tuesday, the 29th of August, and especially by his failure to call in. I told him I was particularly worried that he had gone back on the booze."

On September 13, George's birthday, Bill summarized a conversation he'd had with George on September 8: "I told him again that if he starts drinking and loses control we will have to assign him to some other duty. . . . I urged him to seek professional help if he needs it."

It was not just one episode but a pattern of months and years that Bill watched George fall apart. Years he denied to my face.

In the same memos, Bill recounted that though he would reassign George to some other, presumably less sensitive and important job, if the situation did not improve, he "certainly would not recommend termination."

Bill wrote: "I told him that, as I had said before, I would not run him off the job and I would again state that I would not do this, but that I could not justify continuing his employment in this position since it would neither be fair to the Company nor to the people reporting to him."

*I would not run him off the job. Certainly would not recommend termination.* There was loyalty. Nuclear brotherhood. Bill never stopped protecting George. Not even after George's death.

A memo from September 23, 1973, reported that George's security clearance would soon be suspended. Badges granting access to exclusionary areas of the plant had already been pulled. The memo was written by Jack Case, then Y-12 plant manager. His lake house was next door to the Strasser one. What my father remembered about Jack Case was that his was the house of the heaviest drinking, where the men skipped beer in favor of harder stuff.

"If you think Geo is in trouble I'd appreciate you letting me know," Bill Wilcox had written in a letter to Jack Case, detailing the "Strasser business."

In June 1974, George was medically retired from the plant, pronounced by his doctor to be "totally and permanently disabled." George was, by then, fifty-six years old. His children now suspect that his friends covered for him until the magic year when his age and years of service ensured his eligibility for a full pension, until Doris and the kids would be taken care of.

In hiding his mental illness, George's friends might have saved his life or might have hastened its end. It's another example of what powerful white men with powerful friends can get away with, even if it kills them.

Nearly thirty years after his death, long after any revelations about his mental health could hurt him, the forces that protected George remained strong. I didn't know whether Bill lied to me out of his loyalty to George or out of some unnecessary but unshakable adherence to secrecy. But that he did suggested that something of George's story threatened his own narrative of the work he'd devoted his life to, the choices he'd made, and the place to which he'd pledged his loyalty. And if he did not lie? If he, in fact, did forget those letters he wrote to George at the psychiatric hospital, how fiercely must he have suppressed the knowledge to overcome his excellent memory? Something in George broke in Oak Ridge— what would it have cost Bill to admit that?

In 1977, fourteen years after the lithium operations had ended, an internal plant investigation found that more than half a million pounds of mercury had been spilled or lost to the environment. Another nearly two million pounds could not be accounted for. The public was not notified.

On a mild winter Saturday, December 5, 1981, the Gough brothers took a walk in the woods around Y-12. Stephen was a biologist at Oak Ridge National Laboratory (ORNL, the Lab), the World War II weapons plant turned research laboratory postwar; his brother, Larry, worked for the US Geological Survey (USGS). Stephen knew something about elevated levels of mercury in East Fork Poplar Creek, and he wanted to investigate for himself. The brothers knelt at the stream's edge to cut samples of moss, pulling white roots from cool soil. Larry sent them off to USGS to get tested; the results revealed high levels of mercury, more than either had suspected.

On April 12, 1982, the samples were confiscated by the Lab. Stephen was reprimanded for insubordination and ostracized by his peers. He left the Lab in June. "It is an intellectual ghetto, an aberration in which there is enormous peer pressure to conform," he told the *New York Times*.

Shortly after the Gough brothers' samples were confiscated, a local paper submitted a FOIA request for all files on mercury. On May 17, 1983, the paper received the 1977 inventory estimating millions of pounds of mercury lost or unaccounted for.

Three days later, the Y-12 plant manager appointed a Mercury Task Force to compile information on Y-12's mercury operations and possible health and environmental effects. The task force was made up of individuals with Q clearances who had not been involved with the Y-12 lithium operations. The chair of the task force? Bill Wilcox.

If I had known that before he died, would I have had the courage to ask Bill, "How guilty was George?" What would he have told me then?

By the time the mercury leaks came to public attention, George was retired and living full-time at the lake. When I brought it up with my father, my aunts and uncles, they remembered the media storm that followed those first newspaper reports. They remembered George describing the rushed working conditions of the Cold War—represented in the 1983 Mercury Task Force report as "an atmosphere of high urgency." How they took inventory by counting flasks of mercury, but many flasks arrived only partially full so there were no accurate records of how much mercury had actually been used. How the scientists knew that massive amounts of mercury were being spilled and recommended shutting the process down to take a proper inventory, but there was a lot of pressure from above to keep operations going, twenty-four hours a day, seven days a week. George told his son Kurt, a newly minted environmental lawyer, righteous and indignant, "We were scientists. We knew. We should have been more careful."

In George's records from the Oak Ridge Mental Health Center, I found the names of his former doctors and nurses. I called the hospitals where they no longer worked; I called libraries in Nashville, Knoxville, and Oak Ridge for local telephone listings. I left messages for people with the same names and heard nothing back or received gentle messages in return: "I am not the person you are looking for." So, I was unprepared to hear Dr. Walters's dripping drawl after the first ring. I was unprepared for him to say, "Sure, I remember George Strasser." He was happy to talk to me, but first I needed permission, some sort of form from the court, he said, authorizing a release of information.

I was at the lake when I got all my permissions in order. The family was gathered for a triple birthday celebration, really just an excuse to pack the house full. I dug through boxes in the dark storeroom, concrete cool under my bare feet, to retrieve a copy of the will. Karin signed everything between slathering her grandkids with sunscreen and writing up a grocery list. I drove ten minutes down the road to the closest shopping center and faxed everything to Dr. Walters's office from the "business center" of the hardware store.

Back at the house, I kicked off my shoes, dodged my cousins' kids with promises that I'd join them in the water soon, and climbed the parched wooden stairs to the deck behind the carport.

Sitting on the bench at the deck's railing, I called Dr. Walters, half-hoping he wouldn't pick up or would want to schedule an interview for another day.

He picked up immediately. "I don't know if there's that much to remember," he warned. "It's been a long time." But then he launched in before I had a chance to ask anything, as if he had been waiting these thirty years for my call.

"One of the things that really stuck in my memory—it was his obsession with the mercury spill. That's what I remember most. He was just devastated about that."

I stared out at the lake lapping on the shore under a blue summer sky. Below, the kids were taking turns cannonballing into the water, competing for the biggest splash. My uncles sipped beers and heckled from the dock.

They did their best, Dr. Walters told me, tried everything to keep the mercury contained, called every expert, tried every technology available. While for some people that might have been enough, George blamed himself, felt personally responsible. "Guilt led to self-blame and depression," he said.

Guilt. *Guilt* was the word no one had been willing to use for George before. Guilt does not exist in the Oak Ridge lexicon. Guilt admits mistakes, admits consequences, admits conscience, notions that threaten the very existence of Oak Ridge and the narrative so many of its residents have built their lives on.

Dr. Walters, too, was a veteran of Oak Ridge, where no one was responsible and it was always someone else's job. He was willing to let George off the hook. "Somebody might say, 'Well, we did our best, and it just didn't work out.' He didn't." George, Dr. Walters said, had "a chronic sense of 'I'm not living up to other people's expectations.'"

Maybe it came from his parents, Dr. Walters speculated. He was old-school, spoke of George's perfectionist "ego-ideal."

Maybe, yes. Maybe George was a perfectionist. Maybe it did come from his parents. Joseph Henry's unmeetable demands certainly could have given a child a chronic sense of failure. But this was also true: George was at least partially responsible for an enormous environmental disaster in the place he'd made home. He was on the wrong side, and he knew it. If circumstances and the psychology of Oak Ridge and his own limitations did not allow him to admit failure publicly, he did admit responsibility to himself. I, too, would have been devastated.

The edges of the world were sharp—the shiny green of the needles on the pine trees, the grass, yellowed in the heat of summer, the grains in the rust-colored wooden siding of the house, the silvered splinters of the deck below my feet.

I did not immediately tell my family what I had learned. I carried it, heavy in my belly. Later, lying on a rubbery blue float on my stomach, I watched gentle waves bounce ovals of sky on the water, and I thought of mercury.

A congressional hearing on the mercury leaks, led by Tennessee representatives Al Gore and Marilyn Lloyd, began in July 1983. The panel concluded that over the years, the DOE had given the public "ambiguous, incomplete, or misleading" information about mercury discharges. A Tennessee Department of Health study, published in 1999, estimated that more than 350,000 pounds of mercury had evaporated into the air or slipped into the waters of Oak Ridge, more than 60,000 pounds above what was reported by the Mercury Task Force in 1983.

The Tennessee Department of Health study characterized possible "exposure pathways" by which residents of Oak Ridge and surrounding areas could have been harmed: inhalation, fruit and vegetable consumption, milk consumption, livestock consumption, fish consumption, skin contact with soil or water, ingestion of soil or water . . .

The study concluded that three groups were most likely to have been harmed: Children in Scarboro and families living on farms along East Fork Poplar Creek in the 1950s could have suffered damage to their central nervous systems from mercury inhalation or short-term kidney damage from inorganic mercury exposure. Children born to women who consumed fish from contaminated waterways, including Watts Bar Lake, during their pregnancies between 1953 and 1977 were at risk of brain damage.

My grandmother was a pregnant woman during those years, married to a man who loved to fish. So was my aunt Karin. There has been no evidence that my father, Nellie, or Karin's children, the children born in those years, suffered any mercury-related health consequences. But did George ever consider such a possibility? Did he fear it?

Since the 1980s, mercury cleanup efforts have involved removing contaminated soil from the floodplain of East Fork Poplar Creek, from the schools, community centers, and residential areas where it was used as fill dirt; cleaning and repairing Y-12's aging storm sewer systems; and monitoring fish and wildlife downstream of the plant.

But today, mercury still hides in the crevasses of the aging lithium-processing buildings, pools in sumps, lies mixed like silver beads in the soil beneath, and collects in cavities in the earth. Heavy rains disturb the soil, carry mercury streaming silver into the storm drains and out to the creek. Construction has begun on a new mercury treatment plant, contracted at more than $90 million, to be located at the headwaters of the Upper East Fork Poplar Creek, where the Y-12 storm drains discharge their contaminated water.

The DOE and the Tennessee Department of Environment and Conservation (TDEC), which conduct regular environmental monitoring, assert that current levels of mercury contamination do not pose a threat to human health, as long as people do not eat fish out of East Fork Poplar Creek.

Mercury does still threaten the environment in ways that are not entirely understood. In the 1980s, East Fork Poplar Creek, sickened with decades of nuclear pollutants, was barely able to support aquatic life. After decades of cleanup, the ecosystem is bouncing back. Fish dart through clear, cool water that winds past tree-lined banks. But in recent years, ORNL biologists have observed a disturbing trend: though mercury discharges from Y-12 have been declining, fish downstream are testing for higher levels of methylmercury. The findings suggest that the bacteria that convert elemental mercury to the more toxic methylmercury may be thriving in the cleaner water.

Mercury can be found in Oak Ridge's tree rings and spiders, beetles and bats. In the 1990s, researchers estimated that seventy-six metric tons of mercury had accumulated in the sediment of Watts Bar Lake; most of it remains buried beneath layers of cleaner sediment. It's safe, not bioavailable, the environmental reports maintain, as long as it remains undisturbed. According to TDEC, mercury contamination in Watts Bar fish is not a current concern. In the meantime, mercury continues to stream from Y-12 into East Fork Poplar Creek, into the Clinch River, into Watts Bar Lake.

My cousin's boy caught a catfish and kept it in the canoe filled with water. He spent hours observing its soft, sluggish body, its whiskered face. A budding biologist. His older brother learned to drive a Jet Ski. At the end of the day, when they circulated for good-night hugs, they smelled of sunscreen and lake, earthy and clean.

Lithium has been known for its therapeutic properties since ancient times, when Greeks and Romans soaked in lithium-saturated hot springs to alleviate melancholia. Recent studies have affirmed ancient wisdom, finding that communities with naturally higher concentrations of lithium in drinking water have significantly lower suicide rates than comparable communities with lower concentrations of lithium in their drinking water.

Lithium was approved by the FDA as a psychiatric medication in 1970. Today, it is still the most widely successful treatment for bipolar disorder, though scientists still do not really know how it works.

George's last admission to the Oak Ridge Mental Health Center was in September of 1980, nearly a year before the Gough brothers collected their samples. By then, he'd been taking lithium as a mood-stabilizer for several years and had been retired for six.

The report on George's first admission to the Oak Ridge Mental Health Center, from 1972, noted that his psychiatric problems went back fifteen or twenty years. That would put the beginning in the 1950s, just as he was put in charge of Y-12's lithium isotope separation efforts, producing a necessary fuel component for the nation's hydrogen bomb stockpile.

My father said things changed for George when he retired, moved out to the lake, and finally found the right medication. He said lithium saved him. That he found peace, in the end.

For my father's sake, I want to believe that. While I want to believe my grandfather was a man who felt deeply the weight of his work in the world, I hate to think of him dying in the pain in which he lived.

In 1978, one of George's doctors wrote of him: "He seems to view himself in quite non-grandiose fashion: as impaired, as somewhat of a failure, as contagiously sick." But the doctor also wrote, "He has not fallen into despair about all this, and retains some degree of hope that things will work out for him."

My father found a box of letters his parents sent him in the late 1970s and early '80s, when he was living in Knoxville, working at the psychiatric hospital and taking premed classes, then living in Chicago for medical school. His mother sent him the scores of UT basketball games, updates about the families he'd grown up with, and passive-aggressive prods to call more often ("Nellie, as she often does, called yesterday"). His father reported his cattle purchases, advised him on insurance, and asked for the "inside poop" on Chicago politics. He suggested my father, in his early years of med school, should become an adviser on medicine-related investments, "with your Wall Street experience." (My father's "Wall Street experience" consisted of a six-month stint as an administrative temp in his early twenties.) George's obvious pride in his son, his vague but overconfident grasp of his qualifications, and his rather poorly aimed attempt to connect made my heart hurt.

In June 1979, Doris sent my father an uncharacteristically raw letter. "I couldn't talk freely last evening—," she wrote, separating sentences by dashes rather than periods. "Pop is in another depression—"

"Today (Thursday) not good at all—apparently drunk all day—I'll keep you posted."

In July 1982: "Pop doing OK." But she gave him a motherly nudge: "Write him a letter addressed strictly to him—telling him what you are doing or asking for advice or whatever—"

By November: "Disregard anything about us coming at Thanksgiving. I have aborted plans for Chicago several reasons—Pop unstable, weather . . ."

Two weeks later: "I'm glad you'll be here for Christmas and help me evaluate things. This fall has not been good at all. When you call I cannot be as frank as I need to be." This was just over a year before George died. His mother, my dad told me, would have understated things.

The congressional hearing about the mercury leaks began in July 1983.

Six months later, on a January night, Doris woke to a choking sound, then a gurgling, like water filling up a tub; it was fluid filling George's lungs.

"His heart blew up" is the way Nellie put it.

# 15

# BOMBED WITHOUT A BANG

A few days after New Year's, another January, I drove up to the lake again. I realized, as I approached, that I had never stayed in this house alone before. In the summer, it was full of aunts and uncles and cousins rotating through for snacks and sunscreen, dripping water across the living room, retrieving a book to read dockside, or stealing away upstairs in vain hopes of quiet work or rest time. In the off-seasons, Karin and Paul lived here part-time when they were not off cruising the Caribbean in their trawler or working down a bucket list of travels. Now, though, I'd have the house to myself.

I crested the driveway in my little silver rental car and paused. To the left was the apartment above the cool, dark storeroom, to the right, the main house, and stretched between, the carport, which we used mostly as a shaded outdoor seating space for lazy afternoon card games or tuna fish sandwich lunches. From this spot, you could see sky above the carport roof, water below, and it made the whole building seem insubstantial, airy, as if the house was just a breezeway to the elements, just a portal from wherever you'd come from to the slower, sweeter time out here. I glanced at the wide kitchen window, foggy white with age, and for a moment expected to see Meemaw's face framed there, as if time were reeled backward, compressed into this eternal moment of arrival in which I was still a child breathless in the back seat and the dogs were forever bellowing their greeting, rushing toward the car as my father cautiously pulled down the gravel incline, wary of stray tails and paws. But Meemaw's face was not in the window, and this arrival was not joyful but lonely and tentative.

Because now I knew that this lake, really a river slowed and swelled by human hands, was not what I ever thought it was. To this river, I had lost skin cells and strands of hair, fishing lures caught on the rock bottom. How many of my father's baseball caps were snatched from his head by the wind as he stood behind the wheel of the motorboat? As a child, when my father or uncle filled the boat with gas, I worriedly watched the drips that fell to the water and spread as shimmering rainbows across the surface. I was upset by even the smallest signs of pollution. From my happy perch at the bow, wind in my face, my eyes registered each plastic bottle, each crumpled beer can, each floating chip bag, as a desecration. Angered by such carelessness, Julia and I, squished together in front, created a little song to mock this crime. "Litter, litter, litter," we shouted, our high voices rising thin above the wind and the motor, "you're a little kidder!"

But now I knew that the worst pollutants out here, the COCs, or "contaminants of concern," as the environmental reports call them, are the ones we cannot see. After I began searching for information about Oak Ridge mercury contamination, I soon learned what others had learned in the 1980s, as the contamination was first coming to public light—that to tug at one thread, one silver thread of mercury, is to unearth a whole tangled mess left behind by half a century of a rushed and secretive arms race with little regard to the long-term consequences on human health and the environment.

In 1989, the Oak Ridge Reservation was added to the EPA Superfund cleanup list under the Comprehensive Environmental Response, Compensation, and Liability Act (CERCLA); the contaminated area included 35,000 acres spanning 5 watersheds, 247 aging process buildings saturated with chemical and radioactive materials, 56 toxic waste burial grounds, and 52 settlement ponds, in addition to off-site zones where contamination had migrated, including the Clinch River and the Watts Bar Reservoir.

One 1992 report by ORNL scientists described Poplar Creek and the Clinch River as "pipelines" pumping hazardous waste from Oak Ridge into Watts Bar, making the lake a "major zone for contaminant accumulation," including mercury and radioactive cesium-137. Today, the EPA says that eighty-two river miles of the Clinch River and Watts Bar Reservoir are contaminated.

These are the dregs of Hiroshima, of Nagasaki, of more than seventy thousand nuclear bombs built by the US since 1945 and more than five thousand warheads still resting polished and precise in silos, on submarines and Air Force bases, scattered across Europe, lined up in underground bunkers like boxes of monochromatic crayons, the dumb toys of this deadliest game.

Some of the contaminants disappeared into the soil, sank deep into fractured bedrock, slipped into aquifers and streams, or, in the heat of a summer's day, rose silently into the air. There were, for instance, the S-3 ponds at Y-12, unlined pits designed to allow the 2.7 million gallons of liquid waste deposited there—concentrated acids, heavy metals, by-products from uranium recovery processes, and uranium itself—to be absorbed into the soil or evaporate into the air. The S-3 ponds were at one time known as the "witch's cauldron"—see her fingers stretch skyward, twirl in the breeze, tease a lock of child's hair, lift and drop an oak leaf, stretch long and wide toward the bruise of mountains against a carefree sky.

"The more you find out, honey, the more you're going to figure out this is an octopus," one woman warned me. Hydra was what I thought she meant, but I understood her point. That woman, Janice Stokes, is one of the area residents who attributes her suite of mysterious health issues to plant-related exposures.

Janice grew up on Watts Bar Lake, about five miles downstream from our lake house. When the weather was warm, she was in the water before breakfast. "I was a water dog," she laughed, and I laughed with her, remembering the summer days I went from pajamas to bathing suit and back again. Now she thinks that all those waterlogged days contributed to her myriad chronic and debilitating symptoms. "We were bombed without a bang," she likes to say.

None of Janice's family worked in Oak Ridge, and she didn't think about the city much until, in college, she decided to do a paper on the health effects of the Hiroshima bombing. She spent a week and a half in the X-10 library reading accounts by survivors and looking at photographs of the victims' burned and mutilated bodies. She cried as she delivered her oral report to her biology class. "From then on, I knew there was a lot more to Oak Ridge."

She told me she began to get ill in her late thirties: "I started having muscle trouble, fatigue, a little bit of a memory problem." It wasn't until she saw an Oak Ridge oncologist, one Dr. William Reid, interviewed on the news about the high numbers of kidney cancers and autoimmune diseases he was encountering among his patients that she began to wonder whether her poor health could be traced to the place responsible for those same horrific injuries she'd glimpsed in the X-10 library. She went to see the doctor and, through him, met other patients with similar symptoms. They formed a support group; within a year, she told me, they had over one hundred members.

A year or so after we connected over the phone, on my solo trip that January, I drove to meet her on a bright day. From the lake house, it was about thirty miles to the northeast, a forty-minute drive parallel to the tight, narrow ridges that wrinkle this landscape like a wrung rag, past Oak Ridge, and into Clinton, where I stopped for gas at a Marathon that shared a parking lot with Atomic City Computers—its black-and-white sign bore the symbol of an electron's elliptical orbitals enclosing a plump nucleus. This was not the atomic city, just a lonely stretch of highway leading to an older town, but even out here, even now, the bomb apparently maintained a certain glittering mystique.

Janice's spacious brick ranch house was perched on top of a steep hill. I parked in the half-moon driveway and rang the doorbell. Janice was smaller than I expected, shorter than my five feet four, with dark auburn hair and a husky voice. The house was formal but homey, warmly lit.

Perched on a floral couch beneath a window, Janice listed the toxic and radiological contaminants she said had shown up in her blood and urine tests: "It was nickel, cadmium, mercury, lead, uranium, and strontium." And some of the diagnoses she had collected over the years: metal poisoning, chronic fatigue, avascular necrosis, neuropathy, fibromyalgia, immunodeficiency.

Janice told me that, for years, she visited specialists throughout the southeast, seeking treatment for increasingly complex medical problems. Local doctors, she found, were hesitant to treat her or even to confirm another doctor's diagnosis; they feared retribution, she thought, if they implied that her problems could be related to Oak Ridge exposures.

Through the years of doctors' visits, through fatigue and pain and unexplained symptoms, Janice continued to organize alongside other area residents and Oak Ridge plant workers to demand accountability, treatment, and cleanup. They collected reams of records documenting the use and release of various contaminants from the Oak Ridge operations, educated themselves on the possible effects of various exposures, and held countless public meetings. She told me of receiving menacing phone calls and veiled threats, of being followed, of being afraid for her safety and for her job. But she persisted. "It was the most sad and obsessive time of my life," she said.

The group raised awareness and public concern about Oak Ridge contamination and made it easier for others to speak out. Their work supported the efforts of sick nuclear workers fighting for governmental compensation for illnesses that could be related to chemical or radiation exposure, efforts that led eventually to the Energy Employees Occupational Illness Compensation Program Act (EEOICPA) in 2000. But despite findings by public health studies indicating that some residents were likely harmed, the act provided no compensation for nonworker residents, so Janice had no recourse.

"I guess that's why I gave up," she said. "I know that fence does not stop radiation. And I know that little river does not stop groundwater pollution." But she was tired. "I had to accept that I had done something to help."

"Does anything make you feel hopeful?" I asked her.

She shook her head slightly. "It's in the air, and if my grand-children walk through it, then there's nothing I can do." Her voice broke, and she crumpled, covering her face with her hand. "Sorry," she breathed. I stretched my arm toward her across the back of the couch but did not touch her. We sat in a shaky, watery silence.

"It's just," she finally said, "it's too big for me. It's too big for the earth. It'll be the downfall of this earth."

As a child, she used to laugh when she read in the Bible that the earth would be destroyed the second time by fire. "I said, ha, that's not going to happen. I can just see him going around setting little fires, and we'll just go right behind him and put 'em out." But when she read about Hiroshima and Nagasaki, she thought, "Oh my God, that is the fire that will destroy the earth."

I left as afternoon slid into evening, the day dulled to a gray sky portending snow. Janice pressed a piece of homemade peanut butter fudge into my hand and urged me out the door so I'd make it home before the storm hit. The fudge was too sweet to eat all at once, so I put it in a paper towel in the cup holder and took it in small nibbles as I drove through the night coming on in dark sheets, the air beginning to sparkle with snow. I didn't even like the fudge, really, but I was grateful for the small comfort of this too-sweet treat, the gesture of hospitality and friendliness that felt like a patch of mud on a cracking dike, a small shoring-up of human kindness against the too-bigness of what we face. Perhaps we are being poisoned by the air we breathe, the water we drink. Perhaps the world is fated to end in nuclear fire. But in the meantime, let us share peanut butter fudge.

I'd prepared to be alone in the house, a strange quiet after all the crowded summers of my youth. As it turned out, though, I did not have the place to myself. When I arrived, I discovered the unmistak-able signs of a mouse infestation—toilet paper rolls chewed to cozy little nests, droppings on the kitchen counter and across the stove. I cleaned in a frenzy and set traps reluctantly. But at night I heard them scurrying in the air duct above the living room and something larger scrambling in the bricked-up chimney; squirrels, I decided.

The temperature continued to drop, and icy wind swirled flakes of snow as I arrived back at the dark, scuttling house. The house was freezing, the tile bone-numbing on my socked feet. Night pushed in at the windows.

Janice had lent me a VHS of a 1993 CNN broadcast detailing the efforts and persecution of Dr. Reid, the doctor she saw on TV talking about finding a high incidence of certain rare cancers in the area. Luckily, because this house was sort of a time capsule, there was a VCR. It took me about twenty minutes of fussing with the settings, but finally, the stubborn blue screen gave way to a staticky image of a parade accompanied by the eerily distorted sound of out-of-tune trumpets. The scene was, apparently, the celebration marking the fiftieth anniversary of Oak Ridge. I curled tight on the couch under a pile of blankets to watch.

Janice had told me the story of Dr. Reid, how he was run out of town for suggesting that the Oak Ridge plants could have been responsible for making people sick. Now, here was the evidence laid out with all the tropes and drama of cable news. Here was Dr. Reid, the celebrated cancer specialist, new to town after being heavily recruited for his expertise, flooded with patients suffering from rare cancers and immune disorders. He reached out to Martin Marietta, the DOE contractor managing the Oak Ridge plants at the time, for information about the chemicals and heavy metals that workers and residents might have been exposed to. Administrators denied his request. The hospital, originally founded as an army hospital during the war, revoked his parking privileges, cut off his phone lines, threatened his staff. He was called crazy; he was called a drug addict and made to undergo a substance abuse program; he was forced to take a mental competency test and subjected to a peer review process.

Because of the age of the tape, or perhaps the VCR itself, the colors were faded, the image so thick with static that the people were ghostly, eye sockets blank, movements staccato, lending the whole thing a manic quality that did not help my unspooling panic. Sometimes the picture was completely indiscernible, just jerky ribbons of white ascending the screen, or there was merely a vague suggestion of an industrial landscape through an electronic blizzard. The mice were holding relay races above me; the squirrels, I was sure, were chewing away the insulation, preparing to burst through plaster and stone at any moment.

The grim but unshaken voice of correspondent David Lewis was all too clear. Though all allegations against Dr. Reid were eventually revoked, his contract, which expired in August 1992, was not renewed, Lewis informed us. At the time of filming, Dr. Reid was saddled with $170,000 in legal bills. He left town shortly after.

Packaged within the familiar frame of a cable news report, I could almost imagine that this was a story of some other town, this "one industry, one hospital town," where economic dependence and close-lipped company loyalty made criticism an act of betrayal. Yet though the lamplight bounced against the window, sending back a dark reflection of the cluttered living room and my ghostly face, obscuring any view outside, I could not forget the lake was there beyond the glass, yawning wide beneath an opaque sky, the snow carrying who-knows-what from the air, falling crystalline before diffusing into the water's dark depths.

Even the mice were quiet now, and I was thoroughly spooked. I jumped at every click and settling of the old house. What sounded like a ping-pong ball bouncing on a wood floor turned out to be the freezer kicking into gear. I wished the mice would begin their antics again.

I put myself to bed upstairs, in the room that I tried not to remember was the room where George died. I could hear the wind chimes from the carport through the glass of my window, a sound that conjured the restless air before a summer afternoon thunderstorm. I had usually been a child in this house, and now, I longed for someone else to take responsibility. I wanted someone to tell me everything was okay. I wanted to believe them.

In the coming days, I met others who, like Janice, described in brutal and convincing detail the ways this place made them sick. Janet Michel was, ironically, a pollution prevention project manager before she was debilitated by nickel poisoning after only fifteen months working in a contaminated office at K-25 in the early 1990s; the nickel powder was so fine and abundant, she told me, that a finger swiped across the wall came away gray. She described how she went from being an "Energizer Bunny," spending her weekends kayaking, traveling, and cross-country skiing, to falling asleep while driving, while people were talking to her. She said she suffered from weekly migraines so intense the pain made her vomit uncontrollably. The migraines abated a few years after she stopped working, but she still battles chronic pain and fatigue.

Along with other sick nuclear workers from Oak Ridge and across the country, Janet spent much of the 1990s traveling frequently to DC to meet with congressmen and present testimony in support of the EEOICPA. In an astounding reversal after decades of denial, the act passed in 2000, stating: "Since the inception of the nuclear weapons program . . . a large number of nuclear weapons workers . . . who supplied the Cold War effort were put at risk without their knowledge and consent for reasons that, documents reveal, were driven by fears of adverse publicity, liability, and employee demands for hazardous duty pay."

Since the act was passed, more than 130,000 nuclear weapons workers or their survivors have filed more than 330,000 claims for illnesses they attribute to exposures at one of 381 DOE facilities, vendors, or other related nuclear weapons facilities; the Department of Labor, which oversees the program, has awarded nearly twenty-one billion dollars in medical bills and compensation to workers and their survivors.

These numbers offer no total accounting—for many, the process is onerous and can drag out for years while workers get sicker and medical bills mount. Janet told me she was denied twice before her claim for nickel poisoning was finally approved. Often, workers have to rely on the spotty and sometimes falsified records kept by plant contractors to make their case that their illness is related to their work, records that sometimes contradict their lived experiences. A 2015 McClatchy investigation found that more than half of those who applied for compensation between 2001 and 2015 were denied.

Still, imperfect as they are, these numbers give us something to go on, one way of measuring the cost. According to McClatchy, the Department of Labor determined that exposure to radiation or toxic chemicals had "likely caused or contributed to" the deaths of more than fifteen thousand workers whose survivors received compensation between 2001 and 2015. These numbers likely underestimate the death toll and certainly don't account for the physical, financial, and emotional burdens on chronically ill workers and their survivors.

Janet has spent more than twenty-five years fighting for justice for sick nuclear workers, and she has remained involved in advocating for the compensation program's improvement. But she had to take a big step back when her friends, her comrades in the fight, began to sicken and die. "I went to so many funerals," she breathed, just above a whisper. She is doubtful that current plant safety protocol or environmental monitoring have improved enough to prevent others from getting sick.

Certainly, there have been accidents and safety violations since the passage of the EEOICPA. In 2013, the Government Accountability Office criticized the DOE for "persistent safety problems" at its nuclear facilities, driven by "lax attitudes" and poor oversight. And in the last twenty years, there have been multiple documented cases of DOE contractors falsifying exposure records and retaliating against whistleblowers who speak up about safety concerns. At the same time, in their efforts to drive down costs and earn bonuses for quick work, contractors cut corners on safety and push to reduce workers' medical benefits.

Janet has worked to carve out one safe, clean place in this toxic landscape, a haven from a world that often brings her to tears with its injustice. She gets upset thinking about the residents, like Janice, who have no recourse. She gets angry listing the environmental problems that are ongoing. She urged me to look at official reports but warned, "Read 'em with a grain of salt. They're PR. They can hide so much in statistics." She ranted, got teary, caught a breath, laughed, said, "I'm getting on my stump!" Then she giggled like a child.

Now, Janet keeps mostly to her beautiful, sunlit house, filled with plants and Himalayan salt lamps. She's fifteen miles south of Oak Ridge, but she still worries about what can be carried through the air and water to the tree-lined ridge she's perched on. Her house is fitted with a reverse osmosis water filter and a whole-house HEPA air filter. When a radioactive waste incinerator was operating at K-25 between 1991 and 2009, Janet made sure she always knew which way the wind was blowing and stayed inside when she was downwind.

When Janet goes into Oak Ridge to visit friends, she won't drink the water.

I met Janet's friend and fellow advocate for sick workers, Harry Williams. For twenty years, Harry loved his job as a security guard at K-25, until, he told me, a noxious cocktail of toxic and radiological exposures sent his health into a tailspin. In the late 1980s, he said, he began getting "heart attack after heart attack," and by the time he left the plant on disability in 1996, he was suffering from severe fatigue and balance so poor he could barely walk. "It was biting me hard . . . If you'd seen me walk down the sidewalk, you'd've thought I was drunk as a dog." In the years after, in addition to chronic heart disease and extreme fatigue, he suffered from beryllium disease, heavy metal poisoning, and a host of other debilitating symptoms and disorders, a dizzying list he submitted as testimony to Congress in 2003.

"I did have a pretty good job," Harry said. "They just forgot to tell me it was going to kill me." Then he chuckled.

We sat in his dark living room, heavy curtains drawn against the sun. Harry spent his days there in the company of a fuzzy, mouse-brown dog named Sherlock, whom I kept wanting to call Toto. When Harry strained to recall a detail, he pressed his fingertips to his temples or leaned forward, tapping his index fingers against his front teeth.

Harry's wife and daughter worked at ORNL. He worried about what they might be exposed to, especially his wife in her work in waste management. But as much as he wished she would, she wouldn't quit; DOE jobs are some of the highest paying in the region. She called his antidepressants his "happy pills." "All the heavy metal toxicity and things like that lends itself to depression," Harry told me.

His home health nurse arrived as I was getting ready to leave, care provided through his compensation package. "Come in, baby girl," he called to her as the screen door creaked open. "And this is my favoritest nurse of all time," he announced. The health care he received through government compensation had extended his life ten years, he believed.

The nurse set up on the dining room table, portioning out Harry's pills. Before I left, Harry told me to look at the array she'd lined up across the polished wood: "You don't have to look at the prescription, just at the number." I took in the long line of amber plastic cylinders.

"One of these days they're going to declare Oak Ridge uninhabitable," he pronounced. "As science goes along and they learn more, bah bah bah. I wouldn't buy a house in Oak Ridge if my life depended on it, and I probably shouldn't have bought this one." We sat in a suburb of Knoxville, eight miles from Oak Ridge.

I spent days reading environmental reports and sociological studies and newspaper articles. I was determined to get to the bottom of it, to get to the bottom of something, to find an anchor to tether myself to a waking world in which the numbers added up to some kind of sense, in which cause followed effect and justice was served or at least could be fought for because the crime was clear. I wanted to know—what happened here? And what was still unspooling? I wanted to know what I should be afraid of.

I sat upstairs and pulled open the faded yellow curtains to let the sun stream in through the sliding glass doors. I filled my laptop screen with too many articles, drank coffee too quickly, and darted like an anxious squirrel before an oncoming car, switching frenetically between articles, sometimes mid-sentence, then standing up to stare out at the lake, rippling placidly, a sort of hard, silvered blue beside the white of the snow.

It all gave me a kind of emotional whiplash. I'd gathered a collection of sociological studies published in the late 1990s and 2000s, written by different groupings of the same few researchers plus an odd extra here and there; they described the way Oak Ridgers, protective of their history and economic interests, continued to enforce a code of secrecy and unquestioning loyalty to the town industry that made criticism tantamount to blasphemy. Activists were ostracized by community members, some of whom even organized against what they called "remediation excesses." Workers who raised concerns about safety were reassigned to hazardous tasks. Many, fearing retaliation, remained silent. People who had sought medical care to treat illnesses they suspected were caused by exposures reported that they had been dismissed as mentally unwell, that their medical records had been sanitized, and that doctors had refused to give them appropriate tests and diagnoses for fear of retribution like that visited on Dr. Reid.

Janet told me that during the heyday of her activism, she'd often find anonymous packages in her mailbox or on her front porch, containing documentation of contamination or safety violations people had seen at work. "But they would never speak up in public. They're too afraid of retaliation at work. Losing their benefits. Being harassed. Because they've seen it!"

The extensive environmental reports, produced by various agencies under the EPA Superfund requirements, portrayed a landscape exhaustively monitored: groundwater, surface water, soil, and air filters sampled, contaminants tracked in fish, birds, algae, insects, and microscopic river creatures. I was touched by detailed descriptions of collection methods: wood duck and tree swallow eggs hand-lifted from nests; cattail, watercress, and willow pulled from soggy floodplains. I imagined environmental scientists wading through creeks in tall rubber boots, venturing out with black lights at dusk and midnight to collect swarms of insects.

There is an annual goose roundup, when employees from the DOE and ORNL team up with the Tennessee Wildlife Resource Agency to corral flocks of geese on the reservation and screen them for radiological contamination. During annual turkey and deer hunts, all carcasses are tested. "Good news: No rad deer," reported a *Knoxville News Sentinel* blog on the November 2015 hunt, and "A not-so-hot deer season; only one kept for rad reasons," after the December hunt. I found this detail perversely soothing—one radioactive deer, out of the 244 killed in the 2015 hunt, seemed like a traceable, manageable problem.

The reports designed for public consumption had larger type, bold headings, and colorful pictures of wildlife on their covers: a bumblebee burying itself in a yellow daisy, a pink lady's slipper quivering above the forest floor, a waterbird balanced on a partially submerged tree stump in a still pond. All asserted, in different words, that cleanup was ongoing, that continued monitoring was necessary, that there was no current threat to human health. The tone of the DOE reports was especially cheerful and self-congratulatory.

But I had been given plenty of reasons to mistrust these reports. The DOE still controls most of the information on contamination and worker health, while TDEC, the state agency charged with independent oversight of the DOE's cleanup efforts, relies on funding from the DOE, and levels can fluctuate year to year. At the end of the day, Oak Ridge is still a company town, and the DOE holds huge economic sway in the region; a report by the East Tennessee Economic Council found that in 2020, the DOE and its contractors employed more than fourteen thousand people, created more than twenty-eight thousand indirect jobs, and added more than four billion dollars to the state's GDP. Reports of contamination can affect both employment and property values.

At some point while I was reading, I looked down and realized that the woven cotton blanket I'd been sitting under was decorated with Oak Ridge landmarks—the civic center, the high school, the Chapel on the Hill. In the center, beneath a dove and an atom, were the words, "born of war, living for peace, growing through science." I sat straight up, threw off the blanket, and paced the room, heart pounding.

Someone had rearranged the photographs again, and now there was a larger-than-life-sized headshot of George hanging above the stairs. Every time I ventured down, to refill my coffee or grab a snack, I turned the corner to confront him at eye level, this intelligent, polished, restrained George, impeccable in a black suit, not a hair out of place. One eye was slightly squinted, and he wore a thin, somber smile.

Nellie told me that in the darkest moments in her life, times when she was desperate with rage and despair, suicidal, screaming drunk, and toxic with self-loathing, she would cry out to her father. *Help me. Please help me.*

He was the man who had, in some large part, caused her suffering. It was Nellie who heard her father weeping about his mother's suicide. Nellie who her mother curled beside on the nights when George was drunk and volatile. Nellie who fled to neighbors' houses to escape the chaos of her own. And Nellie who drove home from college time and again to check her father into psychiatric care, to help manage a crisis her mother couldn't bring herself to fully face.

George passed on to his youngest child the genetic predispositions toward alcoholism and bipolar disorder, while his own poorly managed mental health ensured those seeds ideal growing conditions. In her darkest moments, though, Nellie felt he was the one who would understand her. She felt like he was listening, like he was there.

Now I wanted to rage at the grandfather I never knew, to stand on the stairs, eye to eye with that smug portrait and demand the truth. *What do you have to say about all this, George? What about Dr. Reid? What about Janice and Janet and Harry? Where were you, George, when all this was going down? Did you think you could hide all that waste away in the depths of this porous earth until it sank down to poison its very core? Did you think none of it counted?* I wanted to rip out tufts of carpet like grass and throw them at his complacent face, to burst into such an unrestrained temper tantrum that I rocked the ghost from his slumber and surprised him into speech. *What the hell, George, what the hell kind of a mess did you leave us with?*

But I was in my grandmother's house still, and so while I shook my head, I said aloud only, "What the heck, George, what the heck."

At night, I swam through shallow, restless dreams. In a large white room, men were standing behind folding tables, each displaying a plastic bin of water. They were waiting patiently to be assessed for their work, like kids at a science fair. And there was George, the one from the portrait, bald pate shining, face smooth-shaven, narrow tie and short-sleeved button-up tucked into belted pants. I ambled past and leaned close to peer at his container of water. It was from the lake, I knew, though it didn't look right—far clearer than it should have been, fogged only by a whisper of gray sediment. And I knew he was showing off his handiwork, how clean he could make the water look. George stood relaxed, hands behind his back, looking straight ahead. He didn't speak to me, or even seem to see me.

In town, I met a former pastor turned full-time antinuclear activist. I met a risk analyst with more than thirty years of experience assessing the hazards of chemical and radioactive contaminants on human health. I met a scientist for TDEC, the agency tasked with overseeing the DOE's monitoring and cleanup efforts.

I tried to look like a journalist, but really, I was just hoping I wouldn't cry when I asked them, in more sophisticated terms—*But how bad is it, really, now? What should I be afraid of?*

The activist was Ralph Hutchison, a white-haired, elfin man. He is the coordinator for the Oak Ridge Environmental Peace Alliance (OREPA). In the 1990s, OREPA organized with the sick workers and residents advocating for environmental cleanup. Ralph also served as a community representative on a panel of local citizens and experts advising and overseeing the Oak Ridge public health studies conducted by the Tennessee Department of Health (TDH) in the 1990s. Though he has no scientific background or security clearance, he has an impressive and precise command of past and ongoing environmental contaminants.

I noted that he drank the water. We were sipping tea at the Panera Bread just a mile down the road from the gates of Y-12. Across the road, the city's water tower rose through the gray mist of this chilled January day.

The water flows from the Clinch River, upstream of Oak Ridge's DOE facilities and should not be impacted. Still, the pipes cross Y-12 before arriving at the 1940s-era water treatment facility, which was owned and operated by the DOE until 2000, on a ridge top on Y-12 land. I understand why those who've spent decades steeped in the DOE's environmental failures are cautious.

"We live a life of risk." Ralph shrugged. "It's filtered."

Still, he said he would be wary of buying a house downwind or downstream of Oak Ridge. And he wouldn't swim in Watts Bar Lake.

Since the 1990s, though, OREPA has moved away from focusing on issues of health and environment in their fight against nuclear weapons. It is just too difficult to prove anything. "When you work for a small nonprofit like I do, all you have is your credibility."

The risk analyst was a man named Owen Hoffman. After nearly two decades in the Environmental Sciences Division at ORNL, he founded his own company that consults on risks posed to human health by toxic and radiological contaminants. As an analyst and adviser for the National Cancer Institute, the International Atomic Energy Agency, the CDC, the UN, the EPA, and others, he spent decades studying the public health effects of radiological exposure from Chernobyl, nuclear weapons testing, nuclear weapons production, and other sources.

I asked him to help me understand the numbers in the Oak Ridge health studies and environmental reports, and he did. But he cautioned that the reported numbers didn't show the complete picture. He described the way local and national politics influenced what got disclosed and how risk was communicated to the public. That the data, in other words, were politicized and incomplete. "The devil is in the details," he said. He would know.

In the 1990s, Owen worked on the fourteen-million-dollar TDH study of the public health effects of historical contaminant releases from the Oak Ridge nuclear facilities. The studies, which concluded in 1999, found it was "likely that some people were hurt by the releases" in the past and advised further environmental sampling, studies, and public health interventions.

But the subsequent assessments by the Agency for Toxic Substances and Disease Registry (ATSDR), meant to pick up where the TDH studies left off with respect to past exposures and to conduct evaluations of present risks, disregarded many of the TDH recommendations and mostly found no evidence of harm or inconclusive data. The DOE, an agency with a pattern of withholding information from the public and a vested interest in minimizing its culpability, controlled both funding and disclosure of the data on which public health conclusions and cleanup recommendations were based; experts and the public raised concerns that environmental sampling was limited and inadequate; and EPA officials criticized some of the ATSDR's assumptions and methods, including their recommendation to lower the standard of cleanup for mercury-contaminated soils below the EPA's recommended level.

Owen was not involved in the ATSDR studies, but as a local expert who had worked on some of the initial TDH reports on which they were based, he followed them closely and in growing dismay.

For years, he wrote letters to the CDC and the ATSDR documenting his extensive concerns and advocating for improvements.

"I don't give them much credence," he told me. "The funding for ATSDR came from the Department of Energy. And locally there was a lot of interest that these reports not be too critical because they were affecting property values. So there was a lot of attempt to downplay and downgrade any information on health risks."

Owen explained that exposures that do not cause statistically significant health effects might still increase risks to individuals; low exposures in small populations often produce false negatives. But the ATSDR relied on the limits of epidemiological detection to make the claim that there was no harm done in Oak Ridge.

And human bodies are not dominoes, toppled or not by a single push. While an epidemiological assessment might estimate that a certain level of exposure, by itself, would likely cause less than one case of cancer in a given population, that exposure could still be a contributing factor to an individual case of cancer. The compensation program for nuclear workers acknowledges this fact, compensating for exposures that might have caused, contributed to, or aggravated a worker's illness or death. But there is no such program for the public.

Owen pointed out, for instance, that if the criteria set to compensate nuclear workers were applied to the public, then any person who drank cow or goat milk as a child in the continental US during the 1950s nuclear tests and who later developed thyroid cancer would be eligible for compensation. Residents in and around Oak Ridge faced a compounded risk, as they were exposed not only to fallout but also to releases of radioactive iodine from Oak Ridge National Laboratory from 1944 to 1956.

So too, despite recommendations from the TDH, the ATSDR did not study the effects that combined exposures to multiple contaminants might have on a human body, instead treating each exposure in isolation. But to live in Oak Ridge during the decades of highest releases meant being exposed to a myriad of radiological and toxic contaminants.

Still, Owen cautioned against alarmism. "You are going to be pulled into two extremes," he warned. While he believes some people could have been harmed by past exposures from the Oak Ridge plants, he doesn't think there was a large-scale epidemic, and he is skeptical of those who claim otherwise. At the end of the day, he understands the potential health effects caused by Oak Ridge's radiological contaminants to be small compared to other hazards he's studied—radon gas found in homes, fallout from aboveground nuclear tests, and unnecessary CT scans and X-rays. And smoking dwarfs them all.

He was quick, too, to point out that you can't separate contaminants released from the Oak Ridge plants from the stuff put into the water and air and soil by all of the coal burning in the area.

Where, asked Ralph, the activist, would we go to find a truly pristine place in this country? "Maybe you could go to Montana? If Ted Turner hasn't bought it all," he offered.

The other thing he said was, "How do we exempt ourselves?" This was not a logistical "how" but an ethical one. If we could buy ourselves an uncontaminated haven, would it be right to?

The government employee, Kristof Czartoryski, trod carefully. "Let me see how I can avoid answering this question," he said with a laugh. But he explained where TDEC disagreed with the DOE regarding a recent report on groundwater sampling. When few detections of small amounts of chemicals and radioactive elements turned up in monitoring wells, and in at least one case a resident well, both agencies agreed that the amounts were not themselves hazardous, but where the DOE was quick to claim no risk, TDEC cautioned that two rounds of sampling on a handful of wells did not provide enough evidence to come to any conclusions. "If there is something coming from the DOE burial grounds, these very sporadic and small detections might be the first sentinels. You do not know where something might break through," Kristof said. TDEC would continue to monitor the wells, he assured me, with or without the DOE's blessing.

The question he wanted to avoid answering was whether anyone would improve the too-simplistic groundwater model used for monitoring and risk assessment. Groundwater contamination, I'd learned, is a particularly vexing challenge for Oak Ridge environmental management. The geology of this region is highly complex, soluble carbonate bedrock that over time has dissolved into a network of underground drainages, caves, and sinkholes, a topography known by geologists as "karst." "Plume" describes the way contaminants move through the groundwater, leeching out of historic waste burial grounds through cracks in bedrock, filling limestone caverns and underground channels to join aquifers that might eventually make their way to rivers and wells. In some places, "mature contaminant plumes have evolved," reported the DOE's 2015 annual site environmental report; tracking the pathways of these plumes through the karst, the "plume trajectory," is the subject of ongoing monitoring and research.

For a long time, the Clinch River, which cradles the southern and eastern borders of Oak Ridge, was thought to be a hydraulic boundary to off-site groundwater contamination. Boundary, in this case, did not mean, as one might assume, that the river served as some sort of wall, retaining toxic waters within the bounds of DOE land, but rather that, when groundwater eventually converged into the Clinch, it was carried downstream and diluted to levels considered safe. (Downstream means into the Tennessee River, which flows into the Ohio, which flows into the Mississippi, which empties into the Gulf of Mexico.) Recent evidence, however, has suggested that contaminant plumes may be migrating under the river through deep channels in the rock. As a precaution against the possibility of drinking wells becoming contaminated, the DOE has paid to connect a number of homes across the river to the local water utility.

The DOE's 2014 Groundwater Strategy confessed, disturbingly, "Groundwater gradient conditions around and beneath the major rivers of East Tennessee are not well understood."

"Anyone who tells you they know what is going on with groundwater in East Tennessee is lying to you," Ralph told me. According to the EPA, groundwater migration is not under control on the Oak Ridge site.

The truth, Kristof explained after a breath, is that the magnitude of the mess overwhelms the scarce resources available. Though the DOE spends hundreds of millions of dollars every year on Oak Ridge cleanup, "so much money is being eaten by the infrastructure—maintaining securities and guards, regulatory compliance staff here—there is only a token available for actual cleanup work."

He was candid and careful at the same time. There was a delicate balancing act, Kristof explained, in contradicting some of the DOE's claims while not inciting undue public panic over relatively small risks. I was the public he was talking about, and I had been panicking. But I was calmed by the precision with which Kristof parsed risk. And so it did mean something when he said that with everything he knew about Oak Ridge's contamination, the city was home, and he felt safe here. He showed me on a map where he fished, in Melton Hill Lake. "And guess what?" he said. "I eat the fish. And guess what? Ash disposal area. Stuff getting through the quarry here. And here I am fishing for a fish." The exposure was minimal, he said, as long as he was not eating large numbers of fish.

Owen, despite his criticisms of the public health assessments, maintains that the major exposures, and the harm that may have been caused by them, are in the past. He built his life here, raised his kids here. He's adamant that the city's drinking water is perfectly safe, that Oak Ridge, that Watts Bar Lake, do not pose a threat to those who currently swim, fish, and recreate there.

Owen's original love is the outdoors. He was once a park ranger, and he has the broad, cheerful, weather-worn face of someone who has spent days in the sun and wind. On evenings and weekends now, he leads full moon hikes and stargazing at the Obed Wild and Scenic River National Park, an hour west of the city. On his iPhone, he showed me a photo he took of the full moon through a telescope. It was luminous and silvered, textured and heavy like some perfect, damaged metal coin.

I left his office feeling calmed, sad, and wary. One of the sociological studies I read found that people's perception of the danger of environmental contamination in Oak Ridge was linked to their position of power and their investment in community identity. Those with high-level jobs and long ties to the city, who were less likely to be exposed to hazardous materials and who took personal pride in the city's history, tended not to consider contamination to be dangerous as compared to newcomers and those working more dangerous blue-collar jobs. What the sociologists found, in other words, was that what we believe and who we trust are based less on evidence than on who we are, where we come from, and how well we have been served or how far we have been betrayed.

What do we have but piles of numbers and our own gut instinct for how to read them?

And it matters, how we read the numbers, how we tell the stories, who we trust. It matters for our minds, our hearts, our bodies.

Due to its proximity to Y-12, Scarboro, Oak Ridge's predominantly Black neighborhood, has long carried a reputation as the most contaminated residential area. Public health studies have attempted to measure or estimate the chemicals, heavy metals, and radionuclides that could have made their way to the neighborhood from the vents, stacks, drains, and spills of Y-12. This scrutiny of the neighborhood, combined with media attention, anecdotal evidence reported by residents, and general distrust of the government stemming from both a local history of DOE cover-up and the country's history of structural racism, has contributed to the popular perception of Scarboro as highly contaminated.

In 1997, a Nashville *Tennessean* article reporting on perceived high rates of respiratory and other illnesses among Scarboro children seemed to both confirm and inflame residents' fears. A mother of a son suffering from "acute asthma and allergies, an enlarged heart, excessive nosebleeds, ear infections and stomach pains," told the reporters: "Scarboro is our home, the only place we've ever lived. We love it here and would hate to leave. But sometimes, I wonder if I am killing my children by living here." In response to the article, the CDC and the TDH undertook a study that concluded that rates of respiratory and other illnesses were within a normal range.

Some residents expressed relief at the findings; others, pointing out limitations in the studies, expressed mistrust.

A year later, three community members—Al Chambles, a retired Y-12 chemist; L. C. Gipson, a retired ORNL biology technician; and L. C. Manley, a retired ORNL metallurgy technician—wrote a series of long, meticulously researched op-eds for the *Oak Ridger* arguing that the media's portrayal of their neighborhood as heavily contaminated was sensational, irresponsible, and harmful. They cited area sampling that found that Scarboro had significantly lower levels of mercury contamination than other parts of Oak Ridge and pointed out erroneous and misleading reporting by the *Tennessean*, the *Oak Ridger*, and NBC. One of the most obvious and frequently repeated errors was the claim that East Fork Poplar Creek, the heavily contaminated stream that still carries mercury from Y-12 through the city and into local waterways, ran through the center of the neighborhood, when a quick look at a map shows that the creek only skirts the edge of the community, and at some distance from the houses.

Such misplaced negative media attention, the writers asserted, was lowering property values in a community that was already economically disadvantaged, stoking public fears, driving some to move out of the neighborhood, and perpetuating a view of their home as a sick and joyless place. And the perception not only hurt Scarboro residents but also had the effect of suppressing interest and activism among other Oak Ridge residents who, in fact, lived closer to the contaminated creek. "A lot of people who should have been protesting kept quiet, because they thought it was in the Black Scarboro community," Al Chambles told me over the phone.

Among the op-ed writers' requests were that environmental sampling be conducted in other parts of the city to determine whether Scarboro was, in fact, disproportionately impacted.

"Nowhere in Oak Ridge is as pristine as it was in the early 1940s before the Manhattan Project," Al Chambles said, but he did not believe Scarboro was more polluted than other parts of the city.

Six years after the op-eds were published, the ATSDR released its report on uranium releases from Y-12, finding no evidence of past or current negative health effects. The study had used Scarboro as the only reference community, flouting recommendations by the EPA and other experts who contended that prevailing wind patterns and historical sampling suggested that other communities might have been as or more affected. Sampling methods were also criticized as insufficient.

In the community concerns section of the final assessment, many Scarboro residents expressed continuing fear and mistrust:

"We know the soil is contaminated and want someone to prove it. (Just tell us the truth.)"

"DOE MUST remember that many people don't attend these meetings because of fear of retaliation on their jobs."

"There must be something wrong if the government does so many studies, and the newspaper gives it so much attention."

"What experiments were run on us?"

"What secrets are still being kept?"

"We would like for those interested in helping our neighborhood with health and contamination issues to be mindful of the psychological, sociological and economic consequences that can result whether contamination issues are real or imaginary," Al Chambles and his coauthors had written in 1998.

The ATSDR's process and the controversies surrounding it were meticulously documented by a woman named Susan Kaplan for the nonprofit she founded, the Institute for Technology, Social, and Policy Awareness. According to her, the ATSDR's decision to proceed with their assessments without conducting sampling outside of Scarboro was one of the factors that contributed to community distrust of the agency's findings.

Less than a year after Susan completed her report, she died of terminal cancer that Janet told me Susan attributed to her time working at ORNL. "The intent of this report," she'd written, "is to ensure we do not forget what has transpired in this community."

Weeks and months and years later, I would pore again over the latest environmental reports. I would squint at the numbers. I would speak to EPA, DOE, and TDEC representatives.

Jon Richards, a project manager of the EPA Superfund cleanup of Y-12 and ORNL, told me, "I would not have any problem living in and around Oak Ridge in the last thirty years." Before that, maybe. He assured me that the city's water is safe.

David Adler, a division director for the DOE's Oak Ridge Environmental Management program, I learned, is the stepson of one of my grandfather's close friends, who built the house two doors down from our lake house. He answered my questions with the smooth confidence of someone practiced in interfacing with the public, speaking in the language of grants and accomplishments, emphasizing the department's commitment to safety and the integrity of monitoring and cleanup.

The biggest challenge, he told me, is maintaining the momentum and funding to see the massively expensive project through to its completion, decades from now.

He said he understands where public mistrust comes from but hopes people will reach out with their concerns and give the DOE a chance to earn their confidence. He pointed to the EPA, TDEC, and the ATSDR as sources of independent verification.

The TDEC reports are full of statements that seem ominous to me—findings of elevated levels of uranium and other radionuclides in local waterways, leaks from burial grounds, warnings that Oak Ridge contamination has the potential to reach the drinking water of hundreds of thousands of people downstream. Sometimes programs are discontinued or even abandoned midway through due to funding cuts—beetles and birds' eggs, moths and salamanders collected and weighed and packed into glass jars, frozen and shipped overnight, but never tested. Efforts are plagued by mundane problems such as broken equipment and scheduling conflicts.

When I asked Colby Morgan, the environmental program director for TDEC's Oak Ridge Superfund oversight operations, about canceled programs, he explained that gaps are filled by the DOE's own efforts and promised that if the agency sees the need for monitoring not funded through the DOE, the state will find the money elsewhere. He assured me that his office is "not beholden in any way to the Department of Energy." At the same time, he was careful to clarify that the relationship between the agencies is not adversarial.

I spun like a top. Sometimes I was reassured. Sometimes the confident words of these officials sounded like PR. Sometimes the people provided to answer my questions did not appear to have read the reports I was asking about. Sometimes I was promised responses to detailed questions but my follow-up emails went unanswered. Sometimes I read all of this generously—these officials must project confidence in order to secure funding and continue the work, to navigate the delicate politics. Of course no one can know everything about everything. These offices are overburdened. Sometimes I felt suspicious or at least worried that no one seemed to have the whole picture. But these are, for better or worse, the people closest to the data. Their work is essential and must continue.

When I asked these officials whether it was safe to live in or near Oak Ridge, to drink the water, to fish and swim locally, they told me they lived in the area, drank the water, fished, and swam. They are willing to risk their own bodies, then.

Despite his low opinion of the ATSDR's work on the Oak Ridge health assessments, Owen does agree with the agency's final conclusion that current exposures do not pose a public health risk; that assessment aligns with his own knowledge of and experience with environmental evaluations conducted by ORNL in the 1980s and '90s and with his deep familiarity with the TDH studies, which examined data up to the early 1990s. But without personal experience and technical expertise to rely on and with very good reasons to distrust the agency responsible for the pollution, the monitoring, and the cleanup, where does a person turn?

"The shroud of secrecy associated with Y-12 operations," Owen reflected, "feeds public distrust and speculations that lead to a personal belief about relationships between contamination and disease." Later, when I asked him about the harm caused by damaged public trust, he said, "Integrity of information is everything. If you can't trust the information, how can you function as a democracy?"

In that light, the ATSDR studies were a missed opportunity to establish public trust through transparency and accountability, to live up to the city's idealized image of itself as an enlightened community of superior science, and to do right by the people who loved this place, who loved their work. The assessments could have begun to unravel the insidious secrecy and denial that has been woven into the fabric of Oak Ridge since its inception.

Sociologists Sherry Cable, Thomas Shriver, and Tamara Mix argue that Oak Ridge is a microcosm of the "risk society" that has developed since World War II, a society that is "organized around the environmental hazards created by modern agricultural and industrial production technologies." In such a society, the public is exposed to toxic threats without complete information or consent. When people do raise claims of illnesses caused by hazardous exposures, corporate and government actors, protecting the means of wealth and power, deny such claims through gaslighting, withholding information, and other means. A risk society, they argue, is incompatible with democracy as "ever larger segments of the population become ill, and authorities escalate social control tactics to deny illnesses." In this context, more dangerous than the contamination itself is a culture of secrecy and suppression that protects the interests of the powerful above the public.

The antidote, the sociologists write, is the open exchange of technological information, informed public debates about risk, and public control of technology. Think of what could have been, Janet imagined, with all of this scientific expertise, an army of people ready to take care of each other and the home they loved with the best of what science could offer. "They could have built a world-class environmental health clinic," Janet breathed, voice rising. "A big medical center. A new industry. Instead of it being a friggin' ghost town."

At night, the shift between the city and outside is sudden and startling. One moment there are streetlights and strip malls, and then just past the West Gates, the empty white guardhouses that once controlled access to the K-25 plant, the road is dark, long, and lonely, lined on either side by a gray smudge of trees.

As I left town one night, my headlights flashed against the reflectors on the roadside barrier and the tape in the lane divider, structuring my path with a bright rhythm through the otherwise unnerving stretch of nothing. I turned on the radio, flipped through the channels: top 40s, a local live bluegrass broadcast, several country music stations. Then there was the musical drawl of a radio pastor, and I paused. "Philosophy tells me I can tell you more and more about less and less, but I can't *save* you," he said. "Well, I'm here to tell you there's someone who *can* save you." I turned the radio off, and it was just the sound of my tires on the asphalt, the rush of air past my windows.

Finally, there is no knowing, no certainty in a place with such widespread and complex contamination as Oak Ridge, in a place that has been steeped for years in an oppressive culture of secrecy. It comes down to a kind of faith—in the body, in the numbers, in the institutions meant to protect us.

I don't think the world can be reduced to numbers. In the cracks between the numbers are real lives, real bodies. There are the maybes and fears and what-ifs. There are hazards we did not consent to face.

I believe this land, these people, were hurt. I believe it matters that the fish and the spiders still carry elevated concentrations of mercury that can be magnified through the food chain when eaten by birds and bats, that radioactive materials still trickle into the streams and rivers that flow downstream.

The Superfund-mandated cleanup of Oak Ridge is due to be complete by 2047.

"What," I asked David Adler from the DOE, "does it mean to be complete?"

"That's a good question." He laughed and explained that it meant honoring "all regulatory commitments" to the state, to the EPA.

But yes, he conceded, contaminated groundwater and waste burial grounds will require monitoring indefinitely.

"Toxic disasters," writes sociologist Kai Erikson, "violate all the rules of plot. . . . They never end. Invisible contaminants remain a part of the surroundings, absorbed into the grain of the landscape, the tissues of the body, and, worst of all, the genetic material of the survivors. An all clear is never sounded. The book of accounts is never closed."

One evening, in a closet beneath boxes of arts supplies left by my cousin Wendy and her kids, I found a box of home videos. I popped one in from June 1992 and curled up on the couch. The mice were running their relay races through the air ducts, but they didn't bother me anymore.

Aunt Nellie's sunbathing in a red visor with Samantha, her firstborn, just a year old but already in possession of a prolific head of curls, playing with a bucket beside her. Out in the water, my father struggles with the windsurf board. For a few moments, he's standing, sticking his butt out to counterbalance the sail, all angles and awkwardness. Then the sail billows wider, leans toward the water, and he tips forward, splashes down. The dockside audience claps as he slides his belly back onto the board.

Ignoring everyone, bundled in a life jacket and wedged into an inner tube, I'm drifting around the shallows in dreamy circles. Then, struck with some urge, I begin to chart a course out to sea, passing Uncle Paul stretched out on a blue rubber raft, beer in hand, passing the end of the dock, churning up a frothy wake with my determined kicking. The water is opaque, and I have no idea how deep it is or what might be down there, but despite my father's stories about "the Watts Bar shark," I am not afraid. I fix my eyes on the wooded hills on the opposite shore and charge on.

"Do you want me to tow you back in, Emily?" comes my cousin Laurie's voice from the steps where she's just waded in, the tip of her ponytail darkening in the water.

I do not need anybody to tow me in. I am a strong fish of a swimmer, and this lake is mine. Still, I take the adult hint and curve my trajectory back toward the closer shore. I am four years old.

In another clip, my uncle Kurt stands shoulder-high in the water, an arm around me and his daughter Julia. We're just the blocks of color of our oversized life jackets topped by fuzzy mops of sun-lightened curls.

"We're two mermaids," announces Julia. "We have tails."

"We don't have feet," I concur.

"You want me to be the sea witch?" offers Kurt, breaking into Ursula's song, wildly off-tune like an operatic dying slug. We shriek in indignation.

"No," Julia tells Kurt. "I can be Ariel, and she can be Ariel."

"And you can be Flounder," I offer generously.

"Flounder? How about I be Sebastian? I'd like to be able to sing like Sebastian." And he revs up again, swinging us through the water as we squeal with delight.

My chest went gauzy, and I curled tight around the tender place. How happy we were, how bright and confident, little mermaids in the water. And my parents, my aunts and uncles, how much the same. A little younger, hair and glasses a little bigger, waistlines higher, but their voices so much their own that when my mother, with a tight edge of worry in her voice, calls to me to stand further from the edge of the dock, the hair on the back of my scalp rises. "Emily. Emily. Step back from the edge. Emily." She doesn't raise her voice, but the tone cuts through the chatter like some sort of primal, preverbal dog whistle, straight from mother's mouth to child's ears. I had to turn to make sure she was not in the room with me.

How much it all changed, and how much it stayed the same. I could recognize this bit of earth from just an angled edge of dock over murky green water, just the blurred shape of the forested shore opposite. But this liquid sun-soaked moment, it was gone forever. Cradled in the sameness, the absences pulsed. Meemaw with her throaty, matter-of-fact cheekiness. Doug, our little white Jack Russell terrier, bouncing like a tiny rabbit behind my wobbly toddler brother.

More than anything though, I ached for that younger me, the one who trusted the water and my own body in it. I climbed the stairs to bed, my chest hollow and fragile as a bubble. I did not look at the portrait of George as I passed under it.

After I'd been alone in the house for a week or so, my mother joined me. She and my father were building a house on George's farm up the road from the lake house, and she needed to meet with the contractor to go over the final touches. A few days later, Karin and Paul drove up from Florida. They were meeting with an architect to discuss remodeling the lake house; the family was quickly out-growing this place. I was relieved to no longer be alone, and yet, I wasn't sure how to talk about what I'd been learning.

One night around the dinner table, we discussed the cleanup of the Kingston Fossil Plant ash spill. In June 2015, six years after the midwinter night when the waste containment pond ruptured, releasing more than a billion gallons of toxic coal fly ash onto the lake and surrounding shore, after enough ash had been dredged from the water to fill the Empire State Building two and a half times, the EPA declared cleanup complete. Yet half a million cubic yards of toxic fly ash remained in the lake; it was feared that too-aggressive dredging would stir up the mercury and radioactive cesium long since settled in the sediment on the lake floor.

I worked myself into a state. "Explain it to me again," I asked Paul. "Tell me why we're not worried about all that stuff still in the bottom of the lake?"

He said what he always says, what the reports all say. The mercury and cesium are insoluble, buried beneath clean sediment, harmless as long as they stay put.

"What about groundwater?" I said. "Nobody really knows where it's going. What about the fact that methylmercury is increasing in fish populations downstream of Y-12 despite success-ful remediation? Why aren't we worried about what might happen in the future?"

He was quiet a long time, unusual for him. "Because we're too stupid to know any better," he finally said.

Paul and Karin had reclaimed the comfortable bed in George and Doris's old room, and I'd been punted back to the cubbyhole, where I began. Paul was fighting off a sinus infection turned bron-chitis, and his coughs, reverberating through the thin door of their bedroom, kept me awake at night.

A few weeks after we all departed, Paul told me that he had begun to wonder if his severe and frequent pulmonary infections might be related to years of chemical exposures from his time at Y-12. "It's finally caught up to me," he said.

# 16

# HIROSHIMA

It was July 2015, and I was on the train from Tokyo to Hiroshima. In a few weeks, the city would mark the seventieth anniversary of the bombing, and I would be there. For years, I had known that I would need to go to Hiroshima. I had written grants outlining my plan and purpose. I had made lists, contacted an interpreter, planned interviews. But now, I struggled to think of the word to describe what I was doing here.

I was on the Nozomi Super Express. The sleek, white bullet train made the nearly five-hundred-mile journey in less than four hours; out the window, the scenery moved so quickly it was dizzying, a blur of bright-green rice fields and nondescript cities, blocky, modern, gray, broken here and there by the tiled roof of a temple or traditional house.

I liked the word *pilgrimage* in the sense of putting one's body in respectful reverence toward a place, but I was uneasy with the expectation of a blessing at the end. Perhaps *atonement*? One who went to atone gave rather than received. Yet *atonement* implied that amends could be made and balance restored—a presumption that felt absurd in this case. *Witnessing* seemed obvious but not adequate, suggesting that to see and record were sufficient responses. I wanted some word that lay at the intersection of these three.

I'd brought a photograph of George with me, but I didn't need to take it out to see the bald head, the watery smile, the too-small glasses. Instead, I looked out the window and saw my own translucent reflection floating above the rushing scenery.

Evening was falling by the time we pulled into Hiroshima. On the streetcar to my hotel, I caught my first glimpse of the A-Bomb Dome, the now-iconic skeletal ruins of the one-time Hiroshima Prefectural Industrial Promotion Hall, the only brick structure that remained standing so close to ground zero. The bare scaffolding of the dome drew dark lines against the liquid blue of dusk. I realized with a shiver that we were traveling over the rebuilt T-shaped Aioi Bridge, the distinctive landmark sighted as a target from 31,600 feet above by the crew of the *Enola Gay*.

I was familiar with the geography of the city from above, as the plane saw it. The Ota River fans out to the sea like an outstretched hand, dividing the city into long fingers of land. An aerial photograph of Hiroshima before the bombing shows a landscape textured by whites, grays, and blacks. In the same view after the bombing, the white lines of the streets are softened and blurred, the blocks smoothed to monochrome squares, nearly all distinction but the dark ribbons of rivers wiped away, as if the whole city were drawn in chalk.

Most of the maps I'd studied overlaid the city with concentric circles measuring the distance from the explosion, called the hypocenter. Working inward from the outermost ring, each circle represented an increasingly severe level of destruction. On the ground, this geography of devastation was tracked by historical plaques marking the structures that survived the bombing. A temple 1.75 kilometers from the hypocenter sustained severe roof damage but was structurally sound enough to serve as a relief station. The wooden buildings of the Fukuro-machi elementary school, 460 meters from the hypocenter, all collapsed and burned, but the outer shell of one reinforced concrete building survived. The Bank of Japan, an imposing neoclassical building designed to withstand earthquakes, remained standing just 380 meters from the hypocenter while everything around it lay in blackened ruins.

The Hiroshima Peace Memorial Park is a wedge of land anchored at its northern point by the Aioi Bridge and the A-Bomb Dome and cradled between two tidal distributaries of the Ota River. As I walked from my guesthouse that first morning, I counted the rivers I had to cross—one, two—and I counted down through the rings of destruction. It was so hot and humid that my clothes hung limp by the time I arrived at the park. Of course I always knew that the bomb was dropped in August, but I had never thought about what that meant—how the fires that raged through the city all day and all night fanned the heat of a season that was already blistering. No wonder so many died crying for water. These rivers were choked with bodies.

But today was bright, the park lush and green and thrumming with cicadas like I'd never heard, and such suffering felt remote.

I began at the cenotaph, a stone tomb containing volumes inscribed with nearly three hundred thousand names of deceased A-bomb victims, those who died on August 6, 1945, and those who had died since; one volume was dedicated to all whose names remained unknown. The cenotaph rested in the shadow of a saddle-shaped arch that framed the Flame of Peace and the A-Bomb Dome behind. I tried to take on a prayerful silence while other visitors took turns posing in front of the arch. Their gesture struck me as strange, but I didn't know how to be in this place, either.

To the north was the Memorial Mound, a grassy hill covering unclaimed ashes of the dead; beside flowers wilting in the heat rested bottles of water left in offering, labels faded from the sun.

What does it mean to walk through a landscape that has seen such death? I had imagined some ritual of catharsis. I had imagined falling to my knees, crying. I had imagined that once I was here, I would know what to do. But there were clusters of uniformed schoolgirls racing around to each monument, taking turns reading explanations aloud in bright, distant voices, and there were people posing for photographs, and I didn't know what I was doing here. I didn't know what any of us were doing here.

This park, this city—they were supposed to be about peace. And maybe it was the heat or the jet lag or the sinus infection I had developed from the travel, but I couldn't seem to figure out what that meant, exactly. There was the Peace Fountain and the Peace Pond and the Children's Peace Monument, and I began to feel the way I do if I say a word over and over and over again until it becomes unstuck from its meaning, a strange sound lost to the cicadas' buzzing.

I was drawn north through tree-shaded pathways by a long, low tolling. A boy and girl, in a blue baseball cap and straw sun hat, were laughing as they ran up and down the steps to the Peace Bell, tugging the rope that swung the heavy metal clapper to make it ring again and again.

Two people whom I guessed were their grandparents watched in amusement from the stairs, while, partially hidden through the trees, a film crew recorded the scene. As the family began to leave, the cameraman approached and spoke to the grandfather. Receiving permission, he arranged the children side by side, each with a hand on the rope. On the cameraman's signal, they swung the clapper then put their palms together in prayer and bowed their heads, standing still as the deep reverberation lingered.

In the lotus pond around the bell, the frogs croaked irreverently.

When a survivor, Kasaoka Sadae, told me of that day, she closed her eyes and clawed the air with upturned palms. "I was standing in front of the glass window. It flashed red. It was a beautiful color, like the sunrise mingled with orange. With the flash, the glass broke, and shattered in pieces." The force of the blast knocked her to the floor; when she woke, her head was slick with blood.

We sat on cushions around a low table in the common room of my guesthouse, sipping green tea. Out of a folder full of maps and photographs, Sadae pulled a simple silhouette of a man cut from black construction paper, pasted on a white background. This, she told me, was what her father looked like when he stumbled home from the city center that day. When she touched his skin, it peeled.

Lifting a strip of the black, she revealed bright red beneath. The hospitals, overwhelmed, turned him away, deeming him a hopeless case. With no medicine, Sadae tried to cool his burns with grated cucumbers and potatoes. The festering wounds attracted flies, and soon he was crawling with maggots. He died two days later.

After days of searching the city for their mother, her brother returned with a paper packet containing hair and ash. She had died at a temporary first aid station where bodies had been cremated in piles, and it was impossible to separate the remains of one person from another.

Sadae didn't speak of her experience for more than half a century, until renovations at her grandchildren's elementary school uncovered human bones that had been buried just as long. The children wanted to know what had happened there, and so survivors were called. The memories came back then, burning and insistent. She wept as she broke her silence. An image of her father's ghost appeared before her as she spoke.

Silence among survivors is common. As they age, more are moved to speak before it is too late. Still, most survivors, *hibakusha*, do not speak and never will. My interpreter, Sawada Miwako, by her own reckoning, had translated thousands of survivor testimonies. The one story she had not heard was that of her ninety-four-year-old mother, who lost her entire family to the bombing; she still could not bear to tell the story of that day, not even to her daughter.

We know more of the terrors of the bombing than the suffering of the survivors. In the postwar years, hibakusha, literally "bomb-affected people," were used as research subjects by American doctors and scientists who offered no treatment in exchange for invasive examinations. A-bomb orphans and others left destitute without health or family made homes in crowded, makeshift neighborhoods in the heart of the destroyed city, starved or stole or fell prey to gangs. Many hibakusha were shunned by employers and potential marriage partners, who feared crippling health problems and genetically damaged children. Some moved away, where their pasts were not known. Some still hide from the shame.

But it would be easy not to know that, easy to assume that the story of the bombing is well and thoroughly told. At the Peace Park and museum, I could listen to seemingly endless video testimonies that followed the same ritualized pattern; survivors began by stating their distance from the hypocenter on the morning of August 6 and ended with a plea for world peace. The English subtitles lingered on the screen for what felt like minutes sometimes—they seemed to be summaries rather than direct translations.

So I watched the hibakusha's bodies, listened to the rise and fall of their voices. A woman with short black hair closed her eyes and scrunched her face as her voice got high. The tendons in her neck strained. A man, when asked if his family survived, clasped and unclasped his hands in his lap. The footage was scored with cheesy eighties synth music, the testimonies sandwiched between images of doves in flight, the sunny Peace Park, the eternal flame flickering against a blue sky.

Lisa Yoneyama, a scholar of the politics of memory in postwar Japan, writes that many hibakusha who tell their stories publicly become painfully aware of the inadequacy of language to convey their most traumatic experiences. Confronted by the great gulf between their truths and their audience's understanding, they experience "a sense of hollowness and pointlessness," expressed by the Japanese word *munashisa*. Some become discouraged from speaking. Those who continue may have to become resigned to this gap between meaning and understanding. "By casting themselves in narrative performances before haphazard and skeptical audiences, storytellers make the communicative performance itself a higher priority than the authenticity of original meanings," writes Yoneyama.

Hibakusha who give formal, public testimony are often called *kataribe*, meaning "storytellers." In preliterate Japan, kataribe were performers who recited memorized myths and legends. It's a designation some hibakusha reject as reductive, but today, the tradition of the Hiroshima kataribe is well-established.

The systems in place to facilitate such exchanges made it easy for someone like me—without local connections or Japanese language—to meet survivors. My guesthouse was run by peace activists who considered the dissemination of hibakusha testimony central to their mission. When I arrived, the helpful custodians asked, "How many hibakusha do you need?"

In the basement of the Peace Museum, my interpreter helped me reserve hibakusha. I could request my preferred attributes as if ordering from a menu: male or female, A-bomb orphan or in utero survivor, transit worker, schoolchild, mother and daughter pair. I asked for those who had only recently begun telling their stories; I wanted to understand how silence functioned here.

I'd pay the equivalent of $50 for each one, Miwako told me, which would cover their transportation and their time. Someone else would explain that the money was considered a gift in exchange for their stories. I was happy to pay, but when Miwako used the word *reserve*, I was reminded of how, weeks before my trip, I ordered a rental cell phone and portable Wi-Fi connection to be delivered to my hotel in Tokyo. It was all too convenient. I felt numb and vaguely sick.

I had thought a lot about how I would introduce myself to the survivors, what I would tell them about George. I wondered whether they would see me as an enemy. I wondered if they would become angry or quiet. Maybe, I thought, they would not want to talk to me at all.

When I told Sadae George's story, I began, "He grew up on a farm." I told her about the secrecy of Oak Ridge—how many of the workers had no idea what they were building until they heard news of the bombing over the radio on August 6, 1945. I told her that decades later, George struggled with deep depression.

I asked her what she would say to my grandfather if he were alive and she could meet him. And I wanted to bite back the question as soon as it left my mouth.

"He didn't have the whole story. And he just did what he was told to do," she said. "He had some deep injury in his mind. It was not him, but war." She compared him to her father, who, she said, knew Japan would be defeated but would not speak for fear he would be imprisoned.

Her answer was kind, but I was hot with shame. I thought I could not have asked anything worse. How could I meet a hibakusha and make the conversation about my grandfather's pain? The question invited, expected, forgiveness. And I had framed the story to collapse the distance between victim and perpetrator.

I imagined George's hands big-knuckled, like my father's and mine, but thicker and rough from work outdoors, burned, perhaps, from chemical exposures. I had traced those hands to this place, to a hot summer morning seventy years ago, to flash, burn, melt. To what made other hands drip skin like wax.

Months earlier, when I was arranging my trip, I spoke to an American man who had been deeply involved with the Hiroshima peace movement for years; he lived part-time in Hiroshima and was well-connected among hibakusha and their advocates. He helped me find an interpreter and advised me where to stay. He asked me how I wanted to be received in Hiroshima.

"I could make you a minor local celebrity," he offered, "with your grandfather's background." He told me how, when President Truman's grandson Clifton Truman Daniel went to Hiroshima a few years earlier to attend the commemoration ceremony and hear hibakusha testimony, the media staked out his hotel like he was some kind of rock star.

I briefly considered what kind of access such status might afford me but dismissed the idea. No, no, I assured him. I'd rather be anonymous.

Still, as I walked through the Peace Park and attended commemoration events, I noticed men with press badges and large cameras taking my picture as I lit a candle or stood in front of a flower-heaped memorial. Servers in cafes around town and patrons sitting at neighboring tables told me, unprompted, how good it was that I had come to Hiroshima, how good *I* was for coming. I could not move without being reminded that my white American body here, even without the context of George's story, meant something beyond what I intended. Once or twice, I gave brief interviews to eager newscasters or documentarians who sidled up to me. When they asked why I'd come to Hiroshima, I told them about George and then wished I hadn't. I feared they were making something of this story that was too easy, too simple.

Clifton Truman Daniel first visited Hiroshima for the commemoration ceremony in August 2012. When asked, he said he'd come not to apologize but "in the name of reconciliation."

At interviews and commemorative events around town, people kept telling me I'd just missed Ari Beser, the grandson of the only man to fly in both the Hiroshima and Nagasaki missions. When we finally met, I learned that he was interviewing hibakusha for a Fulbright-National Geographic Storytelling Fellowship and that the name of his project, and also the name of his self-published book, was *Nuclear Family*—which was what I had been calling my book for several years.

When I met a woman at my guesthouse who told me she was writing a book about her grandfather's work in Hanford, Washington, Oak Ridge's West Coast twin dedicated to the production of plutonium, I just started laughing. "It's not—I'm sorry. It's not that your story is funny," I tried to explain.

How to account for this urge to trace personal, familial guilt to this place? If not to atone, then at least to confront the sins of our grandfathers? What good does it do?

In the States, people's eyes widened when I told them that I was going to Hiroshima because my grandfather worked on the Manhattan Project, but here, almost no one was surprised. The hibakusha had spoken to others like me. I did not ask again what they would say to my grandfather, but my very presence, and the barest outline of George's story, played to an established narrative. They said, *Many of the scientists felt guilty.* And *He didn't know. He was only doing his job.*

Only one, a man named Ota Kaneji who had been telling his story for just four months, seemed caught off guard. When I told him that my grandfather enriched uranium for the bomb, he began to laugh.

"He thinks it is a little bit difficult to talk about his experience because of your grandfather," Miwako explained. "You don't care?" And I took her question to mean—you won't be upset? I assured them that I was here to hear the "whole story," but even as I said it, I wondered what that meant.

"Bomb is," he said, pausing now after every phrase to let her translate, "radiation; flash; heat ray; blast—these were released, at once."

In the Peace Memorial Museum, I stood in front of a child's tin lunch box, the contents burnt black. His mother had identified the body, burned beyond recognition, by his name carved into the metal. The boy's lunch that day was soybeans and barley with stir-fried vegetables, the first harvest from his own garden.

In a plexiglass case, there was a girl's school uniform, trimmed with lace, one sleeve scorched and tattered. It was beige, marked by reddish-brown stains that might have been blood or might have been mud. The thirteen-year-old sewed the uniform herself. She died late on the night of August 6.

One display case contained "nails and skin left by a junior high student."

I had felt numbed and distant by the magnitude of suffering, but now I felt the horror in my stomach. This child. That mother. That one and that one, all as vibrantly human and warmly living as I was now, standing outside of a glass case, looking at what remained.

Alongside my horror, I began to notice something strange. The context of the bombing, the reason these tattered dresses and human remains lay in glass cases like secular relics, was framed entirely in the passive voice, without reference to who dropped the bomb or why. *At 8:15 on the morning of August 6th, 1945, the world's first atomic bomb was dropped on Hiroshima. It is estimated that approximately 350,000 people were directly exposed to the bomb. The atomic bomb was delivered by a total of three B-29 bombers.*

*Moto Mosoro (then 54) was exposed to the bomb at her house*
. . .

*Kazuhiko Sasaki (then 12) was exposed . . .*
*Toshiko Sekoika (then 13) was exposed . . .*

Here, there was no war. No American planes or American flight crews or American generals picking out Japanese targets on maps in war rooms. No Oak Ridge or Los Alamos or Hanford. Just a bomb sprung from the sky like divine wrath, like a lightning bolt, presented, writes Ran Zwigenberg, a scholar of the politics of atrocity commemoration, "like the scene of a natural disaster."

During this seventieth anniversary, galleries detailing a wider historical context were closed for renovation.

I wandered in a daze to a display of melted glass bottles and blackened ceramic roof tiles, blistered in the heat of the blast. "Feel free to touch these items," a plaque invited. And then smaller, in parentheses, "They are safe."

The words were meant to reassure visitors that the melted items contained no residual radiation, yet they also seemed to promise: *This place is safe. It will not change you.* Safe, I thought, for people like me. People who might have been prone to feel guilt over an inherited responsibility. Or people from a different stock, a military heritage, who might have felt attacked, who might have become defensive, the people who said, *The bombing saved my life* or *my grandfather's life.* The people who said, *The bomb is why I am here today.*

Was peace, I wondered, all about soothing our consciences, writing a history in which no one was held responsible?

I watched an older Japanese man stroke one of the bottles, back and forth, his fingers dipping into the collapsed middle and out again. He stood there for several minutes, the lines of his face lit by the dim glow of the display light.

Before I arrived, I had imagined standing beneath the A-Bomb Dome, looking up at a blue sky cut into wedges by the scorched iron bones of the building. A blue sky from which, seventy years ago, a single plane dropped a heavy package, just a dark speck in a cloudless expanse tumbling toward an earth that would never be the same again. I imagined that to look at that sky through the bombed-out dome, I would understand something.

But when I made it to that northern point of the park, I saw that the building had been fenced in so that I could look at it only from a distance. The windows were all glassless, the walls half-collapsed and jagged on top. But I could see places where cracks had been filled in by fresh concrete and sturdy new scaffolding suspended further decay while maintaining the state of partial ruin.

This history, the way it is told in Hiroshima, begins and ends on August 6. As I stood in front of the A-Bomb Dome, I was reminded of a short historical film I saw in the Bradbury Science Museum in Los Alamos in a theater that smelled distinctly of Subway sandwiches. Most of it was as one would expect: black-and-white footage of Nazis marching in lockstep to ominous orchestral music; the introduction of the main scientific players—Einstein, Teller, Fermi, Szilard, Oppenheimer—and then a story in broad strokes, similar to the Oak Ridge story. There were men and women called by their nation to move to a remote corner of the country and work under a shroud of secrecy; a bustling camaraderie, patriotism, sacrifice, victory.

The cheery swing music gave way to eerie repeated minor chords as the narrative built to the Trinity Test, scientists disappearing into the New Mexican desert to witness the first reckoning of their work. Over the rolling thunder of the explosion, the narrator's voice came in—"Thoughts and feelings as powerful as the explosion rushed through the exhausted witnesses." A seething gray cloud consumed the screen for a few moments before Oppenheimer's voice delivered his famous lines, quoted from the *Bhagavad-Gita*: "Now I am become Death, the destroyer of worlds." The narrator remained silent as the screen showed a circle of bombed desert, a plane taking off, a bomb falling, a white mushroom cloud rising from an indeterminate land mass.

Then—victory parade music, people cheering in the street, and a soldier swinging a woman down for a kiss. A total of seven wordless seconds were given to the actual consequence of the work of Los Alamos. The words *Hiroshima*, *Nagasaki*, and *Japan* were never uttered. A person who did not know the history could see the film and believe that the war ended because the Trinity Test was successful.

In Los Alamos and in Oak Ridge, the story of the bomb is told without Hiroshima, and here, the story is told without the war. There is no conjunction between these histories. No cause. No guilt. No blame.

In postwar occupied Japan, American officials censored information related to the atomic bombings and particularly to the disturbing, ongoing effects of radiation, under the vague justification that such material might "disturb public tranquility." In the name of tranquility, what is left in the gap between these stories?

George is in the gap. If he felt guilt about Hiroshima, it was buried deep and never spoken. And the hibakusha who do not speak? We cannot know what they hold in their silence. "We cannot study silence," one Hiroshima scholar reminded me. "We deal with those who speak."

Granddaughter of a man who helped build the bomb, I stood before a building destroyed by that bomb, and my body insisted on a conjunction. Let my tranquility be disturbed.

From a distance, colorful strands of paper cranes, bundled by the thousand, looked like racks of kimonos. They were everywhere—lining the railing around a statue of a mother carrying a dead child at the edge of the Peace Park, draping the neck of the stone turtle of the Korean victims memorial—but by far the most were around the Children's Peace Monument, where a bronze statue of a girl, Sasaki Sadako, stood atop a tall, rounded pedestal, holding a large gold crane above her head.

Sadako was two at the time of the bombing, but she grew up a healthy and bright child. In 1954, the fall of her sixth-grade year, she came down with what appeared to be a mild cold. Within months, lumps on her neck had swollen large, and in February, she was diagnosed with leukemia, given at most a year to live.

An ancient Japanese legend had it that the person who folded one thousand paper cranes would be granted her dearest wish. Sadako creased squares of colored paper between thin fingers; when she ran out of paper, she used cellophane wrapping paper, candy wrappers, medicine labels. She folded one thousand cranes and kept on going. Sadako died in October 1955. Her family distributed paper cranes at her funeral. In the wake of her death, her classmates organized a fundraising campaign that led, eventually, to the building of the monument dedicated to the child victims of the bombing.

I learned to fold paper cranes at my Quaker elementary school. I remember clear plastic bags in the hallway outside the art room filled with the rainbow flocks. I suppose the bags were sent to Hiroshima—since Sadako's death, paper cranes have become an international symbol of peace. Her memorial is cradled by a semicircle of plexiglass shelters whose sides bulge with some of the ten million cranes sent from around the world each year.

Sometimes the hibakusha gave me paper cranes after our interviews. We bowed to each other and touched hands, and they said, *Thank you for coming to Hiroshima.* And I thought I deserved none of it.

I kept the picture of George tucked into an envelope at the back of my journal. I had thought I would show it to my interviewees, but once I arrived, I could not bring myself to take it out. I did not want to ask them to see his humanity. Let them be angry, if they would.

I sought the places where the narrative broke down. But these were difficult to find. The Japanese government has an interest in maintaining an alliance with the United States, while the United States has an interest in maintaining a narrative of moral righteousness. Robert Jacobs, an American professor at Hiroshima City University who studies the social and cultural effects of radiation on communities, explained to me how official channels and international politics constrain the types of stories that will be heard by outsiders. "If you were a hibakusha in this town, and you were giving testimony, and you talked about how angry you were against the United States for killing your family, you wouldn't be asked to give testimony . . . So there comes to be an accepted narrative." A narrative of forgiveness.

"Places like this are set up for people to come here and consume it as peace culture," he said.

When I went to the bank to change money, the banker invited me to pick out a crane from a box—I chose a black one with small white and violet flowers. At Starbucks, there was a neat stack of origami paper on the counter—I folded a crane while I waited for my order. Even at the baseball game—the Hiroshima Carp versus the Hanshin Tigers at the Mazda Zoom-Zoom Stadium—there were tables for folding paper cranes. These were all red, and they'd be sent to Obama along with letters urging him to visit Hiroshima.

"The world should come to Hiroshima," I heard over and over again, from the hibakusha, from peace activists, from the mayor of the city at a nuclear abolition symposium. The city espoused the belief that to stand in this place, to see the city that was destroyed, to hear the stories of hibakusha, to touch the melted roof tiles, was to know and to be transformed. "As though," said Robert Jacobs, "the reason we have nuclear weapons is because people don't know that they have a horrific impact."

The world had come to Hiroshima for this seventieth anniversary. As August 6 approached, the park filled. White tents with swooping roofs cast wave-like shadows on the grass. Massive groups of peace activists in matching T-shirts waited in sweaty clumps to enter the museum. The World Scout Jamboree, a gathering of scouting groups from around the globe, was meeting this year a couple of hours from Hiroshima; every day, thousands of scouts in collared uniforms and neckerchiefs color-coded by country flooded the park. They gripped perspiring water bottles as they loped the paths between the monuments, joking loudly. One day, I watched a Lithuanian choir in thick plaid skirts and corseted tops promenade silently around the park.

Across the city, there were special art shows, film screenings, plays, and concerts to commemorate the bombing. For this anniversary, all the English-speaking hibakusha had been booked for public testimony.

But what did one see in Hiroshima today? Wide streets and covered shopping arcades and multistory high-end department stores. On a Sunday, I wandered through a public park and into a girls' kickball game. Families sipped from bottles of chilled green tea and cans of vending machine coffee while they cheered from the bleachers. The girls looked intent in oversized uniforms. I wondered how many of them were grandchildren of hibakusha.

Certainly Hiroshima has something to teach us about human resilience. "I am happy now," Kasaoka Sadae told me as I was packing up to leave. With four healthy grandchildren in their twenties, she stopped worrying so much about how her radiation exposure would affect her descendants.

A hibakusha named Nishida Goro seemed to be one of the most genuinely joyful people I had ever met. When we discovered we shared a birthday, he threw back his head and laughed. He'd been to the US several times, both as a tourist and on business. In the Smithsonian, he saw a model of the Hiroshima bomb, the bomb named by its makers "Little Boy."

Just shy of four years old on the morning of August 6, 1945, Goro was playing in the mud with two friends when a bright flash lit up the sky. He ran to take cover in his house just before the roof caved in. He escaped to the river with a woman from his neighborhood.

In the nights after, he watched people carry the dead on corrugated metal sheets to be cremated in parks, schoolyards, by the river. He was frightened to see the open spaces fill with the fires of burning bodies. The Japanese worked in silence, but to this day, Goro remembered the laments of the Koreans from the opposite bank of the river. "Aigoo! Aigoo," a cry of deep sorrow.

Goro survived with minor burns and scrapes, but one of his playmates passed away that night from severe burns. The other was burned badly on his back but survived—now the two were golfing buddies.

I asked Goro what it was like to see the model of the "Little Boy" bomb.

No special feeling, he told me. He'd seen pictures. It was smaller than he'd expected. I believed him when he said he bore no anger toward Americans. "What is bad is war. Not American people, not American government, but war itself."

The Japanese novelist Oe Kenzaburo, in his essays on Hiroshima, speculates that the bomb droppers counted on the resilience of the people of Hiroshima both to lessen their own burden of guilt and to save humanity from a hell "so completely beyond the possibility of human recovery that all mankind will despise their humanity merely at the thought of it."

Humanity needed the hibakusha's grace and resilience, argues Oe, in order to survive the darkest possibilities of human cruelty that the atomic bombings made manifest. In surviving, in recovering, in simply living day to day without succumbing to despair, writes Oe, the hibakusha "were concerned to salvage their own lives, but in the process they also salvaged the souls of the people who had brought the atomic bomb" and ultimately, "the souls of all human beings alive today."

When I read Oe, I realized what I had been ashamed to admit to myself—that part of me wanted to see how Hiroshima had recovered because I wanted to know that the destruction George helped bring about was not total, not final. I wanted to lessen my own guilt. And when Goro grinned and reached his hand for mine across the table, my heart felt lighter. I wanted the hibakusha's forgiveness, even though I believed I had no right to it.

When the parents of the girl he loved forbade their marriage, Kawamoto Shoso fell into despair. Because he was a hibakusha, the girl's parents feared their grandchildren might be born disabled from the genetic imprint of the bombing. Though studies to date have not shown any measurable genetic effects in the children of survivors, the stigma and fear, fed by censorship of information about the effects of radiation, and mistrust of the scientists who studied but did not treat the victims, have overshadowed the lives of many hibakusha.

Shoso was not in Hiroshima on August 6. Like many other children, he'd been evacuated some months before to a temple outside of the city because of the threat of firebombing. Days after the bombing, his older sister came to pick him up, and they returned to the city together. Under Japanese law, those who entered the city shortly after the bombing are considered hibakusha for their exposure to residual radiation and are thus entitled to medical benefits.

Months later, Shoso's sister began to sicken—her hair fell out, bleeding blisters formed on her feet. She died within a week, leaving Shoso, just eleven years old, alone. He was passed among relatives; the orphanages were full. Thousands of A-bomb orphans wound up on the streets, starving and desperate. Some learned cruelty and crime as the only means of survival. They moved like wraiths, stripped the dead of clothing and food, sucked stones and chewed newspaper to stave their hunger, died in the streets of thirst. Many survived only by joining gangs who would house and feed them in exchange for menial work or petty crime.

Shoso was lucky. The owner of a soy sauce company in a village outside of the city offered him room and board in exchange for work. After twelve years, the owner fulfilled his promise to build Shoso a house, and Shoso, ready to start his independent life, asked his love to marry him. Crushed by her parents' rejection, realizing he might never be able to marry, to have a family, he returned to Hiroshima.

He found it overrun by gangs that had moved into the destroyed city during the chaotic years after the bombing. My translator called that time a "dark age" in Hiroshima's history. "We don't talk about it," she said. "Actually, we don't know about it."

He became wild and reckless. He gambled, tried to join a gang. After ten years, angry and hopeless, he thought he might as well kill himself.

Wanting to go where no one knew him, he boarded a train and disembarked in Okayama. Passing a help wanted sign at a noodle shop, he decided he might as well start over. He got the job and poured himself into work.

For nearly thirty years, Shoso told no one where he was from. He could not forget the place where he had lost his entire family, but he did not speak of it. He worked hard and had no close friends. Eventually, Shoso started his own business packaging lunch boxes. It pleased him to see the customers smile.

Then one day, he received an unexpected phone call from an old classmate. The fiftieth anniversary of the bombing was approaching, and their school was organizing a memorial. The classmate had tracked him down through decades of silence to invite him to return.

When I met Shoso in an empty conference room in the basement of the Peace Museum, he'd been telling his story for twenty years. He wore a slight smile the entire time he spoke.

He was passionate about telling the story of the A-bomb orphans, though many of his former classmates urged him not to speak of those years. They did not want their children to know how they had to survive. "We are alive today," he said, "because we hurt someone else that day." These stories threatened their carefully guarded happiness. But Shoso thought of his friends who died on the streets. He wanted them to be remembered.

He wanted people to know about the children who were not exposed to the atomic bomb but were killed by it, nevertheless. "That is real war, a fact of war." But he understood his classmates' fears; he wouldn't tell this story if he had a family, he admitted.

At the end of the interview, Shoso gave me two paper cranes, folded with shiny gold and silver paper. They were shaped a bit differently from the others, the tails thick, wings angled forward. He showed me how to wiggle the necks and make the wings flap. He grinned. These were the special paper cranes he brought to schoolchildren.

"The more I know the history, the more I hate," Hataguchi Minoru told me of his anger toward my country for dropping the bomb on his. I was stunned by his bluntness, so contrary to the careful narrative I had come to expect here. And I was quietly thrilled.

"I can't forgive that part," he said of the targeting of a civilian population. "They used us as a guinea pig."

At one point, he stopped for a breath to assure me, with a laugh, that he did not hate me. He resisted the personalization of this history. He told me he was glad my grandfather suffered for his work, but he did not seem all that interested. He did not like to tell his personal story either.

We'd been talking for more than two hours despite the fact that Minoru, as the former director of the Peace Museum, was in high demand these few days before the anniversary. In fact, Minoru never wanted to be in demand on such a day, to be director of the museum, to talk about the bomb at all.

To Minoru, the bomb meant growing up without a father; it meant his mother's sadness and his loneliness as a young child when his older sisters left for school and his mother for work, leaving him, just five years old, home alone for breakfast and lunch. When, at age twenty-one, he received the lavender booklet that entitled him to free health care as a hibakusha, he stuffed it into a drawer and refused to use it.

He told no one he was an in utero survivor, exposed to the radiation four days after the bombing when his two months' pregnant mother ventured into the city to seek out her husband who hadn't returned from work on August 6. Instead of her husband, she found his pocket watch and belt buckle, the face of the watch burned off, the metal buckle blackened and corroded. On the fiftieth anniversary of his father's death, Minoru, then a grown man, put these mementos under his family gravestone, hoping to be done with them. He hated to be defined by the atrocity that darkened his life before he was born. He hated to be reminded of it.

He kept his silence. He didn't even tell his wife until some time after they were married. He built a career as a civil servant in the city, carefully avoiding all A-bomb-related business for nearly thirty years until, in 1997, he was appointed director of the Peace

Museum. A position many considered honorable and desirable was the last thing he wanted. Yet as a city employee, he was subject to the will of his superiors, required to perform any job to which he was assigned. He asked the mayor whether he had been chosen because he was a survivor. But the mayor hadn't known. The city hadn't known. After the media storm that followed, everyone knew.

Asked why he had hidden for so long, Minoru said he didn't want sympathy. He hated the way hibakusha were automatically treated as heroes just for having been present in Hiroshima on that day. For a while, he attempted to keep his story in the background, to perform his job without reference to his past. But then, after being told his speeches were stiff and unemotional, Minoru, resigned, began to tell his personal story. When he gave museum tours to foreign dignitaries and politicians, he watched them turn from bored to teary when he revealed his past. A US congressman who'd been insisting on the need for nuclear weapons became apologetic and donated flowers to the Memorial Cenotaph in the park. Fidel Castro gave him a hug. He didn't, however, seem all that interested in hearing what Minoru had to say about the Cuban Missile Crisis. Minoru came to understand the power, and limitations, of his personal story, but he never liked using it. After nine years of service, he retired in 2006. Still, he continued to be called on to speak about the bombing, a duty he performed reluctantly.

Before he left, Minoru gave me a handful of the tiniest paper cranes. He tipped them out of a plastic container into my open palm, and they were so beautiful and perfect—each smaller than my pinkie nail, in white, raspberry, sky blue, tangerine, forest green, and indigo—that the interpreter exclaimed in delight, and he gave her some too.

He asked me whether I'd seen Sasaki Sadako's original cranes in the museum. I told him I had. Spread out on a clear conical pedestal, illuminated from beneath, they looked almost translucent. In another display case were three tiny cranes in decreasing size made from red cellophane. The plaque read: "Sadako continued folding paper cranes even after reaching 1,000. From that time on, the cranes became smaller and smaller. Sometimes she used a needle to fold them."

When Minoru met Sadako's father, he asked why she folded smaller and smaller cranes even as her body weakened. Her father didn't know.

I thought of what else we didn't know about Sadako—like how she would have felt about becoming an international martyr after her death. If she had lived, who would she have become, and what story would she have told about herself?

One afternoon during my second week, as I passed through the Peace Park, I did the calculations and realized that I was one year older than George was seventy years ago on the day the bomb was dropped. And I realized, too, that at twenty-seven, I had spent more time trying to tell this story than George, at twenty-six, had spent building the bomb. And still, sometimes I felt I could say nothing for certain.

The constant, metallic drone of the cicadas blanketed all other sound, cocooning me in my thoughts in this crowded park.

My mother met George just once, in the summer of 1983, six months before he died. As a budding antinuclear activist and founding member of the Chicago chapter of Women's Action for Nuclear Disarmament, she was nervous to meet her boyfriend's father, the retired nuclear weaponeer. But her Chicago friends who'd come along for the ride, fiercely intellectual and unconcerned with gaining George's approval, set him pointed questions in low voices, questions about the morality of nuclear bombs, about disarmament.

George, in red suspenders and a striped shirt stretched over a hefty beer belly, was unperturbed. He told them no country should possess nuclear weapons, that the US should disarm, unilaterally, even, if that's what it took. My mom was astonished—it was an extraordinary statement for someone who had spent his life building nuclear weapons. She thought then that he was the most antinuclear person she'd ever met.

The year after George's death, my mother, at twenty-seven, spent the summer organizing a series of free readings, art shows, and concerts in Chicago to mark the fortieth anniversary of the Hiroshima and Nagasaki bombings. Two and a half years later, she held me to her chest and wept in a state of postpartum despair over the possibility that she had brought a child into a world doomed to nuclear annihilation.

I didn't know what to make of her memory. No one else in the family remembered George ever taking such a radical stance on disarmament, adamantly disavowing the industry on which he built his life.

Of course I'd ached to have the story confirmed, to know that, at the end, he had the courage to see what he had done. I was sure now that I'd never know. And the more time I spent here, the less urgent the question seemed. I listened to the stories of the hibaku-sha. I walked the city, pausing in the heat to purchase a green-tea-flavored soft serve, an iced coffee from a vending machine. In an art museum, I was transfixed by Ishiuchi Miyako's photographs of artifacts and clothing left behind by the victims of the bombings, lit from behind and printed larger than life. Hung high on the bright-white wall, a single leather shoe, a stained blouse, became translucent and alive. A dark, long-sleeved dress shone with a burnt sheen; light burst through a tear on the left side, where a heart would be.

Here, the question of George's individual guilt seemed selfish, myopic, and absurdly beside the point. Yes, I had wanted redemption for George, innocence for myself. I did not want to be burdened by the guilt of this heritage. Yet as I walked through a city that seemed designed to soothe my conscience, I became suspicious of the desire for innocence. I began to think that not only was innocence illusory but that the celebration of it, the pursuit of it, was dangerous.

To prove our innocence, we fill silence with the same worn stories told again and again. In Los Alamos and Oak Ridge, the bomb is glorified while the victims are erased. A fear of acknowledging mistakes, confronting past wrongs, and engaging nuance leads to a culture in which those who criticize are threatened and ostracized. It leads to poisoning the backyard and hiding the evidence.

In Hiroshima, the need to uphold the city as an innocent victim elides certain messier parts of the story—the mistreatment of Korean victims, for instance. In 1945, Hiroshima was home to an estimated fifty thousand Koreans, migrants who'd escaped a homeland ravaged by Japanese occupation or forced laborers conscripted to the war effort by the Japanese army. Living in poor, crowded neighborhoods near the center of the city, working outside, they were especially vulnerable to the bomb's explosion. Between twenty thousand and thirty thousand were killed, some half of the city's total Korean population. Their bodies were neglected in the street, and survivors were denied medical care at overcrowded hospitals as Japanese patients were given preference. In the decades since, Korean hibakusha have struggled to gain the same recognition, compensation, and health care afforded Japanese survivors.

More broadly, removing the bombing from the context of World War II erases both American culpability and the brutalities committed by the Japanese army throughout East Asia and the Pacific. Estimates of the total death toll in the Asia-Pacific War range in the tens of millions; the vast majority were noncombatants, and the vast majority of those were Asian victims of Japan's imperialist aggression. Remembrances of atrocities—such as the Nanjing Massacre, when Japanese soldiers slaughtered hundreds of thousands and raped tens of thousands during the brutal occupation of the Chinese city in the winter of 1937–1938, and the Japanese army's sexual enslavement of hundreds of thousands of women and girls from occupied territories—have been politically charged, fraught with controversy and attempts to sanitize the crimes from official histories.

Lisa Yoneyama argues that the framing of Hiroshima as a universal symbol of peace emptied of specific historical context "has significantly contributed to the forgetting of the history of colonialism and racism in the region" and to "a national victimology and phantasm of innocence throughout most of the postwar years."

Supporters of the atomic bombings point to Japanese wartime brutality—to Japan's non-innocence—as justification for the bombings. Yet, as Yoneyama points out, Western powers were partially responsible for minimizing Japanese war crimes post war; while German war crimes were vehemently and formally condemned, scrutiny of Japanese atrocities was more cursory, due in large part to the fact that the victims of those atrocities were politically powerless and not white and that the winners of the war, colonial powers themselves, overlooked the colonial crimes of the Japanese.

Enshrining Hiroshima as a universal symbol of peace outside of historical specificity served the interests of both American and Japanese leaders who wished not to be held to account. To American military leaders, linking the bomb to global peace upheld the narrative of the bomb's necessity by implying that the bomb had, in ending the war, brought peace; at the same time, it justified the continued production of nuclear weapons under the perverse logic that deterrence preserved peace.

I met Ran Zwigenberg for lunch one day. He was a visiting professor at Hiroshima City University, studying the commemoration of atrocities, war memory, and survivor politics. He said to me, "The emphasis on the personal does a huge disservice to history. You can't argue with suffering." He was talking about the way Hiroshima's story has been framed in tight focus around individual stories of hibakusha, obscuring both the circumstances of war that came before and the mess of the postwar years in which hibakusha suffered in poverty and degrading health, shunned in fear from jobs and marriages, while the city recovered thanks to American military investment during the Korean War. The city of peace was not always so. Perhaps it is not so now; though Japan has so far maintained its vow not to produce nuclear weapons of its own, the country relies on American military investment and the protection of the American nuclear umbrella.

The United States remains invested in a narrative of innocence. In 2010, when John Roos, the US ambassador to Japan, became the first official American delegate to attend Hiroshima's annual commemoration of the bombing, Gene Tibbets, son of the pilot who flew the plane that dropped the Hiroshima bomb, condemned the visit as an implicit apology and "an attempt to 'rewrite history.'" I thought there was something almost desperate in Gene Tibbets's vigilance, defensiveness, and need to absolve his father's legacy.

Nine months after my visit, Obama became the first sitting US president to visit Hiroshima. He did not apologize. And while the visit was much anticipated, thick with symbolism and staged with precise political calculus, it passed without much comment and without change to the American nuclear policy and arsenal. By then, despite receiving the Nobel Peace Prize based in large part on promises to work toward the abolition of nuclear weapons, Obama had authorized a massive nuclear modernization program. Estimated to cost between one and two trillion dollars over the next three decades, it will be the most extensive nuclear weapons upgrade since the Cold War.

I had carried an inherited guilt halfway around the world, but now, the picture of George remained hidden in the back of my journal. Now it felt a relief to say—George built nuclear bombs. After Hiroshima, he built bigger bombs. Yes, he suffered, for the work he did, for the pressure he lived under, and for his own personal traumas, but that did not absolve him or prove what kind of a man he was. Was he a good man underneath it all? I did not know. Maybe I no longer needed to blame or save him.

Seventy years after the first atomic bomb was used, the global inventory of nuclear weapons hovered around fifteen thousand, and the weapons themselves were dozens of times more powerful than the bombs dropped on Hiroshima and Nagasaki. Hibakusha had broken their silence, and yet the world was far more poised to destroy itself than it was on the worst day of their lives. When, nine months later, President Obama would stand in the Peace Park addressing the crowd of dignitaries and hibakusha, a military aide, feet away, would hold the "nuclear football," the black leather suitcase containing the codes enabling the president to launch a nuclear attack within minutes.

It was said after the bombing that no grass would grow for seventy-five years. Yet that summer, the seventieth year, the grass was so green it almost hurt the eyes. Today, the city honors more than one hundred still-living trees that survived the bombing or fell but sprouted anew from their still-living roots. Their trunks are scarred, scorched, or twisted. They are called *hibakujumoku* and are marked with yellow signs throughout the city. The closest to the hypocenter is a weeping willow, just north of the T-shaped Aioi Bridge that was the bomb's target. Just outside of the park and hidden by the bridge, the tree is tucked away from the crowds. I found myself there alone. Its trunk was thick and gnarled, its heavy branches propped up by wooden beams. But the leaves were green. Beneath the welcome shade, I rested my hand on its bark.

Unlike the A-Bomb Dome just on the other side of the bridge, this tree was subject to time. It grew, lipped new bark over old scars, dropped leaves. What lay within its bark? What did its roots take up from this bombed soil?

For decades, the hibakusha lived in fear of the breakdown of their own bodies as they watched apparently healthy survivors suddenly sicken with cancer or other latent health effects. Most frightening, however, was the fear of how radiation exposure might affect the next generation.

Oe wrote of the physical nausea he felt on looking through a microscope at the malformed leaf cells of a flowering plant, "slightly crooked in an unspeakably ugly way." Later, he stated the fear more baldly: "What happened in Hiroshima twenty years ago was an absurdly horrendous massacre; but it may be the first harbinger of the world's real end, in which the human race as we know it will be succeeded by beings with blood and cells so ruined that they cannot be called human. The most terrifying monster lurking in the darkness of Hiroshima is precisely the possibility that man might become no longer human."

Oe's fears about the genetic mutations of the survivors' descendants have not been borne out. The children and grandchildren of the hibakusha have shown no measurable increase in harmful genetic mutations. The grass is growing and the flowers are blooming. If there are subtler effects long-term, we have yet to see them. The question of what the bomb has done to our natural world and our human bodies is still being answered.

Fifty years after his writing, I heard Oe's words differently. How can we maintain our humanity in a world that created and used the atomic bomb? Perhaps that was the question I had been asking all along.

On the night of August 6, after the speeches and the songs, after the ringing of bells and the release of doves, the dedication of flowers and the prayers for peace, after the long blue of an August night pried the grip from the white-hot sun of the day, thousands gathered to float paper lanterns down the Motoyasu River, which flows through the park. Beneath the A-Bomb Dome, jagged walls lit like a stage set, the lanterns cast colored squares of light onto the water.

Other than the light from the dome, the banks of the river were dark, people distinguishable only by foreheads, noses, and cheeks leaned close to the lanterns they carried to the water. Children had decorated their lanterns with drawings of the earth, peace signs, smiley faces. One bore the words "happy" and "smile" beside a drawing of a grinning sunflower. Adults had written messages for peace in their own languages, and the rows of characters or lines of script stood dark against the glowing paper.

Most of the lanterns clumped near the shore, bobbing gently against one another in the slow tidal current. They had to be coaxed farther out by men with long poles standing thigh-deep in the water and then by men in rowboats.

I'd chosen a white paper lantern, flecked with colors; it was made of recycled paper cranes. I wanted mine to move, wanted to see it float past the A-Bomb Dome, under the Aioi Bridge, and disappear into the night. I knelt on the shore, leaned out as far as I could, and gave it a little toss. It landed, rippled the water, bumped against the others, and stopped like all the rest.

I stood and brushed the gravel from my knees. A small child carried a lantern bigger than her head, mother anxious at her elbow as she made her way on the unsteady ground. I climbed the stone stairs that led up from the riverbank, back into the park, winding through the crowd and making my way to the bridge, where I leaned against the railing, looking down.

I'd seen the photographs from years past, the lanterns a golden constellation on the mirrored surface of the water. But the photographs didn't show the men with poles; they didn't show that the lanterns didn't want to move but just knock stubbornly against one another, some tipping over, dousing themselves dark or catching fire. The photographs showed those that were pushed out far enough, tugged from the mass by the fingers of the rising tide, pulled into a long golden ribbon past the A-Bomb Dome, under the bridge, out of the park, inland.

Before I knew that this ritual derived from a Japanese Buddhist tradition in which, at the end of a three-day celebration in honor of the ancestors, the spirits are sent back to their resting places by fires lit on hillsides or floated in lanterns, I already understood it as a ritual of departure and release, already imagined the flames as the souls of the dead. What I did not imagine was that standing there, watching the way the lanterns followed the will of the water despite our human intentions, I would also see bodies. Bodies piled and pushing up against the shore. Bodies burned or bloated. Moaning or already and forever silent. The bodies, too, must have followed the will of the water.

The lanterns were still beautiful, but I could no longer see them in only that way.

I crossed the bridge and continued north, away from the park, away from the crowds. I passed the willow, its leaves hanging in a dark curtain, and sat on the stone wall high above the water. By the time the lanterns had passed under the bridge, some had winked out, and I watched others flicker and die.

Further down the river, a small boat emerged from the darkness, two men aboard. They eased up to a cluster of lanterns caught against the shore, and one lifted a long-handled net, dipped it into the water, and scooped up the lanterns one by one. At first, I thought he was only scooping up the dark ones, but then I saw him drag a lit one under to extinguish the flame. When he pulled it out, the paper was wet and torn. He dropped the mess into the back of the boat.

The small, harmless violence made me want to cry. I supposed it was necessary cleanup—I hadn't thought before about what happened to the lanterns, had seen them only floating, fading into the distance until their lights were like stars on the horizon, but I imagined that when the tide reversed they would be deposited in tangled heaps on the shore or dragged out to the sea, buried, eventually, beneath the waves. Still. Each flame held someone's prayer or someone's memory. I watched for a while, then turned away, as the lanterns passed under the bridge, toward the bombed tree, scarred and weeping, but still green.

# 17

# SIRENS

When I returned to the lake, it would be summer and summer again. We'd gather to celebrate Karin and Paul's fiftieth wedding anniversary, which would be held, actually, five years early, because they wanted to be sure they were healthy enough to celebrate. The whole family would be there, now spilling between two houses—the lake house and a house my parents had just built on the prettiest slice of George's farm, far back on the land that dips and folds, at the end of an old roadbed lined with proud cedars.

I do not feel exactly easy about this house, this additional anchor to a contaminated land. But neither do I feel I can leave this place behind. I think of what Ralph Hutchison, the activist, said to me about finding a pristine place: "How can we exempt ourselves?"

I'd asked Janice why, with all she'd learned about the land, she didn't leave. "My family's been here for hundreds of years," she said. "I was here first." My family hasn't been here as long, of course. We came with the bombs, with the radiation and chemicals, our ties tainted by all of that. Janice wasn't here first either, of course—this land we love was stolen from Native people, maybe farmed by enslaved people, before we made our claims. But she and I have dug stubborn roots into this poisoned earth, despite and because of the crimes of our ancestors.

George knew about the mercury, had helped put it there, and he must have known about much of the rest of it too, but still he loved this land, still he tied his children and grandchildren to it.

Either he did not believe this place dangerous or he denied what he knew; when he died, he left lakefront lots to each of his children, lined up along the inlet to the east of the house. Maybe he meant some sort of atonement when he decided that the lots would be assigned in order of preference starting with his youngest. As it turned out, the lots were difficult to build on and they sat empty and overgrown; still, George's intention, to tie his children to this land, to give them a place to come home to, has held.

In one of the sociological studies I read about Oak Ridge, an activist recounted how a friend had ended a conversation on local contamination: "She said in a shaky voice, 'I don't want to hear this. I don't need to know this. I am stuck here—this is where I have to live. This is the end of the conversation.'"

I recognized my own impulse in the woman's panicked response. How many times have I wanted to stop asking questions, to take someone else's word for it? I do not want to have to live inside all of this knowledge, with all of this scared uncertainty. I understand why Oak Ridgers, out of pride and self-protectiveness, talk around certain stories. We live in our minds more than our houses, and none of us want to be guilty, or sick.

Ghosts, as the lore goes, linger when unfinished business ties them to this earth—guilt, betrayal, or great suffering condemns them to circle the sites of their most traumatic moments. But maybe the living, too, get stuck. We shut our minds on the truths we cannot bear to face, board up our hearts against suffering we cannot admit—both our own and that of others. A woman once told me that sore throats were symptoms of unexpressed desires. At the time, I thought it was a nice metaphor—now, I think it's literally true, the muscles of our jaws and throats straining against what we cannot let out. We fear that truth will force us to give up what is most precious.

But why must love mean love without question? Why must loyalty require blind acceptance?

George lingered for years after his death, Nellie told me. She sensed his presence intuitively. When lights went on and off, or she'd walk into a room and the TV would turn on, she knew it was

George. "You're gonna think I'm a fruitcake," she laughed when she told me.

It wasn't a scary presence, though, but a benevolent one. Sometimes, she had vivid dreams, as if she were awake. She'd open her eyes to find her father standing at the end of her bed.

"You're dead," she'd inform him.

"Well, I know," he'd respond. "I want you to take care of Mom. I really need you to get in touch with Mom. I don't think she's doing well."

Nellie would wake feeling buoyant, transcendent, "like the first time you're in love." For weeks after each dream, she'd fall asleep yearning to slip into that luminous space again.

Nellie, of all her siblings, was injured most profoundly by her father's instability. She saw the worst of what he was. And yet she seems now to be able to hold the most vivid and complicated view of her father. He was a tortured man, she says, sympathetic without excusing him. And though I feared what pain my questioning might unearth, Nellie has never been hurt or angry or defensive in response to my probing of the family's past; she has been grateful to speak of what there has never been much room to say.

I want love to mean that we fight for what is good and true and just with our eyes wide open. I want care to mean we take responsibility—for ourselves, our choices, each other. I want home to be a place where no questions are unbroachable.

Oak Ridge, these days, seems simultaneously obsessed with and embarrassed by its history. An annual Secret City Festival showcases the city's puzzling brand of science, kitsch, and Southern hospitality—baking contests, craft shows, bouncy castles, and robotics competitions. But despite the name referencing the city's wartime history, the bomb is not much in evidence. There's a mug or key chain here or there with an atom symbol, a couple of dusty history exhibits tucked into the library and historical society, but that's about it unless you sign up for the Y-12 bus tour, offered only once a year during the festival.

Even on the tour, though, confined to the bus and the approved path, you don't see much—boxy old tile and concrete buildings that could be anything if it weren't for the relative lack of windows, the tentacles of white pipes springing from the flat roofs, or the periodic signs warning of radioactivity or the use of deadly force beyond certain chain-link fences.

When I took this tour during the city's seventy-fifth anniversary celebration in June of 2018, most of the other twenty or so people on the bus seemed to be in some way connected to Y-12: current employees showing partners or kids where they worked, retirees with grandkids, and a couple of locals who just wanted to peek inside the forbidding nuclear weapons plant. But though we were in the South, where effusive conversations between strangers are common, when I asked them what they hoped to learn from the tour, they glanced at my notebook, and their mouths got smaller as their words faded away. When I asked one woman how old her kids were, squirming bored in the seats across the aisle, she told me, then said nervously, "You're not going to write that, are you? I don't want to get in trouble."

We got out of the bus at the first of only two stops, the 9731 building, the pilot plant for Y-12's World War II uranium enrichment operations. There was a sign on the door that said, "Q Cleared Personnel Only," but we went right in. It was a vast, mostly empty warehouse with high ceilings, gaping air vents, and polished concrete floors, a few historical displays hunched in the corners. An alpha calutron, the machine used for the first stage of the enrichment process, towered above us, tall, gray-painted metal rectangles with pipes sticking out of the tops, looking like nothing in particular. A beta calutron, a bit smaller, bore a yellow sticker reading: "Caution: Internal Contamination."

Our tour guide hammed it up, as if we were all in on the same joke. "We don't glow in the dark," she assured us, "but my vision has improved at night." No really, the plant was big on safety, she promised; you'd get more radiation exposure from flying on an airplane.

Staring down the blunt nose of a thermonuclear bombshell manufactured at Y-12 in the 1960s, our guide praised the efficiency of the weapon. She talked about Hiroshima and Nagasaki, cited an estimated 225,000 killed, and emphasized that the majority died from the thermal heat of the initial explosion, not from radiation. Ongoing studies of the health effects of radiation exposure had produced varied results, she said. "And people live there today." I wasn't sure what her point was. A kid banged his fist on the empty casing, producing a dim, hollow sound.

Two public affairs officials flanked me and asked why I was taking so many notes. I told them that I was interested in the history because my grandfather worked here, and they relaxed a bit and became chatty, but one of them sat in the empty seat next to me when we boarded the bus again.

The Y-12 site is 811 acres scraped dry between two green, wooded ridges. Driving through, it looked mostly desolate and abandoned, a good setting for a zombie movie; the imposing facades of buildings built in the 1940s, '50s, and '60s were streaked and dulled from decades of weather. Everything was rust-colored or dull gray. Here and there, a truck moved, or a guard exited a building, or a car from this decade flashed in the sun, and we were reminded that this was a working facility.

In the center of the complex, there was an incongruous building, a blinding white and starkly new fortress encircled by several layers of fencing, curls of barbed wire sparkling in the sun—it was the Highly Enriched Uranium Materials Facility, where the nation's weapons-grade uranium is stored.

Our guide talked about counterterrorism, subcritical testing, "Stockpile Stewardship," and the "Life Extension Program," all euphemistic nods to Y-12's critical role in maintaining the nation's nuclear arsenal. But the most blatant, and disturbing, reminder of Y-12's legacy came in souvenirs you could purchase in the plant's visitors center: hats and T-shirts bearing bomb silhouettes labeled "Little Boy" and "Fat Man" above the words "Keeping America Safe." There was an actual little boy on my bus sporting the "Little Boy" T-shirt.

"Where did you get that marvelous shirt?" a woman asked the boy's mother. Finding her at the souvenir table later, I asked her what she thought of the tour. She was dewy-eyed with gratitude for what "these people did and are still doing." I blinked at her.

One Sunday, I joined the peace protesters for their vigil outside the gates of Y-12. Weekly, without fail, come rain, shine, or snow, they gather in bright windbreakers and faded tie-dyes and sit in a circle of folding chairs in the grassy shoulder across the street from the plant's entrance. Most are from Knoxville or other surrounding towns, not Oak Ridge itself. It seems easier to remain astonished and upset by the bomb's presence here from a step away.

One of the members of the group, one of the few who actually does live in Oak Ridge, handed out brochures and peace cranes one year at the Secret City Festival. He was shocked to find that most people who approached the table did not know that Oak Ridge still built nuclear weapons. "The government has done a very good job of making it seem innocuous," he marveled.

A family friend who grew up swimming in the lake with my father and his siblings and now teaches sociology at the local community college said she didn't know and assumed it was still secret, "where the nuclear stuff is" these days. "I don't know how much is here in Oak Ridge, how much they still make . . ."

I broke the news to her. I told her that Y-12 holds the nation's store of weapons-grade uranium, possibly the largest single stockpile in the world (amounts, of course, are classified); Nuclear Watch New Mexico has estimated that it is enough to power about fourteen thousand warheads. The plant is one of only five active production facilities within the nation's nuclear weapons complex and the only one to manufacture thermonuclear secondaries, the fusionable cores of hydrogen bombs. I told her that under the Life Extension Program, the plant manufactures new parts for old weapons; technically, it's refurbishment, but some analysts argue that the upgraded parts introduce new capabilities to the weapons, making them effectively new bombs and driving a new arms race. What Y-12 is building is still deadly on a numbing scale.

A year or so later, the same friend began to send me articles about a series of lawsuits brought by the Kingston ash spill cleanup workers against Jacobs Engineering, the TVA contractor that managed the cleanup process. Ten years after the disaster and nearly as long since everyone else had forgotten it ever happened, more than thirty cleanup workers were dead and hundreds more were sick or dying of cancers, blood disorders, strokes, respiratory conditions, and other illnesses. In court, the workers testified that they were assured the ash was safe, denied respirators and simple dust masks, and even ordered to destroy protective equipment; some witnessed managers tampering with air monitors before sending them for testing. Managers mocked workers who complained of deteriorating health. Court decisions in 2018 and 2019 favored the workers, but the plaintiffs rejected settlement offers that fell far short of covering mounting medical bills and years of being unable to work. They keep fighting, keep growing sicker, keep dying.

The Kingston Fossil Plant is not a nuclear plant, just a regular coal-fired power plant. But it was built in the 1950s to serve the energy demands of Oak Ridge's Cold War weapons production. It is hard not to see a parallel between Oak Ridge's culture of secrecy, the longtime cover-up of environmental contamination, and this crime, the scope of which we are only beginning to understand.

Dredging regulations in Watts Bar Lake are meant to ensure that the "legacy waste"—mercury and radioactive cesium—from Oak Ridge remains immobilized beneath clean sediment. But reporting by *Grist* found that TVA cleanup after the ash spill did in fact dig up some of that waste; dredging of one section of the river was halted suddenly one winter night between 2009 and 2010 after testing showed that the waste contained levels of mercury and cesium-137 that could only indicate the decades-old nuclear contamination.

If nuclear waste was found to be mixed with the coal ash, the whole lot would have been categorized as hazardous under federal regulations, obligating the TVA to conduct a more expensive, longer-term cleanup subject to stricter regulations and opening the agency up to legal troubles. Eventually, despite an EPA analysis finding that the ash was "commingled" with nuclear waste from Oak Ridge, despite extremely high levels of uranium reported in and then deleted from a TDEC report, and despite the fact that the waste contained radium levels twice that allowed by the Alabama Department of Health, the ash was still categorized as nonhazardous and dumped in a landfill in the low-income majority-Black community of Union-town, Alabama. Half a million cubic yards of coal ash remain in the bottom of the lake.

I send articles about the lawsuits to my family. I send them articles about disputes between the state, environmental advocates, and the DOE over a new hazardous waste landfill the DOE wants to build in Oak Ridge to replace the nearly full current facility. I urge them to submit public comments calling for more transparency and more stringent environmental requirements. They respond with concern, but I still feel like Cassandra, always bearing unwelcome prophecies.

At the peace vigil, we held hands in a circle and sang protest songs I remember from my Quaker school days. My eyes grew damp with embarrassment or emotion, I wasn't sure which. I was nervous about who would see me here and ask me what I was doing, holding vigil outside of Y-12. I was not sure what we were doing here. While this group objects in other, more tangible ways—lobbying Congress and suing the government to halt further nuclear production—this weekly gathering presents no challenge to policy or status quo. Still, I am grateful that they are here, every Sunday, witnessing. Saying, with their bodies, we protest this bomb and all it stands for. We are willing to look foolish for it.

When they are not holding vigil, the Oak Ridge Environmental Peace Alliance (OREPA), with Ralph Hutchison at the helm, focus their resources on fighting to halt the production of new weapons at Y-12. The US expects to spend well over $1 trillion, and as much as $2 trillion, on nuclear modernization over the next several decades;

a new Uranium Processing Facility, budgeted for $6.5 billion, is set to be completed at Y-12 by 2025. OREPA, along with the National Resources Defense Council and Nuclear Watch of New Mexico, won a suit against the DOE and the National Nuclear Security Agency over failing to consider grave seismic and environmental hazards that could compromise the safety of the planned facility, but the agencies continued construction anyway.

In the meantime, Y-12's contaminated World War II–era buildings are crumbling, posing a daily threat to workers, area residents, and the environment. A 2015 audit by the DOE's inspector general identified hundreds of excess high-risk facilities across the nuclear weapons complex; Y-12's Alpha 5 was dubbed "the worst of the worst." Water damage, roof degradation, and pipe corrosion have made the building a toxic time bomb with "potential for an explosion or reaction associated with remaining contaminants."

Such aging facilities pose "ever-increasing levels of risk" to workers and the public, warned the inspector general's audit.

"Now, I've been doing this for thirty years," said Ralph, and "I've never before seen a DOE official document that said anything presented a risk to the public, let alone an ever-increasing risk." His eyes widened, still incredulous after all these years. "But we can't get in to clean them up because we're still building bombs there, and there's a security fence. You can't clear every worker and driver." Still outraged, still fighting.

On the Fourth of July, I watched fireworks from the bow of the motorboat, snuggled between my cousins' kids. The next afternoon, I drove into Oak Ridge. I wanted to hear the emergency siren that was tested on the first Wednesday of every month, the siren that would sound in the case of an accident at one of the DOE facilities.

I wandered around Walmart while I waited for it to begin. I studied a picked-over display of July Fourth merchandise: flag-decorated, light-up tumblers; red, white, and blue M&M's; banners and bows and leis for cars, mailboxes, doorways.

We were a mile and a half from the site of the Hiroshima bomb's manufacture, a mile and a half from the fortress where workers, that day, were doing whatever they do to build hydrogen bomb cores "in decades-old buildings near or past the end of their expected life spans," as described on Y-12's own website. Mercury dripped into the groundwater.

Later, when I was back at the farm baking a pie with my nine-year-old cousin Komal, Wendy's youngest, she asked me, "Did you go to the crime scene?"

"Crime scene?"

"I thought because you said a siren, there was a crime." She shrugged.

At noon, I stepped outside of the Walmart just in time to hear a brassy, high, frenetic note rise above the drone of the summer day. A woman exiting the store stopped for a moment. "Is that that alarm?" she asked. "The first time I heard it, it scared the life outta me!" She shook her head and walked on.

The alarm crested and fell in waves, as if someone was actually wailing, pausing now and again to catch their breath.

When other people exited, they looked momentarily startled, but soon incorporated the shrill sound and moved on. A young boy wearing a monster truck shirt that said, "Let's roll out!" did not ask his mother about the noise.

I was reminded of another siren. At 11:02 a.m. on August 9, 2015, I stood in the Nagasaki Peace Park, head bowed, as the chiming of the Peace Bell marked the exact moment, seventy years before, that the American plane called *Bockscar* dropped a nuclear bomb on the city. After a few moments, the high keen of an air-raid siren took up the call, a discordant, chilling undertone beneath the bright, metallic chime of the bell. There was, that day, no plane in the hot blue sky, no actual threat of violence to this peaceful gathering, but still, my neck prickled in alarm.

I'd gone to Nagasaki only as an afterthought, with little prior planning or research. Hiroshima was where the uranium George enriched ended up; Nagasaki was a plutonium bomb, its deadly fuel manufactured in Hanford, Washington. And like many scholars and journalists, I was guilty of using Hiroshima as shorthand for both bombings. Perhaps we ignore Nagasaki, too, because its legacy is even more uncomfortable than Hiroshima's, its bombing crueler and more unnecessary. Even those who still claim the bombing of Hiroshima was justified struggle to endorse Nagasaki.

But perhaps what is most unsettling about Nagasaki is the precariousness of its legacy: while Hiroshima will always be the first city destroyed by a nuclear bomb, Nagasaki may not remain the last. As long as we have nuclear bombs and working weapons plants, Nagasaki's legacy could change in a moment. While much of the city's commemoration ceremony mirrored Hiroshima's—there were hibakusha testimonies, dignitaries offering garlands of flowers, a mayoral address—the siren was unique. That long cry, relentless minor note, a reminder of the threat we live under every day.

I stepped back into Walmart, and the siren dulled to a low whistle you had to strain to hear. A woman purchased a Twix bar. Another, a nonstick pan, a welcome mat, a box of Cheerios. Thirty feet in, the alarm was indiscernible above the humming static of the store.

# Acknowledgments

To all of my teachers and mentors, especially M. Mark, Paul Russell, and Paul Kane, for early belief in this project. In particular, I owe this book's existence to Dean Crawford, my earliest reader and editor, who told me this was a book before I was brave enough to dream it could be.

To the University of Minnesota MFA faculty and staff, whose conversations, careful readings, and encouragement helped shape this book—including Holly Vanderhaar, Kim Todd, Ray Gonzalez, V. V. Ganeshananthan, and especially my thesis advisers, Julie Schumacher and Patricia Hampl. To my cohort and colleagues who became my editors and friends.

To the many friends, too many to name, who wrote with me, thought with me, talked with me, cried with me, laughed with me through these years—I love you fiercely. To those who read these pages and helped me make them better, especially Kendra Atleework, Erica Berry, and Carolyn Byrne. To Nathalie Bellin for cake and pep talks. To Hannah White for making me laugh till I snort, for hand-drawn pick-me-up cards at all the right moments. To Alice Domby for well-timed brownies. To Gabe Frumkin for craving deviled eggs. To Jenny Middleton for reading for science. To Emma Domby for road trips and singing loudly out of tune. To Ndinda Kioko for dancing in our office and crying on the floor together. To Ellie Garran, for reading this beast maybe more times than anyone else, for your editorial eye, and for your big love and patient support through the final, difficult stretch.

To the many, many people who responded to the emails or calls of a stranger and shared your time, expertise, stories, resources, and connections, including Peter Raynor, Alan Zelicoff, David Schuster, Alex Wellerstein, Hannah Horowitz, Ran Zwigenberg, Bo Jacobs, Valeria Roberson, Al Chambles, and so many others. To Dylan Miettinen for research and fact-checking assistance. D. Ray Smith deserves special thanks for endlessly answering the most obscure questions about Oak Ridge history and always connecting me to the right people. Owen Hoffman pushed me toward greater nuance and precision about health risks and environmental contamination. To Steve Leeper for sharing your love and knowledge of Hiroshima and working for a more peaceful world, even when it seems so dark. To Ralph Hutchison for your generosity, deep knowledge of Oak Ridge, and the work you do in the world.

A big thanks, also, to all of the librarians, archivists, and FOIA officers who've helped me dig up obscure documents and navigate byzantine systems. In particular, I'm grateful for the patient and knowledgeable assistance of Shane Bell at the National Archives at Atlanta, Martha DeMarre at the Nuclear Testing Archives, and Justin Schell at the University of Minnesota.

To everyone who granted me an interview, who shared your knowledge and stories with me—this book could not exist without you. I am especially grateful to Janice Stokes, Janet Michel, Harry Williams, and the hibakusha—Kasaoka Sadae, Ota Kaneji, Nishida Goro, Kawamoto Shoso, and Hataguchi Minoru. To my Japanese interpreters—Hiraoka Sachiko, Ikeda Miho, Yamane Michiko, and especially Sawada Miwako—for giving your time and hearts to communicating these stories that must not be forgotten. Some interviews that did not ultimately appear in the book nevertheless deepened my understanding in fundamental ways. I also want to remember those who have passed away in the course of my writing this book: Colleen Black, Dot Wilkinson, Bill Wilcox, Harry

Williams, D. H. Johnson, Mary Jane Hibbs, Frankie and Lester Hulett, and Okada Emiko.

Some of the people who have touched this book in some way may not agree with me. I am nevertheless grateful for their time, perspectives, stories, and assistance that have challenged, enriched, and shaped this work. Errors that remain are my own.

Many grants and fellowships enabled me to do this work: the Minnesota State Arts Board; the Metropolitan Regional Arts Council; the Jerome Foundation; and the Judd, O'Rourke, and Graduate Research Partnership Program fellowships from the University of Minnesota. Especially important were the W.K. Rose Fellowship from Vassar College, the Olive B. O'Connor Fellowship from Colgate University, and the McKnight Fellowship. To the grant panelists, writers, and administrators who made these opportunities possible, especially Cristina García for the McKnight, Bao Phi at the Loft, and Jennifer Brice, CJ Hauser, and Peter Balakian for the beautiful gift of a year at Colgate. Much thanks, also, to the residencies that gave me the gift of time and space to write: Write On, Door County, the Anderson Center, the Kimmel Harding Nelson Center for the Arts, and I-Park Foundation.

Portions of this book in earlier iterations have appeared in *Guernica*, *Ploughshares*, *Colorado Review*, *Bulletin of the Atomic Scientists*, *Catapult*, *Nowhere Magazine*, "The Bomb" podcast by *BBC*, *Curbed*, and *The Telegraph*. I'm thankful for their pages, their editors, their readers, their early votes of confidence.

To Janet Silver for being a champion of this project. To Patrick O'Dowd and the entire University Press of Kentucky team—including David Cobb, Meredith Daugherty, Darian Bianco, Lesley Bolton, Kat Lynch, Shannon Li, Jamie McKee, and Tara Dugan—for giving this book a home and a birthday.

To the entire extended Strasser family, who have been unbelievably supportive of this project. To Ben for keeping me laughing. To Julia for your friendship and thoughtful comments on the manuscript. To Paul for answering a million nuclear questions, for always hashing it out with me. To Karin, Kurt, and Nell, for your patience and love as I've plumbed your memories. To my mother for help on every level of this project and for always believing in me and my work. To my father for your love and help along the way and for trusting me with this undertaking.

I wrote these pages on land stolen from Indigenous Peoples across what we now call the United States. A bulk of the work was completed in Minneapolis, Minnesota, which is located in the traditional homeland of the Dakota people taken through genocide, forced land cessions, and broken treaties. Today, Minneapolis is home to people of many Indigenous nations, including Dakota and Anishinaabe people. The land is and will remain Indigenous land.

# NOTES

The majority of the interviews I conducted were recorded, and quotations are as close as possible to the originals, with slight edits for clarity and concision. Occasionally, quotations are reconstructed from notes and memory. In some cases, I combined multiple conversations for concision. Interviews took place in person and over the phone between 2010 and 2021.

Interviews with hibakusha were conducted in July and August of 2015 with Japanese interpreters. I am indebted to the following individuals, who generously gave their time and emotional energy to interpret these important stories: Hiraoka Sachiko (interpreted for Kasaoka Sadae), Sawada Miwako (interpreted for Ota Kaneji and Kawamoto Shoso), Ikeda Miho (interpreted for Nishida Goro), and Yamane Michiko (interpreted for Hataguchi Minoru). In addition to interpreting several interviews, Sawada Miwako checked quotations against the recorded interviews. For the most part, I have preserved the wordings of quotations as they were interpreted and as I heard and responded to them in real time; where Miwako's translation revealed a discrepancy or misunderstanding, I've edited for clarity and accuracy.

On Japanese names: As per Japanese custom, I have listed family names first in the body of the narrative. After initial introduction, I refer to subjects by their given names, as I do with other interview subjects throughout the book. Names from museum plaques are listed in the order in which they appeared in English.

In the notes, names of cited scholars and writers appear in the order in which they are printed in the referenced works.

For the sake of narrative flow, I have combined the events of two separate trips to Las Vegas in the chapter "Practicing for Doomsday."

I am grateful for the rich resource of the Center for Oak Ridge Oral History, which can be accessed on the Oak Ridge Public Library's Digital Collections. Quotations from that collection are reprinted here courtesy of the Center for Oak Ridge Oral History and the Oak Ridge Public Library.

## Abbreviations

| | |
|---|---|
| AEC | Atomic Energy Commission |
| ATSDR | Agency for Toxic Substances and Disease Registry |
| COROH | Center for Oak Ridge Oral History |
| DOE | Department of Energy |
| FCDA | Federal Civil Defense Administration |
| NARA | National Archives and Records Administration |
| NAA | National Archives at Atlanta |
| ORHASP | Oak Ridge Health Agreement Steering Panel |
| RG | record group |
| TDEC | Tennessee Department of Environment and Conservation |

## 2. Ash

17 **cupholder of his ears** Scott Barker, "The Coal Ash Spill Catastrophe in Kingston—One Year Later," *Knoxville News Sentinel*, December 9, 2009.

18 **7.3 million tons:** Jamie Satterfield, "TVA Coal Ash Spill: 5 Things to Know on 10-Year Anniversary," *Knoxville News Sentinel*, December 20, 2018.

18 **despite environmentalists' recommendations:** Shaila Dewan, "Tennessee Ash Flood Larger Than Initial Estimate," *New York Times*, December 26, 2008.

18 **weaknesses in the dikes:** Barker, "Coal Ash Spill"; Pam Sohn, "Tennessee: Early Warnings on Ash Pond Leaks," *Chattanooga Times Free Press*, January 5, 2009.

18 **more than twice the amount:** Dewan, "Tennessee Ash Flood."

18 **sixteen hundred Olympic swimming pools:** "Tennessee Sludge Spill Estimate Grows to 1 Billion Gallons," CNN, December 26, 2008, http://www.cnn.com/2008/US/12/26/tennessee.sludge/.

18 *Exxon Valdez*: Sean Flynn, "Black Tide," *GQ*, April 20, 2009.

18 **Deepwater Horizon:** Austyn Gaffney, "A Legacy of Contamination: How the Kingston Ash Spill Unearthed a Nuclear Nightmare," *Grist*, December 15, 2020.

19 **damaging or destroying dozens of homes:** Duane W. Gang, "Kingston Coal Ash Spill: 5 Years, $1 Billion Cleanup Tab and No Regulations Later," *Tennessean* (Nashville), December 22, 2013.

# 3. Still Burning

23 **Site X:** For a good overview of the beginnings of Oak Ridge, see Charles W. Johnson and Charles O. Jackson, *City Behind a Fence: Oak Ridge, Tennessee, 1942–1946* (Knoxville: University of Tennessee Press, 1981).

23 **The perimeter of Oak Ridge:** Peter Bacon Hales, *Atomic Spaces: Living on the Manhattan Project* (Urbana: University of Illinois Press, 1997), 128.

24 **asked to show their IDs at any time:** Lindsey A. Freeman, *Longing for the Bomb: Oak Ridge and Atomic Nostalgia* (Chapel Hill: University of North Carolina Press, 2015), 84.

24 **elaborate security apparatus:** Ibid.

24 **some 95 percent:** Ibid., 3.

24 **"What you see here":** Ed Westcott, *Three Monkeys and Uncle Sam*, December 31, 1943, photograph, DOE Photograph Collection, Oak Ridge Public Library Digital Collections.

# 4. Homeplace

34 **even the most mundane details:** Denise Kiernan, *The Girls of Atomic City: The Untold Story of the Women Who Helped Win World War II* (New York: Touchstone, 2013), 163; Johnson and Jackson, *City Behind a Fence*, 152; Freeman, *Longing for the Bomb*, 85.

35 **Personal journals:** Freeman, *Longing for the Bomb*, 80.

35 **mail was censored:** Kiernan, *Girls of Atomic City*, 133, 168.

35 **Acme Credit Corporation:** Johnson and Jackson, *City Behind a Fence*, 150.

35 **as many as one in four:** Janice Harper, "Secrets Revealed, Revelations Concealed: A Secret City Confronts Its Environmental Legacy of Weapons Production," *Anthropological Quarterly* 80, no. 1 (2007): 39–64, 47.

35 **what they knew would be necessary:** Johnson and Jackson, *City Behind a Fence*, 3–8.

36 **In a photograph, the men:** Enclosed in Arthur Compton to Vannevar Bush, Selection of Site for "Power" Project, June 13, 1943, 4NN-326-8505, ARC 1518690, box 54, Formerly Classified Correspondence Files, Series 8505, Records of the AEC, RG 326, NAA, NARA.

36 "unusual occupational hazards": T. V. Moore, Memorandum on the Factors Affecting the Choice of the Plant Site, 1942, 4NN-326-8505, ARC 1518690, box 54, Formerly Classified Correspondence Files, Series 8505, Records of the AEC, RG 326, NAA, NARA, appendix II, 5.

36 "should ever be noticed": Ibid., appendix II, 6.

36 "scattered houses," "very small settlements": Stone & Webster Engineering Corporation, Report on Proposed Site for Plant, Eastern Tennessee, 4NN-326-8505, ARC 1518690, box 54, Formerly Classified Correspondence Files, Series 8505, Records of the AEC, RG 326, NAA, NARA, 5.

36 map the geologic makeup: Ibid., exhibit D.

37 "solemnly guarantee[d]": US Congress, Senate, Committee on Indian Affairs, *Indian Affairs: Laws and Treaties*, vol. II, compiled and edited by Charles J. Kappler, 62nd Cong., 2d sess.-76, 3rd sess., 719-184 (Washington, DC: Government Printing Office, 1904), 30.

37 First Treaty of Tellico: Ratified Indian Treaty 29: Cherokee—Near Tellico on Cherokee Ground, October 2, 1798, IDA Treaties Explorer, the Indigenous Digital Archive, https://digitreaties.org/treaties/treaty/170281481/.

37 families counted for removal: The eviction of pre–Oak Ridge residents is described in Johnson and Jackson, *City Behind a Fence*, 39–45; Freeman, *Longing for the Bomb*, 16–19; Hales, *Atomic Spaces*, 47–57; Kiernan, *Girls of Atomic City*, 23–27.

37 "always the 'homeplace'": Paul Elza, interview by Sibyl Nestor, November 1973, transcript, COROH, City of Oak Ridge Public Library, Oak Ridge, TN.

37 photographed each structure: Hales, *Atomic Spaces*, 50–53.

37 in the rush, abandoned: Freeman, *Longing for the Bomb*, 17; Kiernan, *Girls of Atomic City*, 28.

38 never counted nor compensated: Hales, *Atomic Spaces*, 56–57.

39 to design the townsite: On the design and construction of Oak Ridge, see Johnson and Jackson, *City Behind a Fence*, 12–17; Hales, *Atomic Spaces*, 78–93; Freeman, *Longing for the Bomb*, 45–50. There are some discrepancies in the reported initial population estimates. I have used Johnson and Jackson's number.

39 "All we wanted": Nathaniel Alexander Owings, *The Spaces In Between: An Architect's Journey* (Boston: Houghton Mifflin, 1973), 94.

39 "an ideal plan": Ibid., 95.

39 a system of roads: Johnson and Jackson, *City Behind a Fence*, 21.

40 little country cemeteries: Owings, *Spaces In Between*, 95.

40 the city's population: Johnson and Jackson, *City Behind a Fence*, 25.

40 The roads remained: Ibid., 17.

40 only the most important scientists: Johnson and Jackson, *City Behind a Fence*, 104–105; Freeman, *Longing for the Bomb*, 51; Hales, *Atomic Spaces*, 108–109.

40 empty in case of an accident: Hales, *Atomic Spaces*, 108–109.

41 Residents joked: Theodore Rockwell III, "Frontier Life among the Atom Splitters," *Saturday Evening Post*, December 1, 1945, 45.

41 *that government town*: Johnson and Jackson, *City Behind a Fence*, 17, 50.

41 barbed wire salvaged: Freeman, *Longing for the Bomb*, 20.

42 "Negro Village": Johnson and Jackson, *City Behind a Fence*, 22, 111–113.

42 disregard for the safety policy: Hales, *Atomic Spaces*, 197.

42 10 percent: Ibid.,192.

42 "hutments": Enoch P. Waters, "Negroes Live in Modern 'Hoovervilles' at Atom City," *Chicago Defender*, January 5, 1946; Freeman, *Longing for the Bomb*, 56–59; Hales, *Atomic Spaces*, 194–199; Kiernan, *Girls of Atomic City*, 90–93.

43 only for the duration of the war: Johnson and Jackson, *City Behind a Fence*, 23.

43 life expectancy of just twenty-five years: Ibid., 21.

43 no more than three years: Ibid., 28.

43 no free press: Russell B. Olwell, *At Work in the Atomic City: A Labor and Social History of Oak Ridge, Tennessee* (Knoxville: University of Tennessee Press, 2004), 3; Hales, *Atomic Spaces*, 232–242.

43 union activities were severely restricted: Olwell, *At Work in the Atomic City*, 28–20, 37; Hales, *Atomic Spaces*, 170.

43 "Number of Deaths at the Oak Ridge Hospital": Charles E. Rea, Major Medical Corps, Chief of Clinical Services, to Major H. G. Hoberg, Number of Deaths at the Oak Ridge Hospital, September 20, 1944, 4NN-326-8505, box 80, Formerly Classified Correspondence Files, Series 8505, Records of the AEC, RG 326, NAA, NARA.

43 Instead of bodies: J. H. Coobs and J. R. Gissel, "History of Disposal of Radioactive Wastes into the Ground at Oak Ridge National Laboratory" (Oak Ridge, TN, October 1986), https://doi.org/10.2172/5120611.

43 the cemeteries lie there still: "Historic Cemeteries in Oak Ridge," City of Oak Ridge Public Library, http://orpl.oakridgetn.gov/services/oak-ridge-cemeteries/.

44 With a security escort: D. Ray Smith, Y-12 and Oak Ridge historian, email message to author, February 12, 2022.

45 A funeral home opened its doors: D. Ray Smith, "Historically Speaking: Martin Funeral Homes: A Brief History, Part 2," *Oak Ridger*, January 25, 2011.

46 eleven thousand graves: Number as of February 2022, per Vernon J. Samson, email message to author, February 11, 2022.

46 also ensures perpetual care: Frank Munger, "'Perpetual Care Fund' for Oak Ridge Landfill at $15.5M," *Atomic City Underground* (blog), *Knoxville News Sentinel*, January 1, 2014, http://knoxblogs.com/atomiccity/2014/01/01/perpetual-care-fund-oak-ridge-landfill-15-5m/.

46  **nearing its capacity:** Benjamin Pounds, "Steps toward Landfill for DOE Demolition Debris in Oak Ridge," *Oak Ridger*, July 19, 2021.

46  **a new landfill:** US DOE, Oak Ridge Office of Environmental Management, *Record of Decision for Comprehensive Environmental Response, Compensation, and Liability Act Oak Ridge Reservation Waste Disposal at the Environmental Management Disposal Facility, Oak Ridge, Tennessee,* UCOR LLC, DOE/OR/01-2794&D1 (Oak Ridge, TN, June 2021).

46  **thirty-two historic cemeteries:** G. A. Scott McGill, program analyst, Oak Ridge Reservation Management, email message to author, February 14, 2022.

# 5. Kin

49  **"Whose son":** This and other Oak Ridge billboards' wording from photographs taken by Ed Westcott, official Manhattan Project photographer, during the war, available from the DOE Photograph Collection, Oak Ridge Public Library Digital Collections.

50  **rumors, speculation, and jokes:** Kiernan, *Girls of Atomic City,* 178.

50  **"The bottom half of horses":** Colleen Black, interview by Charles Johnson and Charles Jackson, May 15, 1976, transcript by Jordan Reed, City Behind a Fence Interviews, COROH, City of Oak Ridge Public Library, Oak Ridge, TN, 9–10.

50  **"Eighty cents . . . half of 'em":** Colleen Black, interview by Jim Kolb, February 20, 2002, transcript, COROH, City of Oak Ridge Public Library, Oak Ridge, TN, 25.

51  **Colleen worked:** Colleen Black's and Dot Wilkinson's stories are also told in Kiernan, *Girls of Atomic City.*

51  **"anything funny":** Ibid., 127.

52  **average age:** Freeman, *Longing for the Bomb,* 59.

53  **"a new form of 'kinship'":** Janice Harper, "Secrets Revealed, Revelations Concealed: A Secret City Confronts Its Environmental Legacy of Weapons Production," *Anthropological Quarterly* 80, no. 1 (Winter 2007): 39–64, 47.

53  **high school girls did as well or better:** Cynthia C. Kelly, ed., *The Manhattan Project: The Birth of the Atomic Bomb in the Words of Its Creators, Eyewitnesses, and Historians* (New York: Black Dog & Leventhal, 2007), 205–207.

54  **"perfect machines, in all that they did":** Hales, *Atomic Spaces,* 119.

54  **"leave your doors open":** Betty Stokes, interview by Don Hunnicutt, March 18, 2015, audio, COROH, City of Oak Ridge Public Library, Oak Ridge, TN.

54  **a kind of utopia:** Freeman, *Longing for the Bomb,* 44–45.

54  **"class-unconscious":** Dick Smyser quoted in ibid., 50.

54 "a beautiful enclave": Jay Searcy quoted in ibid., 113.

54 "Camelot": Stokes, interview.

54 "People from every walk of life": John Michael Haffey, ed., *Nineteen Sixty-Seven: 25th Anniversary, Oak Ridge, Tennessee* (Oak Ridge, TN: Oak Ridge Community, 1967), 13.

54 "the whole human race!": Betty Clayton Osborn, "Where Are You From, Mr. Oak Ridger?," *A Thousand Suns: A Musical Story of Oak Ridge's 25 Years* (Oak Ridge, TN: 1967).

55 "the worst place": Kattie Lou Strickland, interview by Chris Albrecht, November 3, 2005, video, COROH, City of Oak Ridge Public Library, Oak Ridge, TN. Kattie's story comes from this interview and from Kiernan, *Girls of Atomic City*.

55 strict hierarchies: Freeman, *Longing for the Bomb*, 50–52; Johnson and Jackson, *City Behind a Fence*, 104–105.

55 Lowest down the ladder: The recruitment and employment of Black workers are described in Waters, "Negroes Live in Modern 'Hoovervilles'"; Freeman, *Longing for the Bomb*, 58, 75–76.

55 obscured blatantly discriminatory practices: Olwell, *At Work in the Atomic City*, 20–24.

55 miserable, swampy hutments: Segregation and housing conditions for Black workers are described in Waters, "Negroes Live in Modern 'Hoovervilles'"; Freeman, *Longing for the Bomb*, 55–59; Hales, *Atomic Spaces*, 193–197; Johnson and Jackson, *City Behind a Fence*, 111–114; and Kiernan, *Girls of Atomic City*.

55 Black nurses: Waters, "Negroes Live in Modern 'Hoovervilles.'"

55 Brilliant Black scientists: Brittany Crocker, "Bias Kept Black Scientists Out of Oak Ridge's Atomic Bomb Work," *Knoxville News Sentinel*, March 1, 2018.

56 "the pen": Freeman, *Longing for the Bomb*, 56–57; Kiernan, *Girls of Atomic City*, 90–91, 170.

56 "back side of the world from my kids": Strickland, interview.

56 "I just liked what I was making": Ibid.

57 "slums that were deliberately planned": Enoch P. Waters, "Negro Kids Can't Go to School at Biggest Brain Center," *Chicago Defender*, December 29, 1945, 1.

57 "actually foreign to the area": Ibid., 6.

57 the Colored Camp Council: Johnson and Jackson, *City Behind a Fence*, 113–114.

58 "retarded the cause of democracy": Waters, "Negro Kids Can't," 1.

58 Ebb Cade: The experiment on Ebb Cade is detailed in Eileen Welsome, *The Plutonium Files: America's Secret Medical Experiments in the Cold War* (New York: The Dial Press, 1999), 83–87, 121. Information about the radiation experiments in general also from Welsome.

59 "the poor, the powerless, and the sick": Ibid., 7–8.
59 Decades after Ebb's injection: Kiernan, *Girls of Atomic City*, 221.
60 white residents would claim ignorance: Freeman, *Longing for the Bomb*, 58.
60 "stick to their knitting": Groves quoted in Hales, *Atomic Spaces*, 118.

# 6. Countdown

63 **Forty-Three Seconds:** Description of the bombing mission comes from
Rhodes, *The Making of the Atomic Bomb*, 25th anniversary ed. (New
York: Simon & Schuster, 2012), and Kelly, *The Manhattan Project*. Small
discrepancies exist in the exact timing of the bombing and the height from
which the bombs dropped—here, I have used Kelly's numbers (329–330)
as excerpted from *Operational History of the 509th Bombardment* (Pease
Air Force Base, New Hampshire).

64 **an eight-year-old boy playing hide-and-seek:** Takashi Thomas Tanemori,
*Hiroshima: Bridge to Forgiveness* (Richmond, BC, Canada: Multicultural
Books, 2007).

64 **"it was a dud":** Van Kirk quoted in Kelly, *The Manhattan Project*, 332.

66 **The primary argument:** The arguments used to justify or condemn the
bombing, including various casualty estimates, are summarized and
analyzed by J. Samuel Walker, "Recent Literature on Truman's Atomic
Bomb Decision: A Search for Middle Ground," *Diplomatic History* 29,
no. 2 (2005): 311–334; J. Samuel Walker, *Prompt and Utter Destruction:
Truman and the Use of Atomic Bombs against Japan*, 3rd ed. (Chapel
Hill: University of North Carolina Press, 2016); Alex Wellerstein, "What
Journalists Should Know about the Atomic Bombings," *Restricted Data:
The Nuclear Secrecy Blog*, June 9, 2020, http://blog.nuclearsecrecy.com
/2020/06/09/what-journalists-should-know-about-the-atomic-bombings/;
Alex Wellerstein, "The Decision to Use the Bomb: A Consensus View?,"
*Restricted Data: The Nuclear Secrecy Blog*, March 8, 2013, http://
blog.nuclearsecrecy.com/2013/03/08/the-decision-to-use-the-bomb
-a-consensus-view/.

66 **inhumane and unnecessary:** Peter J. Kuznick, "The Decision to Risk the
Future: Harry Truman, the Atomic Bomb and the Apocalyptic Narra-
tive," *The Asia-Pacific Journal: Japan Focus* 5, no. 7 (July 12, 2007): 10;
Ronald Takaki, *Hiroshima: Why America Dropped the Atomic Bomb*
(New York: Back Bay, 1995), 30.

67 **Soviet betrayal:** Hibiki Yamaguchi, Fumihiko Yoshida, and Radomir
Compel, "Can the Atomic Bombings on Japan Be Justified? A Conver-
sation with Dr. Tsuyoshi Hasegawa," *Journal for Peace and Nuclear
Disarmament* 2, no. 1 (June 11, 2019): 19–33.

67 *count* **has meant "to tell":** *OED Online*, s.v. "count (*v.*)," updated December 2021.

67 **five hundred thousand Purple Heart medals:** Claims about the number of
Purple Hearts estimated to have been produced in anticipation of the
invasion of Japan vary somewhat. See, for example, D. M. Giangreco,
"75 Years Later, Purple Hearts Made for an Invasion of Japan Are Still
Being Awarded," *History News Network*, August 9, 2020; David Smith,
"'He Felt He Had to Do It': Truman's Grandson on Bombing Hiro-
shima," *Guardian*, August 4, 2020. This story is contested in J. Samuel
Walker, *Prompt and Utter Destruction: Truman and the Use of Atomic
Bombs against Japan*, 1st ed. (Chapel Hill: University of North Carolina
Press, 1997), 118n.

68 **thirty-five thousand Purple Hearts:** Military Order of the Purple Heart,
"Purple Heart Recipients" as of April 1, 2015, https://web.archive.org
/web/20180825031025/http://www.purpleheart.org/DownLoads/Bank
/MOPHInformationalBrochures/MOPHToday.pdf.

68 **some one hundred thousand to one million:** Physicians for Social Responsibility, *Body Count: Casualties after 10 Years of the "War on Terror"—
Iraq, Afghanistan, Pakistan,* (Washington, DC: 2015).

68 **civilians and combatants continue to die:** See database on Iraq Body
Count, Conflict Casualties Monitor, https://www.iraqbodycount.org
/database/recent/.

68 *To reckon* **also means:** *OED Online*, s.v. "reckon (*v.*)," updated June 2022.

69 **two hundred times more concentrated:** Ibid., 43.

69 **forced labor:** Mining conditions are described in Patrick Marnham, *Snake
Dance: Journeys Beneath a Nuclear Sky* (London: Vintage, 2014),
216–217; Susan Williams, *Spies in the Congo: America's Atomic Mission
in World War II* (New York: PublicAffairs, 2016), 6.

69 **While estimates suggest:** Gabrielle Hecht, *Being Nuclear: Africans and the
Global Uranium Trade* (Cambridge, MA: MIT Press, 2012), 193, 335.

69 **locals tell of unexplained illnesses:** Frank Swain, "The Forgotten Mine
That Built the Atomic Bomb," BBC, August 3, 2020, https://www.bbc
.com/future/article/20200803-the-forgotten-mine-that-built-the-atomic
-bomb.; Williams, *Spies in the Congo*, 266.

69 **The secrecy surrounding the mine:** Swain, "The Forgotten Mine"; Tom
Zoellner, *Uranium: War, Energy, and the Rock That Shaped the World*
(New York: Viking, 2009), 170.

70 **freelance miners:** Zoellner, *Uranium*, 11–12; Hecht, *Being Nuclear*,
336–337.

70 **uranium ore made its way:** The path and processing of uranium ore are
described in Williams, *Spies in the Congo*, 6–7; Kiernan, *Girls of Atomic
City*, 99; US DOE, Office of History and Heritage Resources, "Uranium
Milling and Refining," The Manhattan Project: An Interactive History,
https://www.osti.gov/opennet/manhattan-project-history/Processes
/UraniumMining/uranium-refining.html.

70 **fed into calutrons:** Kiernan, *Girls of Atomic City*, and Kelly, *The Manhattan Project*, 205–207.

71 **uranium got stuck:** In addition to my conversation with Bill Wilcox, information about uranium reclamation and reprocessing comes from William J. Wilcox Jr., *An Overview of the History of Y-12, 1942–1992: A Chronology of Some Noteworthy Events and Memoirs*, 2nd ed. (Oak Ridge, TN: self-published, 2009), 13.

72 **packed into gold-lined cylinders:** Kiernan, *Girls of Atomic City*, 131–132; Rhodes, *The Making of the Atomic Bomb*, 602–603.

73 **"two shakes":** "Time of Reaction," AtomicArchive.com, accessed February 15, 2022, https://www.atomicarchive.com/science/fission/time-of-reaction.html.

73 **878 Sailors:** The bomb's journey from Los Alamos and the story of the *USS Indianapolis* are from Rhodes, *The Making of the Atomic Bomb*, 662, 693–695.

73 **total loss of the precious material:** Telephone call from Dr. Oppenheimer, June 21, 1945, Preparation and Movement of Personnel and Equipment to Tinian, Events Preceding and Following the Dropping of the First Atomic Bombs at Hiroshima and Nagasaki, roll 1, target 6, folder 5, subfolder 5C, Correspondence "Top Secret" of the Manhattan Engineer District, 1942–1946, Records of the Office of the Chief of Engineers, RG 77, National Archives at College Park, NARA.

73 **Twelve Airmen:** Flight and arming procedure from Rhodes, *The Making of the Atomic Bomb*, 704–708; John Coster-Mullen, *Atom Bombs: The Top Secret Inside Story of Little Boy and Fat Man* (self-published, 2013), 33–38.

74 **"last one to touch the bomb":** Morris Jeppson, *White Light / Black Rain: The Destruction of Hiroshima and Nagasaki*, directed by Steven Okazaki (Berkeley, CA: HBO Documentary Films, Farallon Films, 2007).

74 **.7 Grams Uranium:** Eric Schlosser, interview by Dave Davies, "Nuclear 'Command and Control': A History of False Alarms and Near Catastrophes," *Fresh Air*, NPR, August 11, 2014.

74 **less than one kilogram:** Alex Wellerstein, "Kilotons per Kilogram," *Restricted Data: The Nuclear Secrecy Blog*, December 23, 2013, http://blog.nuclearsecrecy.com/2013/12/23/kilotons-per-kilogram/.

74 **"war without mercy":** John W. Dower, *War without Mercy: Race and Power in the Pacific War* (New York: Pantheon, 1986), 11.

74 **American firebombing:** Mark Selden, "American Fire Bombing and Atomic Bombing of Japan in History and Memory," *The Asia-Pacific Journal: Japan Focus* 14, no. 23 (December 1, 2016).

75 **"special moral obligation":** The full petition can be found in Harrison-Bundy File, folder 76, Records of the Office of the Chief of Engineers, RG 77, National Archives at Washington, DC, NARA.

75  Military authorities halted: Peter Wyden, *Day One: Before Hiroshima and After* (New York: Simon & Schuster, 1984), 176.

75  some general acting in the stead of another general: Yamaguchi, Yoshida, and Compel, "Can the Atomic Bombings on Japan Be Justified?," 27.

75  "no 'decision to use the atomic bomb'": Wellerstein, "What Journalists Should Know."

75  as efficiently as possible: Alex Wellerstein, "The Height of the Bomb," *Restricted Data: The Nuclear Secrecy Blog*, August 8, 2012, http://blog .nuclearsecrecy.com/2012/08/08/the-height-of-the-bomb/.

76  eighty-two thousand pairs of hands: Johnson and Jackson, *City Behind a Fence*, 168.

76  half a million people: Alex Wellerstein, "How Many People Worked on the Manhattan Project?," *Restricted Data: The Nuclear Secrecy Blog*, November 1, 2013, http://blog.nuclearsecrecy.com/2013/11/01/many -people-worked-manhattan-project/.

76  60 percent of the project's total expenditures: Kevin O'Neill, "Building the Bomb," in *Atomic Audit: The Costs and Consequences of U.S. Nuclear Weapons Since 1940*, ed. Stephen I. Schwartz (Washington, DC: Brookings Institution Press, 1998), 60.

77  dead and injured schoolchildren: Alex Wellerstein, "Counting the Dead at Hiroshima and Nagasaki," *Bulletin of the Atomic Scientists*, August 4, 2020, https://thebulletin.org/2020/08/counting-the-dead-at-hiroshima-and -nagasaki/.

77  Around eighty thousand: Seren Morris, "How Many People Died in Hiroshima and Nagasaki?," *Newsweek*, August 3, 2020.

## 7. Restricted Data

79  "one bomb on Hiroshima": Harry S. Truman, "Statement by the President of the United States," August 6, 1945, The Decision to Drop the Atomic Bomb collection, folder Press Release by the White House, series Subject File, Truman Papers, Truman Library, https://www.trumanlibrary.gov /library/research-files/press-release-white-house.

80  heard the news first: Descriptions of the reaction of Oak Ridgers to news of the bombing are in Johnson and Jackson, *City Behind a Fence*, 164–166; Freeman, *Longing for the Bomb*, 93–94; Kiernan, *Girls of Atomic City*, 249–268.

80  iconic photographs: Ed Westcott, *V-J Day at Jackson Square*, August 14, 1945, photograph, DOE Photograph Collection, Oak Ridge Public Library Digital Collections.

81  the first official statements: Robert Jay Lifton and Greg Mitchell, *Hiroshima in America: Fifty Years of Denial* (New York: Putnam, 1995), 7, 24.

81  the city began to empty: Johnson and Jackson, *City Behind a Fence*, 168–169.

81  machining of uranium weapons parts: Wilcox, *An Overview of the History of Y-12*, 22.

82  psychiatric service: Johnson and Jackson, *City Behind a Fence*, 109–110; Freeman, *Longing for the Bomb*, 90–92.

83  "acute anxiety neurosis": Eric Kent Clarke, "Psychiatric Problems at Oak Ridge," *American Journal of Psychiatry* 102, no. 4 (1946): 437–444, 438.

83  determined the file to be "restricted": For more on this process, see Matthew M. Aid, "Declassification in Reverse: The US Intelligence Community's Secret Historical Document Reclassification Program," *National Security Archive*, February 21, 2006.

84  Scotch tape or sealing wax: S. J. Vaughn, special agent, CIC, Memorandum to the Officer in Charge: Safeguarding Military Information, March 15, 1944, 4D0-326-97-001, box 1, folder 1, Security Division Files, Series 34, Records of the AEC, RG 326, NAA, NARA.

84  "Destruction of Classified Documents—1945": Memo found in 4D0-326-97-001, box 1, Security Division Files, Series 34, Records of the AEC, RG 326, NAA, NARA.

85  "waste burial ground here": Samuel R. Sapirie, manager of Oak Ridge Operations, Memo Route Slip, 4D0-326-97-001, box F-390, Assistant Manager for Operations Files, Series 86, Records of the AEC, RG 326, NAA, NARA.

88  Restricted Data: "42 U.S. Code § 2275—Receipt of Restricted Data," Legal Information Institute, Cornell Law School, https://www.law.cornell.edu/uscode/text/42/2275.

88  extreme and illogical classifications: Jennifer Sims, "A Half Life for Historical Formerly Restricted Data (FRD)," *Transforming Classification* (blog), National Archives / Public Interest Declassification Board, April 19, 2011, https://transforming-classification.blogs.archives.gov/2011/04/19/a-half-life-for-historical-formerly-restricted-data-frd/.

89  scientists have been pressured: William J. Broad, "Hydrogen Bomb Physicist's Book Runs Afoul of Energy Department," *New York Times*, March 23, 2015.

89  the heftier the perceived burden: Michael L. Slepian et al., "The Physical Burdens of Secrecy," *Journal of Experimental Psychology: General* 141, no. 4 (November 2012): 619–624.

89  the cognitive strain of secret-keeping: Julie D. Lane and Daniel M. Wegner, "The Cognitive Consequences of Secrecy," *Journal of Personality and Social Psychology* 69, no. 2 (1995): 237–253.

89  "unconscious conspiracy of silence": Thomas F. Howard, "Secrecy in the Fifties," in *These Are Our Voices: The Story of Oak Ridge 1942–1970*, ed. James Overholt (Oak Ridge, TN: Children's Museum of Oak Ridge, 1987), 278.

90 "far beyond the capacities": Eric K. Clarke, MD, chief psychiatrist, to Stafford L. Warren, Monthly Report for the Psychiatric Department: March 1945, April 10, 1945, 4NN-326-8505, box 54, Formerly Classified Correspondence Files, Series 8505, Records of the AEC, RG 326, NAA, NARA, 1–2.

90 "being human": Morris Zelditch, Family Welfare Association of America, director of war services, to district engineer, Clinton Engineering Works, *Report on Social Services in Oak Ridge*, 4NN-326-8505, box 54, Formerly Classified Correspondence Files, Series 8505, Records of the AEC, RG 326, NAA, NARA, 2.

90 "saturation point": Eric K. Clarke, MD, chief psychiatrist, to Stafford L. Warren, Quarterly Report for the Psychiatric Department: April–June 1945, July 6, 1945, 4NN-326-8505, box 54, Formerly Classified Correspondence Files, Series 8505, Records of the AEC, RG 326, NAA, NARA, 1.

90 treated in isolation: See Clarke, "Psychiatric Problems at Oak Ridge," 440.

90 warn the emperor of Japan: Kiernan, *Girls of Atomic City*, 197–201.

90 berated him: Johnson and Jackson, *City Behind a Fence*, 164.

91 "killing all those people": The story of Ruth Huddleston is told in D. Ray Smith, "Atomic Bombs Dropped 75 Years Ago: A 'Calutron Girl' Remembers," *Oak Ridger*, June 15, 2020.

91 "anticipated a flood of acute anxiety": Eric K. Clarke, MD, chief psychiatrist, to Stafford L. Warren, Quarterly Report for the Psychiatric Department: July–September 1945, November 5, 1945, 4NN-326-8505, box 54, Formerly Classified Correspondence Files, Series 8505, Records of the AEC, RG 326, NAA, NARA, 45. (Hereafter referred to as Clarke to Warren, Quarterly Report for the Psychiatric Department: July–September 1945, Series 8505, RG 326.)

91 through the eyes of six survivors: John Hersey, *Hiroshima* (New York: Vintage, 1989). First published as John Hersey, "Hiroshima," in *New Yorker* in 1946.

92 "glovelike pieces. . . . These are human beings": Ibid., 45.

92 "very few people even spoke": Ibid., 36.

92 "Hiroshima" was reprinted widely: On the reception of Hersey's "Hiroshima" and press restrictions on the coverage of Hiroshima, see Lifton and Mitchell, *Hiroshima in America*, 86–92.

92 "whoopee spirit": Ibid., 88.

92 Joseph Rotblat left Los Alamos: Joseph Rotblat, "Leaving the Bomb Project," *Bulletin of the Atomic Scientists* 41, no. 7 (1985): 16–19.

93 Leo Szilard: William Lanouette with Bela Silard, *Genius in the Shadows* (New York: Scribner, 1992), 259–280.

93 "devastation on an unimaginable scale": The text of the final petition is reproduced in Lanouette, *Genius in the Shadows*, 272–273.

93  **155 scientists:** Kai Bird and Martin J. Sherwin, *American Prometheus: The Triumph and Tragedy of J. Robert Oppenheimer* (New York: Vintage, 2006), 302.

93  **"not bothered by moral scruples":** Rotblat, "Leaving the Bomb Project," 18.

93  **"psychic numbing":** Lifton and Mitchell, *Hiroshima in America*, xvi.


# 8. Lying

95  **petty and accidental thefts:** Various memos found in 4D0-326-97-001, box 2, last folder: Personnel 2–7 Employment, Security Division Files, Series 34, Records of the AEC, RG 326, NAA, NARA. (Hereafter cited as various memos, Series 34, RG 326.)

95  **a statement of intent:** Editorial and Records Committee, Statement of Intent, September 14, 1945, Association of Oak Ridge Engineers and Scientists, records, box 1, folder 5, Hanna Holborn Gray Special Collections Research Center, University of Chicago Library.

95  **engineers at K-25 put it:** Cuthbert Daniel to Walter E. Cohn, November 6, 1945, Association of Oak Ridge Engineers and Scientists, records, box 1, folder 4, Hanna Holborn Gray Special Collections Research Center, University of Chicago Library.

96  **Association of Oak Ridge Engineers and Scientists:** This and subsequent history of the Association of Oak Ridge Engineers and Scientists from "Guide to the Association of Oak Ridge Engineers and Scientists Records 1945–1952," Hanna Holborn Gray Special Collections Research Center, University of Chicago Library, 2000, https://www.lib.uchicago.edu/e/scrc/findingaids/view.php?eadid=ICU.SPCL.AORES; Jessica Wang, *American Science in the Age of Anxiety: Scientists, Anticommunism, and the Cold War* (Chapel Hill, NC: University of North Carolina Press, 1999).

97  **"intend to continue this practice":** Quoted in Wang, *American Science in the Age of Anxiety*, 45.

97  **"Communist fronts":** Parnell Thomas as told to Stacy V. Jones, "Reds in Our Atom-Bomb Plants," *Liberty*, June 21, 1947, 90.

97  **an eager young polygrapher:** Unless otherwise noted, all history of the polygraph, in Oak Ridge and otherwise, comes from Ken Alder, *The Lie Detectors: The History of an American Obsession* (New York: Simon & Schuster, 2007).

98  **"insofar as possible":** Quoted in Ibid., 206.

99  **Subjects of the exams were rated:** Various memos, Series 34, RG 326.

99  **"uninterpretable charts":** S. R. Sapirie to F. P. Callaghan, *Report on Polygraph Program, April 1, 1952—September 20, 1952,* February 25, 1953, Records of the AEC, RG 326, National Archives at College Park, NARA, 70.

99 "Revelation of the mental stability": Carroll L. Wilson to J. C. Franklin, Continued and Extended Use of the Polygraph, October 10, 1947. Obtained through a FOIA request.

99 Latin *integritās*: *OED Online*, s.v. "integrity (*n.*),", updated June 2021.

99 questionable polygraph results: Various memos, Series 34, RG 326.

101 widely scientifically discredited: Stephen E. Fienberg and Paul C. Stern, "In Search of the Magic Lasso: The Truth About the Polygraph," *Statistical Science* 20, no. 3 (2005): 249–260.

101 whether the polygrapher believes: A conversation with Dr. Alan Zelicoff (February 10, 2014) helped inform my understanding of polygraphs.

102 by deterrence: Ken Alder, "America's Two Gadgets: Of Bombs and Polygraphs," *Isis* 98, no. 1 (2007): 124–137.

102 "enforce a new form of loyalty": Alder, *The Lie Detectors*, 207.

102 "confused his 'isms'": Ibid.

103 neither posed much of a threat: Various memos, Series 34, RG 326.

103 Operation Open Sesame: Freeman, *Longing for the Bomb*, 114–115.

103 "a recalibration so to speak": Alder, *The Lie Detectors*, 208.

104 Nearly half a century: Alder, "America's Two Gadgets."

105 Neurasthenia: David G. Schuster, *Neurasthenic Nation: America's Search for Health, Happiness, and Comfort, 1869–1920* (New Brunswick, NJ: Rutgers University Press, 2011), and correspondence with the author.

107 a capacity for just fourteen: Clarke to Warren, Quarterly Report for the Psychiatric Department: July–September 1945, Series 8505, RG 326, 3.

107 "association with the psychiatric service": Ibid., 12.

# 9. Practicing for Doomsday

108 May 5, 1955: Details about the Apple II / Operation Cue nuclear test (here and subsequently) come from Jean Ponton, Martha Wilkinson, and Stephen Rohrer, *Shot Apple 2: A Test of the TEAPOT Series, 5 May 1955*, report number AD-A-113538, DNA 6012F (Washington, DC: US Department of Defense, Defense Nuclear Agency, 1981); US Federal Civil Defense Administration (FCDA), *Cue for Survival: Operation Cue, AEC Nevada Test Site, May 5, 1955* (Washington, DC: US Government Printing Office, 1955); US AEC, "FCDA Proposal for an Open Shot During Operation Teapot," December 10, 1954, AEC 707/11, Washington, DC; and photographs of the test provided by the Nuclear Testing Archive, Las Vegas, NV.

110 Whether the beer: Alex Wellerstein, "Beer and the Apocalypse," *Restricted Data: The Nuclear Secrecy Blog*, September 5, 2012, http://blog.nuclear secrecy.com/2012/09/05/beer-and-the-apocalypse/.

110 **bomb-fried bacon:** Robert H. Philbeck and Delbert M. Doty, *The Effects of Nuclear Explosions on Meat and Meat Products* (Washington, DC: US FCDA and US Food and Drug Administration, 1956).

110 **"colonized the lived experience":** Patrick B. Sharp, *Savage Perils: Racial Frontiers and Nuclear Apocalypse in American Culture* (Norman: University of Oklahoma Press, 2007), 170.

112 **"shot book":** Information on numbers and yields of tests from National Nuclear Security Administration Nevada Field Office, US DOE, *United States Nuclear Tests July 1945 through September 1992*, DOE/NV—209-REV 16 (Las Vegas: 2015).

115 **Apple II was delayed ten days:** Joint Test Organization (JTO), *Operation Teapot: Report of the Test Manager, Spring 1955*, unclassified extract prepared for Defense Nuclear Agency, accession number A995154 (Washington, DC: 1981).

115 **claimed by them still:** Ian Zabarte, "The Sale of Yucca Mountain Was an Attack," *Indian Country Today*, October 2, 2015; Associated Press, "Native American Land Activist Carrie Dann Dies in Nevada," January 11, 2021, https://apnews.com/article/mountains-reno-nevada-nuclear-waste-native-americans-516fc568a9f8f8afdbc46da31abfb39a.

116 **Task Force Razor:** Ponton, Wilkinson, and Rohrer, *Shot Apple 2*, 11–13.

116 **"face away from the blast":** *Operation Cue*, produced by US FCDA, 1955, film.

117 **"rise like a gas balloon":** Joint Test Organization, *Continental Atomic Tests: Background Information for Observers*, 1955, accession number NV0014474, Nuclear Testing Archive, Las Vegas, NV, 7.

118 **Las Vegas casino hotels:** Ibid., 18.

118 **this city was once illuminated:** On Las Vegas and nuclear testing, see US AEC, *Atomic Tests in Nevada—March 1957* (Washington, DC: Government Printing Office, 1957), accession number NV0006372, Nuclear Testing Archive, Las Vegas, NV; Anthony Turkevich, "Assuring Public Safety in Continental Weapons Tests: AEC Thirteenth Semiannual Report," *Bulletin of the Atomic Scientists* IX, no. 3 (1953): 85–89; National Endowment for the Humanities, "Nuclear Nevada," July 31, 2011, https://www.neh.gov/news/nuclear-nevada; PBS American Experience, "Atomic Tourism in Nevada," Las Vegas: An Unconventional History, accessed June 29, 2022, https://www.pbs.org/wgbh/american experience/features/atomic-tourism-nevada/.

119 **"unlimited ceiling":** Ponton, Wilkinson, and Rohrer, *Shot Apple 2*, 14.

122 **footage has been dubbed:** Alex Wellerstein, "The Sound of the Bomb (1953)," *Restricted Data: The Nuclear Secrecy Blog*, July 13, 2012, http://blog.nuclearsecrecy.com/2012/07/13/the-sound-of-the-bomb-1953/.

122 maps of their hometowns: US FCDA, "Observer Booklet: Operation Cue," redraft, accession number NV0323292, Nuclear Testing Archive, Las Vegas, NV.

123 two hundred other companies: FCDA, *Cue for Survival*, 159–162.

123 framed as both victims and heroes: Sharp, *Savage Perils*.

123 those most likely to be victims: Nathan Hare, "Can Negroes Survive a Nuclear War?," *Negro Digest*, May 1963; Erica X Eisen, "Blackness and the Bomb," *Boston Review*, June 29, 2021.

123 unable to enforce racial hierarchies: Eisen, "Blackness and the Bomb"; Sharp, *Savage Perils*, 198, 206.

123 Downtown Shopping Center: John Huotari, "Photos: Downtown Shopping Center," *Oak Ridge Today*, December 30, 2014.

124 knock a person to their knees: FCDA, "Observer Booklet."

124 the events that followed: Ponton, Wilkinson, and Rohrer, *Shot Apple 2*, 34; JTO, *Operation Teapot*, 108.

125 "It must be borne in mind": *Operation Cue*, US FCDA.

126 Daytime photographs: Peter Kuran, *How to Photograph an Atomic Bomb* (Santa Clarita, CA: VCE, 2006), 71.

128 the Apple II cloud: Ponton, Wilkinson, and Rohrer, *Shot Apple 2*, 14, 62.

128 "allay unfounded fear": JTO, *Operation Teapot*, 86–87.

128 "blinded by fear of the unknown": Joint Test Organization, *Atomic Tests in the Nevada Test Site Region* (Washington, DC: US Government Printing Office, 1955), 32.

128 "make you quite sick," "apparently made good recoveries": Ibid., 34.

129 "uniformly over the earth's surface": Ibid., 17.

129 "too small to measure": "Very Slight 'Fallout' Noted," *Oak Ridger*, May 10, 1955.

129 "does not constitute a serious hazard": Joint Test Organization, *Atomic Tests in the Nevada Test Site Region*, 17.

131 more than seven hundred pigs: Defense Atomic Support Agency, *Operation Plumbbob: Technical Summary of Military Effects, Programs 1–9*, 1962, unclassified extract prepared for Defense Nuclear Agency, WT-1445 (EX) (Washington, DC: 1979).

132 nuclear apocalypse to the frontier: Sharp, *Savage Perils*, 199.

132 There was even a yearning: Ibid., 193; Eisen, "Blackness and the Bomb."

133 racked with chills and vomiting: Accounts of downwinders, especially Patricia George and Virginia Sanchez, interview by Mary Palevsky, September 11, 2004, transcript, Nevada Test Site Oral History Project, University of Nevada, Las Vegas, NV; see also Michael Janofsky, "Cold War Chill Lingers Downwind from a Nuclear Bomb-Testing Site," *New York Times*, January 11, 1994; Patricia George and Abel Russ, "Nuclear Testing and Native Peoples," *Reimagine*, accessed May 6, 2021, https://reimaginerpe.org/node/165.

133 **Among the most heavily exposed:** Eric Frohmberg et al., "The Assessment of Radiation Exposures in Native American Communities from Nuclear Weapons Testing in Nevada," *Risk Analysis* 20, no. 1 (2000): 101–112; Abel Russ et al., "Native American Exposure to 131 Iodine from Nuclear Weapons Testing in Nevada," *Human and Ecological Risk Assessment* 11, no. 5 (2005): 1047–1063.

133 **"We were exposed":** Ian Zabarte, "A Message from the Most Bombed Nation on Earth," *Al Jazeera*, August 29, 2020.

134 **RECA has awarded:** Numbers as of March 2, 2022, "Awards to Date," Radiation Exposure Compensation Act, US Department of Justice, https://www.justice.gov/civil/common/reca.

134 **lower rates than other populations:** Tamar Sarai Davis, "Victims of the US Uranium Boom Pay Substantial Costs despite What They're Owed by the US Government," *Prism*, December 14, 2021.

134 **reached the entire continental United States:** Steven Simon, André Bouville, and Charles Land, "Fallout from Nuclear Weapons Tests and Cancer Risks," *American Scientist* 94, no. 1 (2006): 48–57; F. Owen Hoffman, A. Iulian Apostoaei, and Brian A. Thomas, "A Perspective on Public Concerns about Exposure to Fallout from the Production and Testing of Nuclear Weapons," *Health Physics* 82, no. 5 (2002): 736–748.

135 **"to be used for military experimentation":** Robert Jacobs, "The Bravo Test and the Death and Life of the Global Ecosystem in the Early Anthropocene," *The Asia-Pacific Journal: Japan Focus* 13, no. 29 (July 20, 2015).

135 **fingerprints of atmospheric testing:** Robert Krulwich, "How A-Bomb Testing Changed Our Trees," NPR, November 16, 2008, https://www.npr.org/templates/story/story.php?storyId=96750869; GrrlScientist, "How Nuclear Fallout Helped Identify Longest-Lived Vertebrate on Earth," *Forbes*, August 12, 2016; Nicholas Wade, "Heart Muscle Renewed Over Lifetime, Study Finds," *New York Times*, April 2, 2009.

135 **Our stratosphere:** Sarah Zielinski, "Plutonium from Nuclear Tests Lingers in the Atmosphere," *Smithsonian Magazine*, January 7, 2014.

136 **Sedan:** Richard L. Miller, *The US Atlas of Nuclear Fallout 1951–1970 Vol. I*, Abridged General Reader Ed. (The Woodlands, TX: Legis Corporation, 2002), 329–340; US Department of Health and Human Services, US Centers for Disease Control and Prevention, and the National Cancer Institute, "Chapter 3: Estimation of Doses from Fallout" in *Report on the Health Consequences to the American Population from Nuclear Weapons Tests Conducted by the United States and Other Nations* (Atlanta, 2005), 50.

## 10. Fusion

144 "arousing the hope of mankind": J. Robert Oppenheimer et al., Enclosure 1, Statement Appended to the Report of the General Advisory Committee, October 30, 1949, *Foreign Relations of the United States, 1949, National Security Affairs, Foreign Economic Policy, Volume I*, Document 211, eds. Neal H. Petersen, Ralph R. Goodwin, William Z. Slany, and Marvin W. Kranz (Washington: Government Printing Office, 1976).

144 "an evil thing considered in any light": E. Fermi and I. Rabi, Enclosure 2, Statement Appended to the Report of the General Advisory Committee, October 30, 1949, *Foreign Relations of the United States, 1949, National Security Affairs, Foreign Economic Policy, Volume I*, Document 211, eds. Neal H. Petersen, Ralph R. Goodwin, William Z. Slany, and Marvin W. Kranz (Washington: Government Printing Office, 1976).

145 "so-called hydrogen or superbomb": Harry S. Truman, Statement by the President on the Hydrogen Bomb, January 31, 1950, The American Presidency Project, https://www.presidency.ucsb.edu/documents/statement-the -president-the-hydrogen-bomb.

145 top priority for more than a decade: The history of lithium separation at Y-12 was gathered from Wilcox, *An Overview of the History of Y-12*; interviews with the author; and numerous articles by Y-12 historian D. Ray Smith. See "Historically Speaking: Y-12 Plant Prepares to Separate Lithium Isotopes," *Oak Ridger*, March 13, 2009.

148 the first fusion bomb: Richard Rhodes, *Dark Sun: The Making of the Hydrogen Bomb* (New York: Simon & Schuster, 1995), 509–510.

148 high levels of radioactive contamination: Dan Zak, "The Marshall Islands, Once a U.S. Nuclear Test Site, Face Oblivion Again," *Washington Post*, November 27, 2015.

148 "slaughter a million people": Kenneth W. Ford, *Building the H Bomb: A Personal History* (Hackensack, NJ: World Scientific Publishing Company, 2015), 1n3.

149 "writhe convulsively": John F. Hogerton, ed., *Atoms for Peace: USA 1958* (United States AEC, 1958), 102.

150 "When you're high it's tremendous": Kay Redfield Jamison, *An Unquiet Mind: A Memoir of Moods and Madness* (New York: Vintage, 1995), 67.

150 "cosmic relatedness": Ibid., 37.

## 11. Phantom

165 "the crypt": Nicolas Abraham and Maria Torok, "'The Lost Object-Me': Notes on Identification within the Crypt," *Psychoanalytic Inquiry* 4, no. 2 (1984): 221–242.

166 *nescience*; "familiar and strange": Esther Rashkin, "Review: Tools for a New Psychoanalytic Literary Criticism: The Work of Abraham and Torok by Nicolas Abraham and Maria Torok," *Diacritics* 18, no. 4 (1988), 41.

# 13. Half-Life

180 "persist through several generations": Abraham and Torok, "'The Lost Object-Me,'" 223n1.

182 repression of memory around collective historical trauma: Gabriele Schwab, "Writing against Memory and Forgetting," *Literature and Medicine* 25, no. 1 (2006): 95–121; Gabriele Schwab, "Haunting Legacies: Trauma in Children of Perpetrators," *Postcolonial Studies* 7, no. 2 (2004): 177–95.

182 "pushed into the cultural unconscious": Schwab, "Haunting Legacies," 183.

182 "psychic deformations": Ibid., 181.

182 "cycles of violence": Schwab, "Writing against Memory and Forgetting," 100.

183 fight against racism and colonialism: For more on the antinuclear movement among Black cultural leaders, see Vincent J. Intondi, *African Americans against the Bomb* (Stanford, CA: Stanford University Press, 2015).

183 "a raw nerve": Lifton and Mitchell, *Hiroshima in America*, xi.

184 "Their wrath will be terrible": Arundhati Roy, "The End of Imagination," *Frontline*, August 1, 1998.

184 serve to further encrypt: Schwab, "Writing against Memory and Forgetting," 108–110.

186 the DOE convened panels: Peter C. van Wyck, *Signs of Danger: Waste, Trauma, and Nuclear Threat* (Minneapolis: University of Minnesota Press, 2005); Roman Mars and Matthew Kielty, hosts, "Ten Thousand Years," *99% Invisible* (podcast), May 12, 2014.

187 "must be kept and always disclosed": Wyck, *Signs of Danger*, 24, 5.

# 14. Mercury

191 Lithium-6 was called "aspen": ChemRisk, *Mercury Releases from Lithium Enrichment at the Oak Ridge Y-12 Plant—A Reconstruction of Historical Releases and Off-Site Doses and Health Risks*, task 2 report of the Oak Ridge Dose Reconstruction, vol. 2 (Nashville: Tennessee Department of Health, 1999), 4–3.

191 ancient human magic: See, for example, Michael S. Bank, "Industrial Use of Mercury in the Ancient World," in *Mercury in the Environment:*

*Pattern and Process*, ed. Michael S. Bank (Berkeley: University of California Press, 2012), 19–24.

191 **COLEX (column exchange) process:** Scott C. Brooks and George R. Southworth, "History of Mercury Use and Environmental Contamination at the Oak Ridge Y-12 Plant," *Environmental Pollution* 159, no. 1 (2011): 219–228; D. Ray Smith, "Historically Speaking: Y-12 Lithium-6 Production," *Oak Ridger*, April 17, 2009; Union Carbide Corporation Nuclear Division (UCCND), 1983 Mercury Task Force, *Mercury at Y-12: A Study of Mercury Use at the Y-12 Plant, Accountability, and Impacts on Y-12 Workers and the Environment, 1950–1983*, Martin Marietta for US DOE, Y/EX-21/del rev, Records Center, Y-12 Plant, Oak Ridge, TN, August 18, 1983, 42–44 (hereafter UCCND, Mercury Task Force, *Mercury at Y-12*).

192 **dog tags:** Memories of dog tags, civil defense exercises, and shift-change whistles gathered from the public Facebook group "I Remember When in Oak Ridge, TN . . . Favorite Memories."

193 **Between 1950 and 1963:** Descriptions of mercury leaks here and subsequently from ChemRisk, *Mercury Releases*; Brooks and Southworth, "History of Mercury Use"; Frank Munger, "Secret Cold War Project Results in Largest US Environmental Cleanup," *Knoxville News Sentinel*, December 11, 2011; UCCND, Mercury Task Force, *Mercury at Y-12*; Agency for Toxic Substances and Disease Registry (ATSDR), *Evaluation of Y-12 Mercury Releases, U.S. Department of Energy, Oak Ridge Reservation* (Atlanta: US Department of Health and Human Services, 2012).

193 **eleven billion thermometers:** O'Neill, "Building the Bomb," 42n12.

194 **Workers remember wading:** This anecdote is frequently repeated by knowledgeable sources and was reported in Randell Beck and Terry Williams, "Workers Live and Die with Poison," *Knoxville Journal*, November 30, 1983.

195 **Swallow elemental mercury:** Information about the health effects of mercury exposure primarily from ATSDR, *Evaluation of Y-12 Mercury Releases*, appendix D.

195 **When I requested documents from Y-12:** Documents described here are from the Y-12 Mercury Task Force Files, obtained by request from the DOE Information Center, Oak Ridge, TN.

196 **methylmercury exposure and heart disease:** Giuseppe Genchi et al., "Mercury Exposure and Heart Diseases." *International Journal of Environmental Research and Public Health* 14, no. 1 (January 12, 2017).

196 **"he was everywhere":** Nicholas Culpeper quoted in Allison B. Kavey, "Mercury Falling: Gender Malleability and Sexual Fluidity in Early Modern Popular Alchemy," in *Chymists and Chymistry: Studies in the History of Alchemy and Early Modern Chemistry*, ed. Lawrence M. Principe (Sagamore Beach, MA: Watson Publishing International, 2007), 131.

196 "with our fingers": Bart Bond, interviewed by author, October 2, 2015.

197 to fall on homes and gardens: ChemRisk, *Mercury Releases*, ES-6.

197 metallic beads of mercury: J. Linn Allen, "Atomic Research Casts Shadow on Tennessee Town," *Chicago Tribune*, February 18, 2001.

197 a foot under water: ChemRisk, *Mercury Releases*, 6–12.

198 "Hypomania is mania with a tether": Linda Logan, "The Problem with How We Treat Bipolar Disorder," *New York Times*, April 26, 2013.

199 "changes of mood or mind": *OED Online*, s.v. "mercurial (*n.* and *adj.*)," updated June 2022.

201 nearly two million pounds could not be accounted for: ChemRisk, *Mercury Releases*, 3–6.

201 the Gough brothers: Robert M. Press, "A Look at Mercury Spill at DOE Plant," *Christian Science Monitor*, February 7, 1984.

202 "peer pressure to conform": Ronald Smothers, "Discovery of Mercury Contamination Prompts Dispute in Oak Ridge, Tenn.," *New York Times*, May 26, 1983.

202 "an atmosphere of high urgency": UCCND, Mercury Task Force, *Mercury at Y-12*, 207.

205 "ambiguous, incomplete, or misleading": Congressional panel quoted in Press, "A Look at Mercury Spill."

205 more than 60,000 pounds above: ChemRisk, *Mercury Releases*, ES-2-ES-4.

205 "exposure pathways": Ibid., 6-1—6-26.

205 The study concluded: Oak Ridge Health Agreement Steering Panel (ORHASP), *Releases of Contaminants from Oak Ridge Facilities and Risks to Public Health*, DOE/OR/21981-00 (Nashville, TN: Tennessee Department of Health, 1999), 10–11.

206 mercury cleanup efforts: ATSDR, *Evaluation of Y-12 Mercury Releases*, 26–29; Susan Arnold Kaplan, *Impacts on Oak Ridge Landowners of Off-Site Releases to the Environment from the Y-12 Plant and Associated Long-Term Stewardship Issues* (Knoxville, TN: Institute for Technology, Social, and Policy Awareness, 2005), 17; Frank Munger, "Mercury Discharges Decline at Y-12; Much Work Remains," *Atomic City Underground* (blog), *Knoxville News Sentinel*, November 5, 2015, http:// knoxblogs.com/atomiccity/2015/11/05/mercury-discharges-decline-at -y-12-much-work-remains/.

206 But today, mercury: Frank Munger, "Thanks in Part to Mercury, Y-12 Plant Has Most Studied Creek in Tennessee," *Knoxville News Sentinel*, December 19, 2011; ATSDR, *Evaluation of Y-12 Mercury Releases*, 26.

206 mercury treatment plant: US DOE, Office of Environmental Management, "Crews Mobilize to Build Mercury Treatment Facility in Oak Ridge," July 30, 2019, https://www.energy.gov/em/articles/crews-mobilize-build -mercury-treatment-facility-oak-ridge.

206 **thriving in the cleaner water:** Munger, "Thanks in Part to Mercury"; Vincent Gabrielle, "How Artificial Streams inside This Oak Ridge Lab Are Making Our Nation's Water Safer," *Knoxville News Sentinel*, May 4, 2021.

207 **Mercury can be found:** ChemRisk, *Mercury Releases*, ES-8; URS | CH2M Oak Ridge, *2015 Remediation Effectiveness Report: Data and Evaluations*, DOE/OR/01-2675&D2 (Oak Ridge, TN: US DOE, Office of Environmental Management, 2015), 7–14; Tennessee Department of Environment and Conservation, Division of Remediation (TDEC), *FY 2018–2019 Environmental Monitoring Report* (Oak Ridge, TN: 2020), xvii.

207 **seventy-six metric tons:** C. R. Olsen et al., *Transport and Accumulation of Cesium-137 and Mercury in the Clinch River and Watts Bar Reservoir System*, ORNL/ER-7 (Oak Ridge, TN: Oak Ridge National Laboratory, 1990).

207 **not a current concern:** TDEC, "Bacteriological and Fishing Advisories," February 24, 2022, https://www.tn.gov/environment/program-areas /wr-water-resources/watershed-stewardship/bacteriological-and-fishing -advisories.html.

207 **mercury continues to stream:** Robert Alvarez, "Y-12: Poster Child for a Dysfunctional Nuclear Weapons Complex," *Bulletin of the Atomic Scientists*, August 4, 2014.

207 **Lithium has been known:** Jaime Lowe, "I Don't Believe in God, but I Believe in Lithium," *New York Times Magazine*, June 25, 2015; Anna Fels, "Should We All Take a Bit of Lithium?," *New York Times*, September 13, 2014.

## 15. Bombed without a Bang

211 **the contaminated area included:** Susan Thomas, Laura Frank, and Anne Paine, "Oak Ridge Contamination Even Worse Than Feared," *Tennessean* (Nashville), August 17, 1997; Superfund Site: Oak Ridge Reservation," Environmental Protection Agency, accessed March 6, 2022, https:// cumulis.epa.gov/supercpad/SiteProfiles/index.cfm?fuseaction=second .Cleanup&id=0404152#bkground.

212 **"major zone for contaminant accumulation":** Olsen et al., *Transport and Accumulation*, 9.

212 **seventy thousand nuclear bombs:** O'Neill, "Building the Bomb," 102.

212 **five thousand warheads:** Arms Control Association, "Nuclear Weapons: Who Has What at a Glance," updated January 2022, https://www .armscontrol.org/factsheets/Nuclearweaponswhohaswhat.

212 **"witch's cauldron":** The Oak Ridge Education Project, *A Citizen's Guide to Oak Ridge*, 2nd ed. (Knoxville, TN: The Foundation for Global Sustainability, 1992), 9–10.

214 **menacing phone calls and veiled threats:** On this common perception among activists, see Tamara L. Mix, Sherry Cable, and Thomas E. Shriver, "Social Control and Contested Environmental Illness: The Repression of Ill Nuclear Weapons Workers," *Human Ecology Review* 16, no. 2 (2009): 172–183, 178–179; Harper, "Secrets Revealed," 55.

214 **some residents were likely harmed:** ORHASP, *Releases of Contaminants*, 6.

216 **1993 CNN broadcast:** David Lewis, correspondent, "A Poisoned Atmosphere," *CNN*, February 23, 1993. The story of Dr. Reid is recounted widely. See, for example, Dick Thompson, "Living Happily Near a Nuclear Trash Heap," *Time*, May 11, 1992; Sherry Cable, Thomas E. Shriver, and Tamara L. Mix, "Risk Society and Contested Illness: The Case of Nuclear Weapons Workers," *American Sociological Review* 73, no. 3 (2008): 380–401, 395.

218 **"put at risk without their knowledge":** Energy Employees Occupational Illness Compensation Program Act of 2000, Pub. L. No. 106–398, §1 [div. C, title XXXVI, §3601], 114 Stat. 1654, 1654A-495 (Oct. 30, 2000).

218 **Since the inception of the act:** US Department of Labor, Office of Worker's Compensation Programs, "EEOICP Program Statistics," updated February 27, 2022, https://www.dol.gov/owcp/energy/regs/compliance /weeklystats.htm.

219 **spotty and sometimes falsified records:** Jim Morris and Jamie Smith Hopkins, "Ailing, Angry Nuclear-Weapons Workers Fight for Compensation," *Center for Public Integrity*, December 11, 2015.

219 **A 2015 McClatchy investigation:** Rob Hotakainen et al., "Irradiated: The Hidden Legacy of 70 Years of Atomic Weaponry," *McClatchy DC* website, December 11, 2015.

219 **Government Accountability Office criticized the DOE:** US Government Accountability Office, *Testimony Before the Subcommittee on Oversight and Investigations, Committee on Energy and Commerce, House of Representatives: Observations on DOE's Management Challenges and Steps Taken to Address Them*, GAO-13-767T, July 24, 2013, 9.

219 **multiple documented cases:** Hotakainen et al., "Irradiated."

220 **submitted as testimony to Congress:** *Energy Employees Occupational Illness Compensation Program Act: Hearings before the Committee on Energy and Natural Resources*, 108th Cong., 1st sess. (2003).

221 **some of the highest paying in the region:** East Tennessee Economic Council, *U.S. Department of Energy FY 2017: Economic Impact in Tennessee* (Oak Ridge, TN: ETEC, 2018), 6.

222 **criticism tantamount to blasphemy:** Cable, Shriver, and Mix, "Risk Society and Contested Illness."

222 "remediation excesses": Tamara L. Mix and Thomas E. Shriver, "Neighbors, Nuisances and Noxious Releases: Community Conflict and Environmental Hazards in the Atomic City," *The Social Science Journal* 44 (January 2007): 630–644, 636.

222 reassigned to hazardous tasks: Mix, Cable, and Shriver, "Social Control and Contested Environmental Illness," 178.

222 People who had sought medical care: Thomas E. Shriver, Deborah A. White, and AlemSeghed Kebede, "Power, Politics, and the Framing of Environmental Illness," *Sociological Inquiry* 68, no. 4 (1998): 458–475.

223 detailed descriptions of collection methods: TDEC, *FY 2018–2019 Environmental Monitoring Report.*

223 "Good news: No rad deer": Frank Munger, "Good News: No Rad Deer," *Atomic City Underground* (blog), *Knoxville News Sentinel*, November 6, 2015, http://knoxblogs.com/atomiccity/2015/11/06/good-news-no-rad -deer/.

223 "A not-so-hot deer season": Frank Munger, "A Not-So-Hot Deer Season: Only One Kept for Rad Reasons," *Atomic City Underground* (blog), *Knoxville News Sentinel*, December 12, 2015, http://knoxblogs.com /atomiccity/2015/12/15/a-not-so-hot-deer-season-only-one-kept-for-rad -reasons/.

223 244 killed: "Deer Hunts," Oak Ridge Reservation Hunt, Oak Ridge National Laboratory, accessed March 6, 2022, https://oakridge reservationhunts.ornl.gov/deer-hunts/.

223 levels can fluctuate: Ben Pounds, "Dispute over Funding for Oak Ridge TDEC Office," *Oak Ridger*, December 12, 2019.

224 a report by the East Tennessee Economic Council: East Tennessee Economic Council, *U.S. Department of Energy FY 2020: Economic Impact in Tennessee* (Oak Ridge, TN: ETEC, 2021), 4, 8.

226 the pipes cross Y-12: John Huotari, "New Water Plant Could Cost More than $40 Million," *Oak Ridge Today*, November 13, 2016.

227 "some people were hurt": ORHASP, *Releases of Contaminants*, 6.

227 But the subsequent assessments: For a summary of the ATSDR's findings, see Agency for Toxic Substances and Disease Registry, "Overview: Oak Ridge Reservation," updated May 30, 2012, https://www.atsdr.cdc.gov /sites/oakridge/overview.html. For a summary of the TDH studies and recommendations, see Tennessee Department of Health, "Oak Ridge Health Studies," accessed May 6, 2022, https://www.tn.gov/health/cedep /environmental/oak-ridge-health-studies.html; see also ORHASP, *Releases of Contaminants*.

227 The DOE, an agency with a pattern of withholding: Kaplan, *Impacts on Oak Ridge Landowners*.

228 any person who drank cow or goat milk: F. Owen Hoffman, A. Iulian Apostoaei, and Brian A. Thomas, "A Perspective on Public Concerns

about Exposure to Fallout from the Production and Testing of Nuclear Weapons," *Health Physics* 82, no. 5 (2002): 736–748, 746. Individuals can calculate their own risk of thyroid cancer from fallout exposure on the "Thyroid Dose and Risk Calculator for Nuclear Weapons Fallout for the US Population," National Cancer Institute, Division of Epidemiology & Genetics, https://radiationcalculators.cancer.gov/fallout/.

229 **turned up in monitoring wells:** Frank Munger, "Tracking Groundwater Pollution beyond DOE's Boundaries," *Atomic City Underground* (blog), *Knoxville News Sentinel*, September 2, 2014, http://knoxblogs .com/atomiccity/2014/09/02/tracking-groundwater-pollution-beyond -boundaries-expanded-tests-planned/.

230 **Groundwater contamination:** For more on the groundwater challenges and monitoring efforts in Oak Ridge, see URS | CH2M Oak Ridge LLC and Science Applications International Corporation, *Groundwater Strategy for the U.S. Department of Energy, Oak Ridge Reservation*, DOE/ OR/01-2628/V1&D2 (Oak Ridge, TN: US DOE, Office of Environmental Management, 2014).

230 **"mature contaminant plumes":** UT-Battalle LLC, Consolidated Nuclear Security, URS | CH2M Oak Ridge LLC, James Rochelle, Ben Rogers, and Katara Vasquez, *Oak Ridge Reservation Annual Site Environmental Report: 2014*, DOE/ORO-2509 (Oak Ridge, TN: US DOE, Office of Environmental Management, 2016), 3–85.

230 **thought to be a hydraulic boundary:** Munger, "Tracking Groundwater Pollution"; URS | CH2M Oak Ridge LLC and Science Applications International Corporation, *Groundwater Strategy*; Frank Munger, "Is ORNL's Nuke Waste Migrating Off-Site?," *Atomic City Underground* (blog), *Knoxville News Sentinel*, March 9, 2009, http://knoxblogs.com /atomiccity/wp-content/uploads/sites/11/2009/11/is_ornls_nuke_waste _migrating.html.

230 **"not well understood":** URS | CH2M Oak Ridge LLC and Science Applications International Corporation, *Groundwater Strategy*, 3–6.

230 **groundwater migration is not under control:** "Superfund Site: Oak Ridge Reservation – Health & Environment," Environmental Protection Agency, accessed July 26, 2022, https://cumulis.epa.gov/supercpad /SiteProfiles/index.cfm?fuseaction=second.Healthenv&id=0404152

231 **One of the sociological studies I read:** Mix and Shriver, "Neighbors, Nuisances and Noxious Releases."

232 **"killing my children by living here":** Wendy Walker quoted in Susan Thomas, Laura Frank, and Anne Paine, "16 Sick Kids on One Street Alarms Officials, Residents in Oak Ridge," *Tennessean* (Nashville), November 9, 1997.

232 **illnesses were within a normal range:** Laura Frank and Susan Thomas, "Kids' Ills Normal, Joint Study Finds," *Tennessean* (Nashville), January 31, 1999.

233 **op-eds for the *Oak Ridger*:** L. C. Gipson, L. C. Manley, and Al Chambles, "Guest Column: Reflections on Images of Contamination and Illnesses in Scarboro Neighborhood," *Oak Ridger*, December 2, 1998; Gipson, Manley, and Chambles, "Guest Column: 'Real Consequences' Result of Cries of Contamination, Illnesses," *Oak Ridger*, December 3, 1998; Gipson, Manley, and Chambles, "Guest Column: Scarboro Residents Make Appeal for Accuracy," *Oak Ridger*, December 4, 1998.

234 **ATSDR released its report:** ATSDR, *Y-12 Uranium Releases, U.S. Department of Energy, Oak Ridge Reservation* (Atlanta: US Department of Health and Human Services, 2004).

234 **flouting recommendations:** Kaplan, *Impacts on Oak Ridge Landowners*, 50–58.

234 **community concerns section:** ATSDR, *Y-12 Uranium Releases*, 102, 111, 114.

234 **"real or imaginary":** Gipson, Manley, and Chambles, "Scarboro Residents Make Appeal for Accuracy."

234 **"what has transpired in this community":** Kaplan, *Impacts on Oak Ridge Landowners*, xiii.

235 **The TDEC reports are full:** TDEC, *FY 2018–2019 Environmental Monitoring Report*.

237 **"organized around the environmental hazards":** Cable, Shriver, and Mix, "Risk Society and Contested Illness," 380.

237 **"tactics to deny illnesses":** Ibid., 398.

239 **"The book of accounts is never closed":** Kai Erikson, *A New Species of Trouble: The Human Experience of Modern Disasters* (New York: Norton, 1994), 148.

241 **EPA declared cleanup complete:** Bob Fowler, "It's a Wrap: EPA Calls Ash Spill Cleanup Complete," *Knoxville News Sentinel*, June 5, 2015.

# 16. Hiroshima

247 **used as research subjects:** Maya Todeschini, "Illegitimate Sufferers: A-Bomb Victims, Medical Science, and the Government," *Daedalus* 128, no. 2 (Spring 1999): 67–100; M. Susan Lindee, *Suffering Made Real: American Science and the Survivors at Hiroshima* (Chicago: University of Chicago Press, 1994).

247 **A-bomb orphans:** Yotsumoto Jun, "'Helping Hands': The Lives of Atomic Bomb Orphans," *NHK World*, January 13, 2020; Shoso Kawamoto testimony in Soka Gakkai Hiroshima Peace Committee, *Hiroshima August 6, 1945: A Silence Broken* (Tokyo: Daisanbunmei-sha, 2014).

247 hide from the shame: Sakae Toda, "Hibakusha: Man Who Hid Hiroshima Experience from Son Writing Book for Next Generation," *Mainichi Daily News*, August 8, 2019.

248 "the communicative performance itself": Lisa Yoneyama, *Hiroshima Traces: Time, Space, and the Dialectics of Memory* (Berkeley: University of California Press, 1999), 91.

248 reject as reductive: Ibid., 127.

251 "in the name of reconciliation": Brian Byrnes, "Truman Grandson Plants Seeds of Reconciliation," *McClatchy DC* website, November 23, 2012.

253 "scene of a natural disaster": Ran Zwigenberg, "Never Again: Hiroshima, Auschwitz and the Politics of Commemoration," *The Asia-Pacific Journal: Japan Focus* 13, no. 3 (January 19, 2015).

254 begins and ends on August 6: A conversation with the artist Shunya Asami helped clarify my thinking along these lines, as did Yoneyama's *Hiroshima Traces*.

254 short historical film: *The Town That Never Was*, directed by Elain Rhue (Los Alamos, NM: Bradbury Science Museum), https://www.youtube.com /watch?v=9LLzBWQY7m0.

255 "disturb public tranquility": Monica Braw, *The Atomic Bomb Suppressed: American Censorship in Occupied Japan* (Armonk, NY: M. E. Sharpe, 1991), 41.

255 Sasaki Sadako: Sadako's story comes from the plaques in the Hiroshima Peace Memorial Museum and Masahiro Sasaki and Sue DiCicco, *The Complete Story of Sadako Sasaki and the Thousand Paper Cranes* (North Clarendon, VT: Tuttle Publishing, 2020).

256 ten million cranes: "Children's Peace Monument," Hiroshima for Global Peace, accessed March 5, 2022, https://hiroshimaforpeace.com/en /childrens-peace-monument/.

259 "will despise their humanity": Kenzaburo Oe, *Hiroshima Notes*, trans. David L. Swain and Toshi Yonezawa (New York: Grove Press, 1996). Originally published as *Hiroshima Noto* (Tokyo: Iwanami Shoten, 1965), 115.

259 "all human beings alive today": Ibid., 118.

259 Kawamoto Shoso: I have supplemented our interview with Shoso's story as printed in Soka Gakkai, *Hiroshima August 6, 1945*.

259 measurable genetic effects: Nori Nakamura, "Genetic Effects of Radiation in Atomic-Bomb Survivors and Their Children: Past, Present and Future," *Journal of Radiation Research* 47, Suppl. B (2006).

259 mistrust of the scientists: Todeschini, "Illegitimate Sufferers"; Lindee, *Suffering Made Real*.

266 mistreatment of Korean victims: Kurt W. Tong, "Korea's Forgotten Atomic Bomb Victims," *Bulletin of Concerned Asian Scholars* 23, no. 1 (1991): 31–37; Adam Taylor, "The Forgotten Story of Tens of Thousands of Koreans Who Died in Hiroshima," *Washington Post*, May 25, 2016.

266 removing the bombing from the context of World War II: Yoneyama, *Hiroshima Traces.*

266 "the history of colonialism and racism in the region": Ibid., 12.

266 "phantasm of innocence": Ibid., 13.

267 minimizing Japanese war crimes: Ibid., 11–12.

267 linking the bomb to global peace: Ibid., 20.

267 tight focus around individual stories: See also Zwigenberg, "Never Again."

268 "an attempt to 'rewrite history'": Joshua Rhett Miller, "Son of Pilot Who Dropped A-Bomb Opposes Plan to Send U.S. Delegation to Hiroshima Ceremony," Fox News, December 23, 2015.

268 massive nuclear modernization program: Arms Control Association, "U.S. Nuclear Modernization Programs," updated January 2022, https://www .armscontrol.org/factsheets/USNuclearModernization; Loren Thompson, "Obama Backs Biggest Nuclear Arms Buildup Since Cold War," *Forbes,* December 15, 2015.

268 fifteen thousand: Stockholm International Peace Research Institute, *SIPRI Yearbook 2015: Armaments, Disarmament and International Society* (Oxford: Oxford University Press, 2015).

269 "nuclear football": Justin McCurry, "Hiroshima to Open Up Its Horrors to Barack Obama during Historic Visit," *Guardian,* May 13, 2016.

269 "an unspeakably ugly way": Oe, *Hiroshima Notes,* 126.

269 "become no longer human": Ibid., 182.

## 17. Sirens

274 "'the end of the conversation'": Thomas E. Shriver et al., "The Role of Collective Identity in Inhibiting Mobilization: Solidarity and Suppression in Oak Ridge," *Sociological Spectrum* 20, no. 1 (2000): 41–64, 55.

278 largest single stockpile in the world: Frank Munger, "A Look at Y-12's Uranium Fortress," *Knoxville News Sentinel,* June 9, 2016.

278 fourteen thousand warheads: Nuclear Watch of New Mexico, "Y-12 National Security Complex," accessed March 6, 2022, https://www .nukewatch.org/activemap/NWC-Y-12.html.

278 only five active production facilities: The description of Y-12's role in the nuclear weapons complex comes from Amy F. Woolf and James D. Werner, *The U.S. Nuclear Weapons Complex: Overview of Department of Energy Sites,* R45306 (U.S. Library of Congress, Congressional Research Service, March 31, 2021).

279 more than thirty cleanup workers: Jamie Satterfield's sustained coverage of this story for the *Knoxville News Sentinel* has been essential in bringing it to public awareness. See Satterfield, "TVA Coal Ash Spill" and "Kingston Coal Ash Spill Workers Treated as 'Expendables,' Lawsuit by Sick and Dying Contends," *Knoxville News Sentinel,* July 21, 2017. As of August

2020, more than fifty cleanup workers had died; see Austyn Gaffney, "'They Deserve to Be Heard': Sick and Dying Coal Ash Cleanup Workers Fight for Their Lives," *Guardian*, August 17, 2020.

279 **reporting by *Grist*:** Gaffney, "A Legacy of Contamination."

280 **a new hazardous waste landfill:** Benjamin Pounds, "Steps toward Landfill for DOE Demolition Debris in Oak Ridge," *Oak Ridger*, July 19, 2021; Rebecca R. Bowman, "Open letter: Concerns on EMDF in Oak Ridge," *Oak Ridger*, September 26, 2019; Benjamin Pounds, "Environmental Group Has Concerns for Future Landfill," *Oak Ridger*, March 1, 2022.

281 **won a suit against the DOE:** Oak Ridge Environmental Peace Alliance, Nuclear Watch of New Mexico, and Natural Resources Defense Council v. US DOE and National Nuclear Security Administration, 3: 18-cv-00150-PLR-DCP, doc. 63 (Ed. Tenn. 2019); John Huotari, "Judge Voids UPF Decision, Requires More Seismic Hazard Analysis," *Oak Ridge Today*, September 24, 2019.

281 **A 2015 audit:** Frank Munger, "IG Identifies More than 200 High-Risk Facilities That Are Dirty and Degraded; 'Worst of Worst' Is at Y-12," *Atomic City Underground* (blog), *Knoxville News Sentinel*, January 28, 2015, http://knoxblogs.com/atomiccity/2015/01/28/ig-identifies-200-high -risk-facilities-dirty-degraded-worst-worst-y-12/.

281 **"ever-increasing levels of risk":** US DOE, Office of Inspector General, Office of Audits and Inspections, *Audit Report: The Department of Energy's Management of High-Risk Excess Facilities*, DOE/IG-0931, January 2015, 2.

282 **"end of their expected life spans":** "Processing," Y-12 National Security Complex, accessed March 6, 2022, https://www.y12.doe.gov/mission /nuclear-deterrence/weapons-production/processing.

# INDEX

## About the Author

Emily Strasser's award-winning essays have appeared in *Plough-shares, Guernica, Colorado Review,* the *Bitter Southerner, Bulletin of Atomic Scientists,* and elsewhere. She has received support from grants and fellowships including the Olive B. O'Connor Fellowship, the Jerome Foundation, the McKnight Foundation, and the Minnesota State Arts Board. Emily earned her MFA in creative writing from the University of Minnesota. She teaches at Tufts University.